ISBN 978-1-5278-3911-3
PIBN 10892035

1 MONTH OF
FREE
READING

at

www.ForgottenBooks.com

By purchasing this book you are eligible for one month membership to ForgottenBooks.com, giving you unlimited access to our entire collection of over 1,000,000 titles via our web site and mobile apps.

To claim your free month visit:
www.forgottenbooks.com/free892035

English
Français
Deutsche
Italiano
Español
Português

www.forgottenbooks.com

Mythology Photography **Fiction**
Fishing Christianity **Art** Cooking
Essays Buddhism Freemasonry
Medicine **Biology** Music **Ancient**
Egypt Evolution Carpentry Physics
Dance Geology **Mathematics** Fitness
Shakespeare **Folklore** Yoga Marketing
Confidence Immortality Biographies
Poetry **Psychology** Witchcraft
Electronics Chemistry History **Law**
Accounting **Philosophy** Anthropology
Alchemy Drama Quantum Mechanics
Atheism Sexual Health **Ancient History**
Entrepreneurship Languages Sport
Paleontology Needlework Islam
Metaphysics Investment Archaeology
Parenting Statistics Criminology
Motivational

Historic, archived document

Do not assume content reflects current
scientific knowledge, policies, or practices.

AFRICAN VIOLETS *Everybody's Flower*

PETUNIAS

Grow them in pots, porch or patio boxes; enjoy them in little beds, big beds, long beds; plant them along fences, driveways or paths; use them in tree stumps, wagon wheels or wheelbarrows. No matter what the use, there is a Petunia to fit.

Why? Because they grow "most anywhere," except in dense shade, and are not fussy as to soil. Because there are compact, mound-like varieties only 9 inches high, all the way to semi-trailing forms 4 to 5 feet long. Because they are covered with flowers from 1½ to 6 inches in diameter. Because you can have colors in almost any conceivable shade of white, pink, rose, crimson, blue and purple, even a deep cream that passes for yellow. Choose the Petunias that suit your purpose. Enjoy their jaunty beauty from June to heavy frost.

Prize-winning All-double Petunias

Mrs. Dwight D. Eisenhower, Alldouble, 3419. Silver Medal Winner, 1947. Luminous salmon, lightly veined with deeper salmon. Pkt. $2.00; 2 pkts. $3.75.

Rose Marie, Alldouble, 3421. Bronze Medal Winner, 1947. A beautiful clear rose-pink, exquisitely veined with deeper rose. Pkt. $1.00.

Orchid Beauty, Alldouble, 3422. Orchid flowers, deeply ruffled and fully double. Individual blooms are 4 to 4½ inches across. Pkt. $1.50.

Colossal Shades of Rose, Alldouble, 3416. Silver Medal Winner, 1946. Over 5 inches across. Delightful shades from salmon-pink to rose-pink. Pkt. $1.00; 3 pkts. $2.75.

America, Alldouble, 3412. Compact plants with 2½-inch flowers of sparkling rose-pink. Pkt. 50c; large pkt. $2.25.

African Violet (Saintpaulia)

African Violets

America's Favorite House Plant

You will find more African Violets on window sills than any other flower. Most of these have been raised from leaf cuttings, since seed has been unobtainable.

This year we have seed from a famous European grower, and we feel there are endless possibilities for raising new varieties from this stock. Grow your own—**1038.** Pkt. 75c; 3 pkts. $2.00.

For complete success buy the most authoritative book on the subject: The African Violet, by Helen Van Pelt Wilson. $2.75, postpaid.

> **WIK-FED-POTS**
> Self watering, self draining. Ideal for African Violets. 4 in. $1.15 each; 2 for $2.00, postpaid.

Petunia, Snowstorm Improved

Single Dwarf Giants of California

A magnificent strain with flowers measuring 4 to 6 inches across, beautifully ruffled and fringed. 18 in.

Crimson Glory, 3391. Brilliant carmine-red with contrasting deeper veins.

Glamour, 3400. Huge salmon-rose with cream throat.

Salmon-Rose Shades, 3393. A delightful blend of choicest salmon-rose shades.

Any of the above: Pkt. 50c; large pkt. $1.25

Dwarf Giants of California Mixed, 3394. Short stocky plants with huge fringed flowers. Solid colors, many with intriguing veining. Pkt. 50c; large pkt. $1.50.

Single Large Flowering

Hybrida Grandiflora—Plain-edged but huge flowers.

Burgundy, 3364. Deep burgundy-red with purple-veined white throat. Pkt. 25c; large pkt. 75c.

Dwarf Elk's Pride, 3366. Bears a great profusion of velvety, deep purple blooms. Very dwarf and compact. Pkt. 25c; large pkt. 75c.

Elk's Pride, 3365. Large, well-formed blooms of brilliant rich purple-blue. Bright foliage. Pkt. 25c; large pkt. 75c.

Snowstorm Improved, 3368. Covered with well-formed, pure white flowers. Pkt. 25c; large pkt. 75c.

The last two are fine in combinations in porch or patio boxes.

Petunia, Fire Chief

WINS THE GOLD MEDAL, ALL-AMERICA SELECTIONS

Brilliant, startling firecracker-red—a mound of fire when in full bloom. Dwarf, compact plants for beds, borders or boxes. No wonder it was the unanimous choice of twenty judges and the first Gold Medal Winner in 11 years.

3336 Pkts. only, 25c

Gold-Medal Petunia, Fire Chief

II

Balcony Petunias

Bedding Petunias

More bloom per square foot. Eighteen-inch plants that bloom all summer.
General Dodds, 3331. Rich crimson flowers.
Heavenly Blue, 3349. Glorious silvery blue flowers.
Howard's Star Improved, 3335. Rose-crimson with five-pointed white star.
Periwinkle Blue, 3339. Bright blue flowers.
Pink Sensation, 3348. Bronze Medal Winner, 1948. Uniform light rose-pink.
Rose of Heaven, 3343. Luminous rose.
Rosy Morn Improved, 3345. Soft rose-pink with white throat.
Snow Queen, 3351. Pure white blooms.
Violet Queen, 3353. Velvety violet.
　　　　　Any of the above: **Pkt. 15c**
Fine Mixed, 3360. Pkt. 15c; ¼oz. $1.00; oz. $3.00.
Pelletized Seed, P3360. Pkt. 20c.
Dreer's Peerless Mixture, 3362. Hand-made mixture of the best bedding varieties.
　　Pkt. 25c; ¼oz. $1.50; oz. $4.50.

Balcony Petunias

A splendid, large and free-flowering type for window boxes, vases, hanging baskets,
etc. The flowers measure 3 inches in diameter. **Pkt. 20c; large pkt. 60c.**
Black Prince, 3269. Deepest maroon.
Balcony Blue, 3271. A very fine rich blue with a velvety finish.
Cornflower Blue (Blue Wonder), 3273. Magnificent cornflower-blue.
Balcony Crimson, 3275. A glowing color set against rich green leaves.
Balcony Rose, 3277. Always greatly admired for its purity.
Balcony White, 3279. Excellent pure white blooms.
　　COLLECTION 4902: One pkt. each of the above six colors, for $1.00
Balcony Mixed Colors, 3280. Pkt. 20c; large pkt. 60c; ⅛oz. $1.00.

Dwarf Compact Bedding Petunias

Compact, mound-shaped plants 9 to 12 inches tall.
Bright Eyes, 3321. Bronze Medal Winner, 1946. Rose-pink
　with white throat. Pkt. 15c.
Celestial Rose Improved, 3305. Bright rose. Pkt. 15c.
Cheerful, 3334. Bright salmon-pink. Pkt. 25c; ⅙oz. $2.50.
Cream Star, 3330. Creamy white, star-shaped blooms. Pkt. 15c.
English Violet, 3332. Bright purple-violet. Pkt. 15c.
Glow, 3309. Rose-red with lighter throat. Very free flowering.
　Pkt. 15c.
Igloo, 3308. Bronze Medal, All-America Selections, 1943. Dainty
　creamy white blooms with light yellow throat. Pkt. 25c.
King Henry (Dwarf Flaming Velvet), 3312. Brilliant velvet,
　blood-red. Pkt. 15c.
Peach Red, 3322. Honorable Mention, 1946. Deep salmon with
　light red tints. Pkt. 25c.
Radiance, 3341. Brilliant rose. Borne profusely and con-
　tinuously. Pkt. 20c.
Dwarf Compact Mixed, 3320. Includes a wide range of beauti-
　ful colors. Pkt. 20c; large pkt. 60c.

Dwarf Compact Single Ruffled

Dwarf, compact, but vigorous plants covered with extra-
large, single frilled blooms.
Martha Washington, 3327. Flesh-pink flowers with deep wine-
　red center. Pkt. 25c.
Ruffled Grandiflora Mixed, 3328. A grand mixture including
　many fine colors. Pkt. 25c.

Giant Single Fringed

Bushy, branching, 18-inch plants
with 3 to 4-inch blooms.
Lace Veil, 3373. Large, fringed, pure
　white flowers.
Scarlet Beauty, 3377. Scarlet
　blooms with fringed edges.
Violacea, 3383. Fringed blooms, vel-
　vety violet-blue.
White Beauty, 3385. Graceful large,
　pure white blooms.
　　Any of the above:
　　Pkt. 25c; large pkt. 75c
**Fringed Ruffled Giants (Fluffy
　Ruffles), 3396.** Large ruffled
　blooms with finely fringed edges.
　Pkt. 35c; large pkt. $1.00.
Ruffled Monsters Mixed, 3398.
　Magnificent in every way. Many
　colors. Pkt. 35c; large pkt. $1.00.

Dreer's Own Superb
GIANT SINGLE
AND DOUBLE PETUNIAS

Dreer's own marvelous strains *plus*
the finest of the newer varieties.
Mixtures unsurpassed in size and
diversity of colors.
**Dreer's Superb Single Fringed
　Mixed, 3390.** Pkt. 25c; large pkt.
　75c.
**Dreer's Superb Double Fringed
　Mixed, 3420.** Pkt. 50c; 500 seeds
　$2.00.

Dreer's Giant
Single and Double
Petunias

Candytuft

Portulaca

This is the stuff from which "edges" are made, and rock gardens and ribbon beds, too—Ageratum, Alyssum, Brachycome, Candytuft and Portulaca. All are dwarf, compact and long blooming—and don't forget your porch, window and patio boxes! Sow the seed right where you want the plants to bloom, in shallow drills. A couple of weedings is all the care they'll need for a summer of beauty. A packet will sow 10 ft.

AGERATUM · Floss Flower

Compact, annual plants with tuft-like blooms, June to heavy frost. Start indoors in February or March, or sow outdoors in April, or May.

Blue Ball, 1045. Compact, ball-shaped plants. Deep Ageratum-blue, 6 inches. Pkt. 15c; 2 pkts. 25c.

Blue Cap, 1047. Rich deep blue, 5 inches. Pkt. 20c; 2 pkts. 35c.

Blue Perfection, 1049. Amethyst-blue, tall enough for cutting. 10 inches. Pkt. 15c; 2 pkts. 25c.

Imperial Dwarf White, 1053. Compact plants with pure white flowers. 6 inches. Pkt. 20c; 2 pkts. 35c.

Lasseaux, 1056. Another tall enough for cutting; clear pink. 12 inches. Pkt. 15c; 2 pkts. 25c.

Blue Ball Improved (Blue Boy), 1046. Scarcely 4 inches tall but perfect in form. Rich blue. Pkt. 20c; 2 pkts. 35c.

Fairy Pink, 1052. Compact plants; bright rose-pink. 5 inches. Pkt. 20c; 2 pkts. 35c.

Midget Blue, 1058. Truly midget plants with brilliant blue flowers. 4 inches. Pkt. 25c.

Golden Ageratum (*Lonas inodora*), **1054.** Bright golden yellow flowers resembling Ageratum. Fine for cutting. 20 inches. Pkt. 25c.

ALYSSUM (Annual)

The most popular edging plant. Dwarf, compact and literally covered with blooms. Sow where they are wanted as soon as ground is fit. Good in porch and window boxes. An ounce will sow 100 feet of row.

Carpet of Snow, 1071. Dwarf, spreading plants. In full bloom they resemble giant white pancakes. Pkt. 10c; ¼oz. 50c; oz. $1.25.

Little Gem, 1077. Mound-shaped, dwarf plants. Pure white blooms. 6 inches. Pkt. 10c; ¼oz. 50c; oz. $1.25.

Lilac Queen, Improved, 1075. Dwarf, compact with bright lilac-lavender flowers. 6 inches. Pkt. 10c; ¼oz. 50c; oz. $1.25.

Sweet Alyssum, 1079. The taller old-fashioned variety. Pure white and really "sweet scented." 9 inches. Pkt. 10c; ¼oz. 25c; oz. 75c.

ALYSSUM, Lutescens, 1072. Pastel, creamy yellow. 6 inches. Pkt. 20c; 2 pkts. 35c.

Violet Queen, 1078. Upright, bushy plants with violet-blue flowers. Thin this one out a bit to give individual plants a chance to develop. 6 inches. Pkt. 15c; ¼oz. 75c; oz. $2.25.

BRACHYCOME
Swan River Daisy

Annual Daisies in pastel shades of blue, pink and white on 12-inch bushy plants. One of the easiest to grow. Sow seeds where you want plants to grow. Flowers all summer.

Blue Star, 1521. Clear lavender-blue flowers. Pkt. 15c; 2 pkts. 25c.

Mixed, 1530. As fine an assortment of miniature Daisies as you will find. White, pink and lavender shades. Sow them for edgings or beds or in rock gardens. 12 inches. Pkt. 15c; 2 pkts. 25c.

CANDYTUFT (Annual)

At home in any surroundings—as edgings, beds, borders or broadcast in the perennial garden. Umbellata varieties have flat flower heads; the hyacinth-flowered types are massive spikes on 18-inch stems. An ounce sows 100 feet of row.

UMBELLATA VARIETIES

Carmine, 1723	Lavender, 1729
Crimson, 1725	Rose-Cardinal, 1731
Flesh-Pink, 1727	Pure White, 1733

All Colors Mixed, 1740
Pkt. 10c; ¼oz. 25c; oz. 75c

Buy one 10c packet each of the six colors for 50c. Collection 4774.

NOTE: Rose-Cardinal is a particularly fine shade

GIANT HYACINTH-FLOWERED White, **1721.** Bushy, well-branched plants 18 inches tall. Each branch is terminated by an immense white spike. Pkt. 10c; ¼oz. 40c; oz. $1.25.

TOM THUMB Mixed, 1750. Dwarf and compact. 6 inches. Pkt. 15c; ¼oz. 35c.

PORTULACA · Sun Plant

Like miniature roses in a bed of bright green moss. They need only a bright sunny spot and an occasional weeding until they get started. 4 to 6 inches. A quarter ounce sows 50 feet of row.

Double Mixed, 3660. White, pink, red and yellow, miniature full-double rose-like flowers. Pkt. 20c; ¼oz. $1.50.

Single Mixed, 3670. The same array of color but flowers resemble big buttercups. Pkt. 15c; ¼oz. $1.00.

Single Jewel, 3671. Gem-like flowers of ruby-red. Pkt. 20c; ¼oz. $1.50.

ZINNIA, Dwarf Mixed, 4520. Pkt. 10c.

Brachycome

Alyssum

Ageratum and Zinnias

ANNUAL SCABIOSA

(Mourning Bride; Pin Cushion Flower)

An old-time favorite bred to modern requirements. Plants are well branched and bear ball-shaped flowers on long, wiry stems. Colorful and long lasting as cut stems. 3 feet tall.

Blue Cockade, 3875. Rich blue.
Cattleya, 3876. Lavender-orchid.
Fire King, 3877. Bright red.
King of the Blacks, 3879. Blackish purple.
Loveliness, 3881. Salmon-rose.
Peach Blossom, 3883. Peach-blossom-pink.
Rosette, 3885. Deep rose, suffused salmon.
Shasta, 3889. Pure white.
Yellow, 3882. Creamy yellow.

Pkt. 10c; ¼oz. 50c

Buy one 10c packet each of the nine colors for 80c. COLLECTION 4948.

Giant-Flowered Mixed, 3890. A wonderful mixture of giant-flowering types that includes shades not yet offered separately. Pkt. 10c; ¼oz. 60c.

SUMMER LONG CUT-FLOWER COLLECTION

Ten Mixtures of the best varieties to give you a constant supply of cut flowers from June to frost.

Aster, Late Branching, 1330. Pkt. 15c.
Baby's Breath, 2539. Pkt. 10c.
Bachelor Buttons, 1880. Pkt. 15c.
Cosmos, Early Giant Sensation, 2040. Pkt. 15c.
Chrysanthemum, Merry Mixture, 1931. Pkt. 25c.
Marigold, African Double, 2900. Pkt. 10c.
Larkspur, Imperial, 2740. Pkt. 15c.
Scabiosa, Double, 3890. Pkt. 10c.
Snapdragon Maximum, 1200. Pkt. 20c.
Zinnia, Dahlia Flowered, 4540. Pkt. 15c.

COLLECTION 4811: One packet each of the 10 Cut Flowers for · · **$1.25** (Value $1.50)

"Tall Stuff"

is the answer to that most-asked question, "What can I grow with the least trouble to give me lots of colorful flowers for cutting from June until frost?"

Grow them in groups, along fences or property lines, or use them to fence off the vegetable garden—and remember, the more you cut 'em the more they bloom.

Chrysanthemum, Merry Mixture

Annual Chrysanthemums are one of those carefree flowers that "grow most anywhere." Sow seed in shallow drills where you want them to bloom, thin to 10 or 12 inches apart, and they will yield flowers by the armful. Plants grow 3 feet and bear daisy-like flowers on long stems. See illustration for range of color. 1931. Pkt. 25c; ¼oz. 75c.

Chrysanthemum, Merry Mixture

BACHELOR BUTTONS

(Centaurea Cyanus)

The old reliable but larger, fuller and longer stemmed for cutting. Plants are bushy and upright, 2 feet tall.

Make one sowing as soon as the ground can be prepared and another May 30 for succession, and you'll have boutonnieres all summer and fall.

Double Black Boy, 1884. Dark maroon.
Double Blue Boy, 1881. True cornflower-blue.
Double Pinkie, 1882. Bright rose.
Double Red Boy, 1886. The finest red.
Double Snow Man, 1883. Pure white.
Double Rose, 1885. Rose-pink.
Double Mixed, 1880. All colors.
Pkt. 15c; ¼oz. 30c; oz. $1.00

Buy one 15c packet of each of the six colors for 75c. Collection 4788.

Dwarf Double Centaurea

The new boutonniere centaurea

Jubilee Gem, 1867. A new dwarf, bushy form only 12 inches tall. Flowers are true cornflower-blue. Pkt. 15c; 2 pkts. 25c.

Cosmos, Radiance

COSMOS

Early Giant Sensation

Easiest of all to grow. Tall, colorful and free flowering. Extra Early Giant Sensation starts to bloom in July. 3 to 4 feet tall.

Radiance, 2059. (Illustrated.) Rose-pink with crimson band at the center. Pkt. 25c.

Dazzler, 2046. Crimson.
Pinkie, 2038. Light pink.
Purity, 2039. Pure white.
Mixed, 2040. All colors.

Pkt. 15c; ¼oz. 75c.

Autumn Giant Cosmos

Late but worth waiting for. Tall plants, 5 to 6 feet, bearing extra-large, single flowers 4 to 5 inches across.

Giant Crimson, 2041.
Giant Pink, 2042.
Giant White, 2043.
Giant Mixed, 2045.

Pkt. 10c; ¼oz. 25c; oz. 75c

Giant-Flowering Scabiosa

Bachelor Buttons

V

Snaps (left to right), Copper Shades, Crimson, Yellow-Giant, Campfire, Alaska, Loveliness

NOTE: Other complete Selections of Snapdragons, Zinnias and Marigolds in their regular order in the General Catalog, Flower Seed section.

Snapdragons. Six glorious colors to bloom in your garden and for your indoor arrangements from June to November. May be wintered over in a coldframe.

Alaska, 1187. Giant pure white.

Campfire, 1189. Dazzling, luminous scarlet with golden yellow lip.

Copper Queen, 1194. Delightful copper shades from gold to orange-copper.

Crimson, 1195. Rich mahogany-crimson, a delightful contrast to the lighter colors.

Loveliness, 1197. Rose-pink, shading lighter, for pastel effects.

Yellow Giant, 1199. Deep buttercup-yellow with golden highlights.

Maximum Mixed, 1200. Our own blending to insure proper color proportions.

Any of the above: Pkt. 20c; ¼oz. $1.25

COLLECTION, 4717. For "Snaps" by the armful buy a packet each of all six colors, for only $1.00.

That's a Zinnia— Not a Dahlia

It's California Giant Zinnia, Scarlet Queen, 4558. Its popularity is measured by the fact that we sell more Scarlet Queen than any other Zinnia. Huge in size, dazzling scarlet in color and up to 4 feet tall. Use with discrimination or it will dominate your garden. Pkt. 15c; ¼oz. 60c.

Marigold Yellow Supreme

The perfect Marigold for cut flowers or garden. Pure sulphur-yellow blooms 3 inches in diameter; long stems for cutting; pleasing fragrance. 2½ feet tall. 2897. Pkt. 15c; ¼oz. 75c.

Marigold Guinea Gold

Betty. 2½ ft. Early October. 60c each; 3 for $1.50;
6 for $2.40

Carnival. 2½ ft. Mid-October. 75c each; 3 for $2.15;
6 for $3.90

Lola. 2½ ft. September. 60c each; 3 for $1.50;
6 for $2.40

Spoon Mums

A Dreer original from way back when. Again in great popularity. Each petal forms a miniature spoon.

Bronze Spoon. Bronze.

Jasper Spoon. Yellow tubes, red spoons.

Orchid Spoon. Pinkish lilac.

Red Spoon. Late blooming.

White Spoon. Pure white, creamy center.

Yellow Spoon. Bright yellow.

Any 3 for $1.50; 6 for $2.40; 12 for $4.75, postpaid.

Spoon Mums

12 of America's Best Mums

Chrysanthemums and Autumn are synonymous. Now you can enjoy their beauty indoors and out from August on, year after year.

We have selected these 12 for variety of color, size, and type; bloom from early August until late fall.

Plants that we will supply are from 2½-inch pots, guaranteed to bloom. By fall they will have developed into large clumps that can be divided in the spring. Many other varieties can be shipped on request. Shipped in May; date depends on the season.

Bronze Pyramid. Deep glowing bronze. Late blooming. 2½ ft.
Courageous. Large, double flowers. Dark ruby-red. 2 ft.
Fred F. Rockwell. Pat. 718. 2 ft. A gorgeous blend of bronze and orange-scarlet.
Glowing Coals. 2½ ft. Cherry-red with orange on back.
Hearthfire. 2 ft. Double, bright red flowers showing a small yellow center when fully opened. Excellent for cutting.
Korean Princess. Pat. 640. 2 ft. Shapely blooms 2½ inches across, of rich bronze-red with golden bronze cushion center.
Mellow Glow. 2½ ft. Suffusion of soft orange-buff, peach-pink and bronze-nasturtium tints. Splendid for cutting.
Oriental. 2 ft. Beautiful and brilliant oriental red. Very free blooming.
Twilight. 2 ft. Large, double, fuchsia-purple blooms.
Valiant. 2 ft. Semi-double flower with long petals of bright rose-scarlet and bright golden center.
White Wonder. 3 ft. Exquisitely formed, ball-shaped blooms of soft creamy white, opening to a clean white. Very sturdy plant.
Yellow Avalanche. 2 ft. Large, fluffy, double flowers of brilliant soft yellow. A sport of the popular Avalanche.

75c each; any 3 for $2.00; any 6 for $3.75; any 12 for $7.00, postpaid.

"Buttons"

Lovely, free blooming and indispensable for cut flowers. Four of the best that start to bloom early in October. Blooms up to 1½ inches across; plants 2 feet.

Irene. Pure white.

Judith Anderson. Buttercup-yellow.

Ouray. That rich bronze button you've been looking for.

Yellow Irene. Canary-yellow; blends with any color.

3 for $1.50; 6 for $2.40; 12 for $4.75, postpaid.

ALL FOUR SURE!
One of each $1.75, postpaid; 3 of each $5.00.

PLEASE NOTE: We cannot accept C.O.D. orders, nor orders for less than $1.00 for plants.

Lavender Lady. 3 ft. Early October. 60c each;
3 for $1.50; 6 for $2.40

Your Garden 1950

Good gardens don't "just happen." Planning is half the fun of gardening. Dreer's all new 1950 Catalog has been completely revised to help you "plan your garden right," and enjoy your gardening to the fullest extent.

Sixteen pages in full natural color—the "cream of the crop" in Flower Seeds, Bulbs, Plants, and Roses and Lawn Seed.

And 64 more pages profusely illustrated, offer as comprehensive a selection of the "Best in Horticulture" as you will find. We hope you like our new Catalog and we shall appreciate your orders, which will be filled to "your entire satisfaction or your money back," Dreer's Century-old Guarantee, backed by 112 years of Reliability for Top Quality and Fair Prices.

The Newest Development in Horticulture

Dreer's *Pelletized* Seeds

Offered to Dreer's Customers for the first time last spring, met with immediate, spontaneous acceptance. We were hard pressed throughout the spring season to keep up with the demand. ORDER EARLY.

Results in our own trials were excellent and showed the importance of following cultural directions (particularly barely covering the Pellets). Where we purposely planted at the regular depth for bare seed, germination was irregular. Reports from all over the country praised the ease of planting and superior results. A few reports from different sections:

Eastern Penna.—My Tomatoes from Pelletized Seed not only ripened earlier, but yielded more fruit than those grown by our gardener. C. E. J., Faulke and Long Institute.

Iowa—Garden Editor of Household Magazine wrote: "I didn't have to wait until harvest to be swept off my feet by their (Pelletized Seed) speed in germination and rapid growth."

Pelletized—Lettuce Seed—Plain

Pelletized Seeds were developed:
(1) To save labor and expense on the farm and back-breaking thinning out and transplanting in the home garden. They can be planted individually right where you want the seed to grow.

(2) To produce sturdier growth and higher germination through protection against soil borne disease and weather conditions. Pelletized Seeds may be planted earlier.

Pelletized Seeds are definitely past the experimental stage; tons of Tomato, Carrot, Lettuce and Sugar Beet seed to name a few, were processed and planted last year, with even bigger production scheduled for 1950.

Ohio—"Pelletized Seed that I received from you last spring gave every satisfaction." J. H. D.

Oregon—"Last spring I bought some Pelletized Seed from you and had good luck with all of them. The Zinnias and Asters were especially fine." A. S. E.

Western Penna.—"The Pelletized Calendulas I bought from you last spring were wonderful." L. W. C.

Pelletized Seeds are offered in many varieties for 1950. Improved formula gives a coating that immediately attracts and absorbs soil moisture.

Pelletized Seeds are fresh, new, carefully selected seeds coated with a special material to increase the size, protect the seed and stimulate early growth.

Important—Planting Directions

(1) Do not cover as deeply as ordinary seeds. Cover only enough to hold the Pellets in place.

(2) Although Dreer Seeds are the best obtainable, no seeds germinate and grow 100%. Pelletized Seeds for plants that require spacing of six inches or more apart, should be planted two at a time and later thinned to the stronger plant. For spacing less than 6 inches apart, plant one Pellet at a time.

(3) Do not pack or firm soil after planting. Pellets expand when in contact with moisture and packing prevents full expansion.

(4) Pelletized Seeds, being protected, may be planted outdoors in the open ground earlier than ordinary seeds.

Pelletized Flower Seeds	Pelletized Vegetable Seeds
For full description of varieties see general list.	For full description of varieties see general list.
Pkt. 20¢ each; 12 for $2.00.	Pkt. 20¢ each; 12 for $2.00.

Pelletized Flower Seeds

For full description of varieties see general list.

Pkt. 20¢ each; 12 for $2.00.

ASTER, Late Branching Mixed. P 1330.
BACHELOR BUTTONS, Mixed. P 1880.
CALENDULA, Double Mixed. P 1600.
CARDINAL, Climber. P 1757.
COSMOS, Radiance. P 2059.
ESCHSCHOLTZIA, Mixed. P 2400.
HOLLYHOCK, Double Mixed. P 2650.
LARKSPUR, Giant Imperial Double Mixed. P 2740.
MARIGOLD, African Double Mixed. P 2900.
MARIGOLD, French Dwarf Double Mixed. P 2940.
MARIGOLD, French Double Spry. P 2943.
MORNING GLORY, Improved Heavenly Blue. P 3029.
PETUNIA, Bedding Mixed. P 3360.
PETUNIA, Rosy Morn Improved. P 3345.
PHLOX, Large Flowering Dwarf Mixed. P 3440.
PORTULACA, Double Mixed. P 3660.
PORTULACA, Single Mixed. P 3670.
SWEET PEAS, Summer Flowering Mixed. P 4180.
VERBENA, Giant Flowering Mixed. P 4370.
WALLFLOWER, Extra Early Single Mixed. P 4456.
ZINNIA, California Giant Mixed. P 4560.
ZINNIA, Dwarf Double Mixed. P 4520.
ZINNIA, Lilliput Mixed. P 4580.

Pelletized Vegetable Seeds

For full description of varieties see general list.

Pkt. 20¢ each; 12 for $2.00.

BEET, Detroit Dark Red. P 149.
BROCCOLI, Sprouting Calabrese. P 179.
BRUSSELS SPROUTS, Long Island Improved. P 185.
CABBAGE, Copenhagen Market. P 193.
CABBAGE, Danish Ballhead. P 195.
CARROT, Chantenay Red-Cored. P 232.
CARROT, Danvers Red-Cored. P 234.
CAULIFLOWER, Snowball X. P 254.
CUCUMBER, Improved Early White Spine. P 392.
EGGPLANT, Black Beauty. P 404.
LETTUCE, Black Seeded Simpson. P 442.
LETTUCE, Great Lakes. P 457.
LETTUCE, White Boston. P 458.
ONION, Southport White Globe. P 584.
ONION, Yellow Globe Danvers. P 568.
PARSLEY, Champion Moss-Curled. P 607.
PEPPER, Ruby King. P 740.
RADISH, Scarlet Globe. P 813.
RADISH, White Icicle. P 786.
TOMATO, Break O' Day. P 896.
TOMATO, Rutgers. P 937.
TURNIP, Purple Top White Globe. P 966.

SEE FOR YOURSELF how quickly the coating absorbs moisture. Place Pellet on a drop of water and almost immediately the coat will take up moisture and swell to more than twice its size.

Achillea—The Pearl

Achillea—*Milfoil, Perennial*

Filipendula, Cloth of Gold, 1012. Strong, vigorous plants with vivid yellow flowerheads through the summer. 3 ft. Pkt. 15¢.

Ptarmica, The Pearl, 1015. Heads of pure white, double flowers from June until frost. 2 ft. Pkt. 15¢; 2 pkts. 25¢.

Abutilon, Choicest Hybrids, 1009. (Chinese Bellflower.) Tender perennial. Bushy plants with bell-shaped white, rose, yellow and orange flowers. Blooms through the summer. 18 in. Pkt. 25¢.

Acroclinium, Giant Double Mixed, 1030. (Everlasting.) Double daisy-shaped flowers in shades of pink and white. 15 in. Pkt. 25¢.

Adlumia, Cirrhosa, 1035. ·(Allegheny Vine.) Hardy biennial climber or trailing ground cover. Small lavender flowers. 8 to 10 ft. Pkt. 25¢.

Ageratum. Illustrated in color, page IV.

Agrostemma, Coronaria, 1065. (Mullein Pink.) Soft, whitish, felt-like leaves. Glowing crimson flowers like single pinks. Perennial. 2 ft. Pkt. 15¢.

Amaranthus—Sunrise

Aconitum—*Monk's Hood, Perennial*

Wilsoni, 1025. Large, rich violet-blue flowers on spikes 5 to 6 ft. tall. Blooms in late fall. Flowers like Delphinium without the spur. Pkt. 25¢; 2 pkts. 45¢.

Napellus, 1023. Stately spikes with attractive rich blue flowers. Blooms May-July. 3-5 ft. Pkt. 20¢.·

HARDY-ALYSSUM

Saxatile Compactum, 1085. (Basket of Gold.) Hardy perennial. Dwarf plants with so many bright yellow blooms that the foliage cannot be seen. It is perfectly hardy for borders or rock gardens. Blooms May-June. 1 ft. Pkt.· 15¢; 2 pkts. 25¢.

Silver Queen, 1087. A pretty white perennial Alyssum. Pkt. 15¢; 2 pkts. 25¢.

Alyssum, Annual. Illustrated in color and listed on page IV.

Ampelopsis, Veitchi, 1099. (Boston Ivy.) Hardy ·perennial climber with olive green leaves which turn bright scarlet in the autumn. Clings to any surface. Pkt.·20¢.

Anemone—*Windflower*

Magellanica, 1114. Nodding bell-like creamy white flowers on 18-inch stems, from May to August. Perennial. Pkt. 25¢.

St. Brigid, 1117. Glorious· semi-double and double flowers in pinks, blues, and white. Blooms in June. 18 in. Perennial. Pkt. 15¢.

Pulsatilla, 1118. (Pasque Flower.) Violet-purple blooms. Grows 9 to 12 inches tall. Blooms in May. Pkt. 25¢.

Amaranthus

Annuals with brilliant foliage thriving best in a warm, sunny location. 3 to 5 ft. tall.

Aurora, 1089. Brilliant carmine head above red, yellow, and dark green foliage. 3 ft. tall. Pkt. 25¢.

Sunrise, 1091. Bronzy crimson foliage with a large tuft of bright scarlet-carmine leaves at the top. Pkt. 15¢.

Tricolor Splendens, 1093. (Joseph's Coat.) Showy foliage, variegated with shades of bronze, green, scarlet and gold. Pkt. 15¢; 2 pkts. 25¢.

Pygmy Torch, 1092. Brilliantly colored dwarf Amaranthus for edging or boxes. Pkt. 25¢.

Amsonia, Tabernaemontana, 1098. Hardy perennial with panicles of soft blue, star-shaped flowers. 2 ft. Pkt. 25¢.

Anoda—*Lavateroides*

Opalcup, 1121. Delightful annual with pretty opaline blue-violet, cup-shaped flowers. Blooms all summer. 48 in. high. Pkt. 15¢.

Snowcup, 1122. Snow-white flowers. 30 in. high. Pkt. 15¢.

Anagallis, Grandiflora Mixed, 1100. (Pimpernel.) Showy ·dwarf annuals that bloom June to frost. Star-shaped flowers cream, pink and orange on bushy 9 in. plants. Pkt. 15¢.

Argemone, Hybrida Grandiflora, 1241. (Prickly Poppy.) Satiny, crinkled, Poppy-like blooms in white, cream and old-rose. 2 ft. Pkt. 15¢.

Aconitum—Monk's Hood

Anchusa

Capensis Blue Bird, 1103. (Cape-Forget-Me-Not.) Brilliant indigo blue, five-petalled flowers on compact plants 15 in. tall. Blooms throughout the summer. Annual. Pkt. 10¢; 3 pkts. 25¢.

Italica Grandiflora, Dropmore, 1105. Rich, Gentian blue flowers on plants 3 to 5 ft. tall. Perfectly hardy. Pkt. 15¢; 2 pkts. 25¢.

Myosotidiflora, 1111. Dwarf, hardy, 10 to 12 in. high. Forget-Me-Not-like flowers of rich blue during April-May. Pkt. 25¢.

Armeria

Sea Pink, Perennial

Giant Pink, 1244. Globular bright pink blooms on plants 2½ ft. tall. Grassy foliage. June. Pkt. 25¢.

Alpina, 1245. Little tufts of grassy foliage covered with bright rose flowers, 4 in. June. Pkt. 25¢.

Formosa, Giant Flowered Mixed, 1246. Many lovely rose shades, 1½ ft. Blooms all summer. Pkt. 15¢.

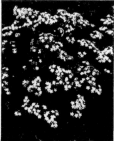

Anchusa—Myosotidiflora

Antirrhinum–SNAPDRAGONS

The cut flower supreme, they bloom and bloom and bloom from early summer until heavy frost. Lovely colors, strong stems and the bugs don't like them. All our Snapdragons are rust-resistant. Annual.

MAXIMUM VARIETY, The Biggest! See in full colors, page VI.

Tall Large-Flowered Snaps

Well branched plants with long nicely-formed spikes. 2½ feet tall.

Orange Shades, 1186.

Padre, 1180. Rich brilliant crimson.

Pinkie, 1181. Clear translucent pink.

Rosalie, 1182. Delightful deep rose.

Shasta, 1183. Snowy white.
Yellow Jacket, 1184. A deep canary yellow.

Pkt. 20¢; 2 pkts. 35¢.

COLLECTION, 4713. One 20¢ pkt. each of the 6 colors, only $1.00.

Tall Large-Flowered Mixed, 1185. Pkt. 20¢; large pkt. 60¢; ⅛ oz. $1.00.

Half-Dwarf Snapdragons

Bushy plants, about 18 inches tall with stems long enough for cutting.

Antique Gold, 1152. Old-gold, copper and orange.

Carmine-Rose, 1158. Bright carmine.

DuBarry, 1156. Salmon-rose.

Garnet, 1160. Velvety crimson.

Indian Girl, 1161. Brilliant old-gold.

Wild Fire, 1168. Orange-scarlet.

Pkt. 15¢; 2 pkts. 25¢.

COLLECTION, 4715. One 15¢ pkt. each of the 6 colors, 75¢.

Large-Flowering Half-Dwarf Mixed, 1170. Pkt. 15¢; large pkt. 40¢; ⅛ oz. 75¢.

Velvet Giant, 1188. Bronze Medal Winner 1947. Majestic in size of flower and plant. Deep velvety crimson blooms on 2½ ft. spikes. Base-branching. Pkt. 50¢.

Rock Hybrids, Magic Carpet, 1130. Compact, free and early flowering plants. 6 in. high. Use in Rock and Wall Gardens. Pkt. 25¢.

THE NEW TETRAPLOID-ANTIRRHINUM

1129. A new race of Giant Snapdragons produced by the wonder drug Colchicine. Largest of all Snapdragons with attractively ruffled flowers more than 2 in. deep and fully as wide. 2½ ft. high and blooming all summer. Mixed only, in magnificent array of colors. Pkt. 25¢; 3 pkts. 65¢.

ASCLEPIAS, Tuberosa, 1249. (Butterfly Weed.) 2 ft. tall. Brilliant orange flower heads from July to frost. Good for dry spots. Pkt. 15¢; 2 pkts. 25¢.

Snapdragon—Antirrhinum

Aquilegia—Longissima

Dreer's Aquilegia
COLUMBINE

Hardy, graceful, free-flowering perennial that always reminds us of fairy or woodland sprites. They thrive in semi-shade and bloom from May until July. Seed is fine and slow to germinate. Do not cover deeply.

Longissima, 1216. Extra-long spurs often 4 in. long. Beautiful well-formed delicate yellow flowers, 2½ ft. tall. Pkt. 25¢.

Longissima Hybrids, 1218. Beautiful, soft-pastel shades all with very long spurs. As graceful as can be. 2½ ft. tall. Pkt. 35¢.

Long-Spurred Columbines

Choose your favorite color or one of the superb mixtures. They bloom freely and are one of the finest cut flowers. 1½ to 2½ ft. tall.

Blue Shades, 1221. The finest strain. Pkt. 25¢.

Copper Queen, 1224. Copper shades from light copper-gold to deep coppery orange. Pkt. 25¢.

Crimson Star, 1215. Rich crimson outer petals with a pure white center. Pkt. 25¢.

Pink and Rose, 1225. Pink and rose with white crowns. Pkt. 25¢.

Snow Queen, 1228. Large-flowered, fragrant, white. Pkt. 25¢.

Mrs. Scott Elliott's Long Spurred Mixture, 1229. Mostly pastel shades, large flowers, long spurs. Pkt. 25¢; large pkt. 75¢; ⅛ oz. $1.00.

Dreer's Long-Spurred, Mixed, 1230. The most complete assortment of Columbine colors. All are long-spurred graceful flowers. Pkt. 25¢; large pkt. 75¢; ⅛ oz. $1.00; ¼ oz. $1.50.

Various Aquilegia

Alpina, 1201. Rich blue. Splendid for Rock Gardens. 1 ft. Pkt. 20¢.

Coerulea, 1213. True Rocky Mountain Columbine. Blue and white. Pkt. 25¢.

Canadensis, 1203. Red crowns, yellow spurs. 2½ ft. tall. Pkt. 25¢; 2 pkts. 45¢.

Chrysantha, 1211. Long-spurred, golden yellow flowers. 3½ ft. tall. Pkt. 20¢.

Double Mixed, 1207. Many colors 2½ ft. tall. Pkt. 20¢; large pkt. 40¢.

$\mathcal{D}$reer's SUPREME ASTERS

Asters will grow 'most anywhere. Full sun is best but they do not seem to mind partial shade. Use them in solid beds or for tall borders or even inter-plant amongst your perennials and shrubbery. As cut flowers they last and last and last. For early August bloom start indoors in March or seed may be sown outdoors in May where they are to bloom. Thin out or transplant to stand at least 12 inches apart. All varieties listed are Wilt-Resistant. Try the New Pelletized Seed, see page VII.

DREER'S SIX FAMOUS AMERICAN ASTERS

For years we have grouped together the best Aster of each color. They are listed below, separately and as a collection. All are thoroughly reliable and all are excellent cut flowers.

Purple Beauty, 1265. Rich glittering purple. 2½ ft. tall. Pkt. 20¢.
California Giant, Deep Rose, 1278. Extra large. 3 ft. tall. Pkt. 20¢.
Crego's Giant White, 1289. An older variety that has defied improvement. 2 ft. tall. Pkt. 15¢.
Late Branching, Azure Blue, 1321. Finest of its color. 2 ft. tall. Pkt. 15¢.
Dreer's Peerless Pink, 1335. The standard for shell pink Asters. 2 ft. tall. Pkt. 15¢.
Sensation, 1337. The nearest approach to a true red in Asters. 18 inches tall. Pkt. 15¢.
COLLECTION, 4752. Buy one pkt. each of the above 6 colors for 80¢.

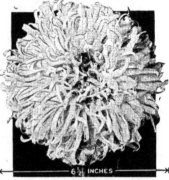

Aster—California Giant

California Giant Asters

Full double flowers with curled and twisted petals 5 to 6 inches across. 3 to 3½ ft. tall. Start to bloom in September.

Pkt. 20¢; large pkt. 60¢; ¼ oz. $1.00.
Appleblossom, 1271. Shell pink.
Crimson, 1272.
Lavender Blue, 1273.
Deep Purple, 1275.
Deep Rose, 1278.
Pure White, 1279.
Finest Mixed, 1280.
COLLECTION, 4740. Buy one 20¢ pkt. each of the 6 colors for $1.00.

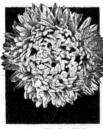

Aster—Giant Sunshine

Giant Crego Asters

Similar to California Giant but not so tall and blooms in August. 2 ft. tall. Pkt. 15¢; large pkt. 50¢; ¼ oz. 90¢.

Crimson, 1281.	Purple, 1287.
Lavender, 1283.	Rose, 1288.
Pink, 1285.	White, 1289.
Crego Mixed, 1290.	

COLLECTION, 4738. Buy one 15¢ pkt. each of the 6 colors for 75¢.

Giant Sunshine Asters

Giant Sunshine Mixed, 1380. Glorious Asters with long, narrow outer petals surrounding a large cushion-like center of tubular florets in contrasting colors. Mid-summer until frost. 3 feet. Pkt. 20¢; large pkt. 60¢; ¼ oz. $1.25.

Giant Single Asters

Giant Single Mixed, 1390. Large Daisy-like single flowers often five inches in diameter. Very effective for borders or for cutting. The plants grow 2 ft. tall and bloom profusely from August until frost. Pkt. 15¢; large pkt. 40¢ ¼ oz. 60¢.

Early Giant Asters

Light Blue, 1255. Big lacy light blue flowers. 1¼ ft. tall. Pkt. 25¢; large pkt. 75¢.
Peachblossom, 1256. Large white blooms flushed pink. 4 to 5 inches across. 1½-2 ft. tall. Pkt. 25¢; large pkt. 75¢.
Rose Marie, 1301. Fine heavy stems with large rich rose fluffy flowers. 1½-2 ft. tall. Pkt. 25¢; large pkt. 75¢.
Extra-Early Navy Blue, 1302. That deep navy blue so hard to get in flowers. Blooms 4 inches in diameter, full double with curled petals. Blooms in August. 20 inches tall. Pkt. 25¢; large pkt. 75¢.

THREE DREER SPECIAL ASTERS

Dreer's Peerless Pink, 1335. Well branched plants 2½ ft. tall. Large, double, rich pink flowers. An old favorite, still among the best of all annual Asters. Pkt. 15¢; large pkt. 50¢; ¼ oz. 90¢.
Heart of France, 1305. The largest of the deep ruby-red Asters. Bushy plants 2 ft. tall bloom from September until frost. Pkt. 15¢; large pkt. 50¢; ¼ oz. 90¢.
Sensation, 1337. Blooms in August and September. Plants are covered with double 3½ inch garnet-red blooms. 18 inches tall. Pkt. 15¢; large pkt. 50¢; ¼ oz. 90¢.

Aster—Peerless Pink

$\mathscr{D}$reer's SUPREME ASTERS

Aster—American Beauty

American Beauty Asters

One of the finest Asters. Starts to bloom in September and continues until heavy frost. Vigorous plants with large, fully double, flat petalled flowers. 3 ft. tall.
Pkt. 20¢; large pkt. 60¢; ¼ oz. $1.00.

Azure Blue, 1261. Purple, 1265.
Crimson, 1263. Shell Pink, 1267.
Deep Rose, 1264. White, 1269.
Finest Mixed, 1270.
COLLECTION, 4736. Buy one 20¢ pkt. each of the 6 colors for $1.00.

Dwarf Hardy Aster, Alpinus, 1394. Mixed. Dwarf plants 6 to 10 inches tall. Daisy-like flowers in shades of blue and white. Blooms during May and June. Good for sunny Rock Gardens. Pkt. 25¢.

Aubrietia—Leichtlini

Royal Asters

An early-flowering type. Blooms from July until frost. Fine for beds and borders and their long-stemmed flowers are ideal for cutting. 2 ft. tall.
Pkt. 15¢; large pkt. 50¢; ¼ oz. 75¢.

Azure Blue, 1351. Scarlet, 1354.
Purple, 1356. Shell Pink, 1358.
Rich Rose, 1357. White, 1359.
Mixed Colors, 1360.
COLLECTION, 4748. Buy one 15¢ pkt. each of the 6 colors for 75¢.

American Late Branching Asters

Fully double flat petalled flowers measuring 5 inches in diameter on well-branched plants 2 to 2½ ft. tall. Blooms during September and October.
Pkt. 15¢; large pkt. 50¢; ¼ oz. 75¢.

Azure Blue, 1321. Deep Pink, 1327.
Deep Crimson, 1323. Shell Pink, 1328.
Deep Purple, 1326. Pure White, 1329.
Finest Mixed, 1330.
COLLECTION, 4744. Buy one 15¢ pkt. each of the 6 colors for 75¢.
Pelletized Seed, Aster, Late Branching Mixed, P1330. Pkt. 20¢.

The Beautiful New Princess Asters

New cutting type of Asters growing 2 to 2½ ft. tall. The flowers have a full, deep, crested center surrounded by several rows of dainty plume-like, ray petals. Blooms from August until frost.

Princess Anne, 1366. Peachblossom. Princess Linda, 1374. Clear rose.
Princess Barbara, 1367. Orchid. Princess Marsha, 1370. Scarlet.
Princess Bonnie, 1368. Salmon-rose. Princess Mixed, 1372.
All colors. Pkt. 25¢.
COLLECTION, 4755. Buy one 25¢ pkt. each of the 5 colors for $1.00.

Aster—Queen of the Market

AUBRIETIA
Rainbow Rock Cress

Beautiful, dwarf rock plant covered with sheets of bright flowers in spring and early summer; 6 inches. Perennial.
Bouganvillei, 1407. Large blue flowers. Pkt. 15¢.
Leichtlini, 1408. Carmine-rose. Pkt. 15¢.
I pkt. each above two varieties, 25¢.
Mixed, 1411. A complete mixture of many fine colors. Pkt. 15¢; 2 pkts. 25¢.

ARABIS
Rock Cress

Alpina, 1231. Delightful compact 6-inch plants covered with showy four-petalled white blooms in April-May. Ideal for Rock and Wall Gardens. Perennial. Pkt. 10¢; ¼ oz. 35¢.
Rosea, 1233. Large rose-colored blooms on 8-inch plants. Perennial. Pkt. 25¢.

Favorite Flowers in Color. 800 natural color photos, 640 pages. $4.95, postpaid.

Queen of the Market Aster

Ballet Queen, 1342. Deep salmon-rose 3½ inch flowers on compact plants. Useful for bedding and cutting. Pkt. 25¢.
Queen of the Market Mixed, 1350. The earliest Aster, starts to bloom in July. Full double, flat petalled flowers 2½ to 3 inches across. 15 inches tall. Pkt. 15¢; large pkt. 50¢; ¼ oz. 75¢.

Arabis—Alpina

11

Arctotis—Grandis

Arctotis

African Daisy

Grandis, 1237. (Blue-Eyed African Daisy.) Large white blooms. Annual daisy with pale lilac-blue on the reverse of each petal. 2 ft. high. Pkt. 15¢; 2 pkts. 25¢.
Hybrids Mixed, 1240. Blooms 2½ to 3 inches across in a variety of showy colors. Does well in dry soil. 8 to 12 inches. July to frost. Annual. Pkt. 25¢; 2 pkts. 45¢.
Anthemis, Kelwayi, 1123. (Golden Marguerite.) Bright yellow daisy-like flowers from June until October. Easy to grow and perfectly hardy. Exceptionally fine for cutting. 2 ft. tall. Pkt. 15¢; 2 pkts. 25¢.
Balloon Vine, Halicacabum, 1419. (Cardiospermum.) Annual climber with airy, small white flowers followed by showy, green balloon-like seed pods. Light green foliage. Pkt. 20¢.
Bells of Ireland, 1507. (Molucella lavevis.) A curious yet attractive plant with deep green calyces attractively veined with lighter green and a two-lipped white flower in each. Blooms during July and August. Dry for use in winter bouquets. 2 ft. tall. Annual. Pkt. 35¢; 2 pkts. 60¢.
Bartonia, Aurea, 1451. (Blazing Star.) Brilliant, large, golden-yellow flowers with prominent stamens and downy thistle-like foliage. 1½-2 ft. tall. Annual. Pkt. 25¢.

Balsam—Double Camellia Flowered

Bushy annual plants with bright green foliage that frames the fully double camellia-like flowers to perfection. Flowers are borne along the stems. Good for shade. 2 feet.
Double Salmon Prince, 1425.   Double Scarlet, 1427.   Double Violet, 1428.
Double White, 1429.   Double Finest Mixed, 1430.
Pkt. 10¢. Any 3 pkts. 25¢.

Double Bush Balsam

Grows 18 inches tall with flowers on end of the stems instead of half hidden by foliage. A lovely taller edging plant.
Rose, 1435.   Scarlet, 1436.   White, 1438.   Mixed, 1433.
Pkt. 15¢; 2 pkts. 25¢.

12

Begonias—Fibrous Rooted
Pkt. 50¢.

Attractive bedding plants. Ideal window garden plants, constantly in bloom. 9 to 12 inches in height. Blooms outdoors from May until frost. Seed is very fine, sow on surface and cover pot with glass.
Christmas Cheer, 1463. Bright crimson-scarlet.
Salmon Queen, 1475. Salmon-pink.
White Pearl, 1478. The best white.
Mixed, 1480. Both green and bronze-leaved sorts.

BAPTISIA, Australis, 1449. (False Indigo.) Spikes of dark blue Lupine-like flowers during June. Pkt. 15¢; 2 pkts. 25¢.

Bellis—English Double Daisy

Bellis and Pansies, the perfect spring bedding and border plants. Sow seed in July-August and transplant before severe cold. Full double daisy flowers on 5-inch plants. Sun or half shade. Blooms in May and June. Pkt. 25¢; 2 pkts. 45¢.

Giant Double Red, 1492.   Giant Double White, 1494.
Giant Double Rose, 1493.   Giant Double Mixed, 1496.

Anthemis

Bellis

BOCCONIA, Cordata, 1511. (Plume Poppy.) Tall hardy perennial. Creamy yellow, plume-like flowers in July and August. 6 ft. tall. Pkt. 15¢.
BRACHYCOME. Illustrated in natural color, page IV.
BROWALLIA, Sapphire, 1535. Compact plants 9 inches tall, covered with dark blue, white-eyed flowers. Blooms continuously. Annual. Pkt. 25¢.
BROWALLIA, Elata, Blue, 1539. Sturdy plants 20 inches tall with pretty violet-blue flowers. Annual. Pkt. 20¢.
CACTUS, Mixed, 1547. Includes many attractive and interesting varieties. Easy to grow from seed sown indoors in pans of very sandy soil. Pkt. 25¢.
CALCEOLARIA, Dreer's Perfection, 1550. (Fisherman's Basket.) Greenhouse or window garden plants with pocket-shaped pink and yellow flowers generally spotted brown. Seed is very fine, do not cover, and water from the bottom. Pkt. 50¢.
CALLIRHOE, Involucrata, 1624. (Poppy Mallow.) Vigorous hardy perennial a foot tall and rambling over the ground. Covered with bright rosy-crimson poppy-like flowers during summer and fall. Pkt. 15¢; large pkt. 50¢.

Bush Flowered Balsam

Colorful Calendulas

Showy cream, yellow and orange, double daisy-like flowers. Bloom best in cool weather. Start early and after their first riot of bloom in June, pinch back for even finer bloom in September and October. Hardy annuals that may be planted outdoors as soon as the ground can be worked. 12-18 inches.

Apricot Queen, 1561. Very large, broad-petalled blooms, bright apricot. Pkt. 10¢.
Lemon Queen, 1591. Rich lemon-yellow. Pkt. 10¢.
Orange King, 1597. Rich orange-red. Pkt. 10¢.
Double Mixed, 1600. All colors. Pkt. 10¢; ½ oz. 35¢.
PELLETIZED SEED, Calendula Double Mixed, P1600. Pkt. 20¢.

Pacific Beauty Calendulas

A new strain that blooms in hot weather. Pkt. 25¢; 5 for $1.00.

Apricot Beauty, 1576. Apricot shades.
Cream Beauty, 1577. Creamy-white shading to soft yellow.
Lemon Beauty, 1578. Lemon yellow.
Persimmon Beauty, 1579. Persimmon orange.
Pacific Beauty Mixture, 1580. All colors.
COLLECTION, 4761. One packet each of the 4 colors, 80¢.

Calendula—Pacific Beauty

Newer Calendulas

Campfire, 1565. (Sensation.) Extra large, rich orange flowers with faint scarlet sheen. Pkt. 15¢.
Chrysantha or Sunshine, 1567. Globular buttercup-yellow blooms with long wide petals. Pkt. 10¢.
Orange Sunshine, 1568. Bright orange of exceptional brilliance. Pkt. 10¢.
Orange Fantasy, 1572. Crested, coppery orange with mahogany red edges. Pkt. 10¢.
Yellow Colossal, 1598. Exceptionally large, fully double, yellow flowers. Pkt. 15¢.
Dreer's Surprise Mixture, 1601. A wonderful assortment of color. Pkt. 15¢; ½ oz. 40¢; oz. 75¢.
COLLECTION, 4760. A packet each of the 5 colors for 50¢.

CARDINAL CLIMBER, 1757. Pretty annual climber with brilliant cardinal red blooms from midsummer until frost. Will grow 20 to 30 feet tall. Does best in full sun. Pkt. 15¢; large pkt. 50¢; ¼ oz. $1.25.
PELLETIZED SEED, Cardinal Climber, P1757. Pkt. 20¢.

Gay and Cheerful Calliopsis

Calliopsis

Hardy annuals of easiest culture. Cosmos-like flowers in shades of yellow with mahogany markings. They bloom in six weeks and if the faded flowers are picked will bloom all summer. Do not confuse with "Coreopsis grandiflora" which is perennial.

Pkt. 15¢; ¼ oz. 25¢; oz. 75¢.
Golden Crown, 1614. Brilliant golden yellow with glossy maroon center zone. 2 ft. tall.
Marmorata, 1615. Bright gold marbled with wallflower red.
Nigra Speciosa, 1616. Reddish maroon.
Tinctoria Splendens, 1617. Large yellow blooms with extra-large brown-black centers. Blooms all summer long. 3½ ft. tall.
Tall Varieties Mixed, 1620.
Alldouble Mixed, 1619. 2½ ft. tall. Pkt. 15¢; ¼ oz. 35¢; oz. $1.00.
Dwarf Crimson King, 1604. Compact plants 9 to 12 inches tall. Covered with large crimson blooms. Pkt. 10¢.
Dwarf Varieties Mixed, 1610. Pkt. 10¢.
COLLECTION, 4762. Buy one pkt. of the 5 named varieties (no mixtures) for 55¢.

Hardy Carnations

Carnations all summer. Seed started indoors in February will bloom the first season.
CHABAUD'S GIANT DOUBLE. Richly clove-scented, double 2-inch blooms. 2 ft.

Blood Red, 1761.	Rose, 1765.	White, 1768.
Deep Salmon, 1764.	Scarlet, 1767.	Yellow, 1769.

Finest Mixed, 1770. Pkt. 15¢; large pkt. 60¢.
COLLECTION, 4780. Buy one 15¢ pkt. of six colors for 75¢.
Giant Marguerite Carnation, Mixed, 1786. Showy, large fragrant flowers. Many fine colors, bloom all summer long. Pkt. 15¢; large pkt. 50¢.
Enfant de Nice, Finest Mixed, 1780. Large double blooms in many showy colors. Often grown as an annual. 15 inches tall. Pkt. 25¢.
GRENADIN. Dwarf compact plants covered during the summer and fall with attractive double blooms. Blooms first year. 1 ft. Pkt. 25¢; large pkt. 75¢.

Bright Scarlet, 1787.	King of the Blacks, 1789.	White, 1793.
Golden Sun, 1788.	Rose Queen, 1791.	Mixed, 1800.

Double Hardy Border, Mixed, 1796. Vigorous plants 15 inches tall. Flowers are full double, sweet scented and include all carnation colors. Pkt. 25¢.
Perpetual Giants, 1797. Almost as large as Greenhouse Carnations. Pkt. 25¢.

Hardy Carnations

13

CAMPANULA – *Canterbury Bells*

Campanula–Medium

Campanula–Medium

Bell-shaped, cup and saucer or double flowers borne on spikes. Bloom June and July. Hardy biennial, blooming the second season. 2½-3 ft. tall. Will generally reseed and come up year after year.

CAMPANULA MEDIUM SINGLE, Bell-shaped flowers.

Dark Blue, 1681.	Rose, 1685.
Light Blue, 1683.	White, 1687.

Pkt. 10¢.

COLLECTION, 4770. Buy one pkt. each of the 4 colors, for 35¢.
Single Mixed, 1690. All colors. Pkt. 10¢; ¼ oz. 60¢.
Double Mixed, 1680. Showy double blooms. Pkt. 15¢; 2 pkts. 25¢.
CAMPANULA CALYCANTHEMA. Cup and saucer-shaped blooms on fine long spikes.

Dark Blue, 1661.	Rose-Pink, 1665.
Light Blue, 1663.	White, 1667.

Pkt. 15¢; 2 pkts. 25¢.

Finest Mixed, 1670. Pkt. 15¢; ¼ oz. 85¢.
COLLECTION, 4768. One pkt. each of the 4 colors, for 45¢.
ANNUAL CANTERBURY BELLS, Mixed, 1700. Annual Canterbury Bells that bloom in six months after seeds are sown. Start seed indoors in February for bloom in July. Pkt. 15¢.

CACALIA Mixed, 1542. (Tassel Flower.) A graceful annual blooming from June until September. Showy little golden yellow and scarlet flowerheads. 1½ ft. tall. Pkt. 25¢.
CANARY BIRD VINE, 1707. Annual climber with fringed yellow blooms during summer and fall. For early blooms start indoors in pots in March. 6-8 ft. tall. Pkt. 25¢.
CORAL FLOWER, 2014. (Talinum paniculatum.) A mass of dark emerald green leaves from which extend 30-inch stems with 5 pointed star-shaped, rose pink flowers followed by coral-like seed pods. Pkt. 25¢.
CATANANCHE, Coerulea, 1811. (Cupid's Dart.) A slender-stemmed hardy perennial with attractive sky blue flowers, in September. 18 inches tall. Good in dry places. Pkt. 15¢.
CENTRANTHUS, Macrosiphon, 1908. Annual with pretty, slender-tubed, pink flowers in dense clusters from June until August. 1 to 2 ft. Pkt. 20¢.

Cheiranthus

Allioni, 1915. (Fairy Wallflower.) Showy biennial about 12 inches tall covered with brilliant orange flower trusses in late spring and summer. Pkt. 10¢.
Linifolius, 1919. (Alpine Wallflower.) Bushy plants, 1 ft. high; covered with showy, light violet flowers in late spring and summer. Pkt. 20¢.
CERASTIUM, Tomentosum, 1911. Pretty, hardy, dwarf, white-leaved edging or rock plant covered with small white blooms. May-June, 12 to 15 inches tall. Pkt. 15¢.

Annual Chrysanthemum – *Painted Daisies*

Bushy, annuals, 2 ft. tall that bear colorful, daisy-like blooms throughout the summer. Easiest culture, sow seed in early May where they are to grow. Pkts. 10¢ each.
Burridgeanum, 1921. Pure white petals zoned rich brownish red and yellow.
Chameleon, 1923. Light yellow to tawny apricot with garnet band and yellow zone.
Eldorado, 1924. Deep canary yellow flowers with black center.
Helios, 1925. Sunflower yellow.
Northern Star, 1928. Pure white with canary yellow zone and brown eye.
Purpureum, 1929. Rich velvety purple with a yellow halo around the center.
Single Annual Mixed, 1930. Pkt. 10¢.
COLLECTION, 4798. Buy one packet each of the 6 varieties for 50¢.
MERRY MIXTURE, 1931. Pkt. 25¢. See page V for full color illustration.

Campanula – Carpatica

Campanula – Garganica

HARDY CAMPANULA. Hardy perennials that bloom year after year. Use the dwarf sorts as edging plants and in Rock Gardens; tall sorts for back ground planting.
Carpatica Blue, 1633. (Harebell.) Free-flowering from June through October. Clear blue, bell-shaped flowers. 12 inches. Pkt. 15¢.
Carpatica Alba, 1631. Snow white. Pkt. 15¢.
Persicifolia Blue, 1643. (Peachbell.) Large blue, bell-shaped flowers in June-July on 2 to 3 foot spikes. Pkt. 15¢.
Persicifolia White, 1641. 2 ft. Pkt. 15¢.
Persicifolia, Telham Beauty, 1647. Immense bell-shaped flowers of pale china blue, on long stems. A very showy tetraploid variety. 2 ft. June-July. Pkt. 25¢; large pkt. 75¢.
Pyramidalis Blue, 1651. (Chimney Bellflower.) Beautiful blue salver-shaped flowers on plants 4 to 5 ft. tall. Pkt. 15¢.
Pyramidalis White, 1649. Pkt. 15¢.
Rotundifolia, 1655. (Bluebells of Scotland.) Masses of large, clear blue flowers from June to August. 1 ft. Pkt. 25¢.
Garganica Major, 1636. Trailing plants with light blue flowers during June and July. Fine for Rock Gardens. Pkt. 25¢.

Cacalia – Mixed

CELOSIA – *Cockscomb*

Easily grown, hardy annuals in bloom from July until frost. For sun or half-shade. Start seed indoors in February-March or sow outdoors April-May.

Dwarf Crested Cockscomb—*Celosia cristata*

Forms massive cockscomb-like flowerheads; splendid for beds and to dry for winter bouquets. 12 inches.
Empress, 1824. Rich deep crimson. Pkt. 15¢.
Golden Queen, 1828. Rich yellow. Pkt. 15¢.
Dwarf Mixed, 1830. All colors. Fine. Pkt. 15¢.
TALL CRESTED COCKSCOMB, Royal Velvet, 1826. Sturdy plants with rich carmine-crimson flowerheads and red-margined bronzy green foliage. 2½ ft. Pkt. 25¢.

Chinese Woolflower

Bushy plants 2½ to 3 ft. tall with showy, rounded, wooly flowerheads. Pkt. 15¢; 2 for 25¢.

Crimson, 1831. Pink, 1833. Yellow, 1837. Mixed, 1840.

Chinese Woolflower

Gilbert's Celosia

A brand new strain with brand new colors. Pkt. 25¢; 3 for 60¢.
Gilbert's Rose Beauty, 1834. Extra-large bright rose flower-heads.
Gilbert's Maple Gold, 1829. Honey-yellow, gold and light orange.
Gilbert's Green Gold. Silvery light rose shaded with gold. .

Centaurea Imperialis—*Royal Sweet Sultan*

Thistle-like blooms on 2½ ft. bushy plants. Lovely cut flowers.
Amaranth Red, 1891.   Deep Purple, 1894.
Brilliant Rose, 1892.   Yellow (Suaveolens), 1901.
Deep Lavender, 1893.   White, 1896.
   Finest Mixed, 1900. Pkt. 15¢; ¼ oz. 75¢.
COLLECTION, 4796. Buy one 15¢ pkt. of each color, for 75¢.

Feathered Cockscomb—*Celosia plumosa*

Gorgeous, red gold and yellow plumes from July until frost.
Magnifica, Golden Plume, 1845. Extra large, bright golden yellow plumes. 3 ft. Pkt. 10¢.
Magnifica, Scarlet Plume, 1847. Graceful, feathery, brilliant scarlet plumes on sturdy plants. 3 ft. Pkt. 10¢.
Magnifica Mixed, 1852. Many fine colors. 3 ft. Pkt. 10¢.
Lilliput, Fire Feather, 1853. Brilliant fiery red. Bushy 18 inch plants. Pkt. 20¢.
Lilliput, Golden Feather, 1855. Brilliant golden yellow. 18 inch. Pkt. 20¢.
Pyramidalis, Flame of Fire, 1859. Compact plants with heavy, rounded plumes of deepest fiery scarlet. 18 inches. Pkt. 25¢.

Hardy Centaurea

Macrocephala, 1903. Large thistle-like flowers, fine for cutting. Plants grow 3 ft. tall and are perfectly hardy bloom in June. Pkt. 15¢.
Montana, 1904. (Perennial Cornflower, Mountain Bluet.) That rare perennial that blooms from July until September. Violet blue flowers on long stems. 2 ft. tall. Pkt. 15¢.

Dusty Millers

Centaurea White-Leaved

Bushy plants with finely cut dusty foliage. For borders, beds and porch boxes. Start indoors in February.
Candidissima, 1861. 15 inches tall, showy, white wooly foliage and yellow flowers. Annual. Pkt. 20¢.
Gymnocarpa, 1863. Hardy in warmer sections with cut-leaf silvery foliage and rosy-purple flowers. 2 ft. Pkt. 10¢.
CENTAUREA, Americana, 1865. Lacy, rose-lavender blooms 4 inches across on sturdy 3-ft. plants. July to September. Unopened buds look like small tightly woven baskets. Annual. Pkt. 10¢.
Americana, White, 1866. Pkt. 10¢.

Cobaea—Scandens

Cineraria Hybrid

House or conservatory plants with daisy-like flowers. Blooms March-April. Sow seed anytime from May to September.
Cremers' Wilt-Resistant Prize Strain, 1954. Free flowering and wide range of colors. Pkt. 50¢; large pkt. $2.00.
Dreer's Prize Super-Giant, Mixed, 1962. Compact plants with immense flowers in many beautiful colors. Pkt. 50¢.

Cléome

CLEOME, Spider Flower, Giant Pink Queen, 1998. Hardy annual 3 ft. tall with huge trusses of bright salmon-pink flowers all summer. Reseeds and comes up year after year.
Lutea, 1996. Perennial Cleome with feathery yellow blooms all summer. 1 ft. Either Variety, pkt. 15¢.

COBAEA, Scandens, Purple, 2001. (Cup and saucer vine.) Rapidly growing climber with canterbury-bell-like, dark blue blooms. Grows 30 to 40 ft. and blooms all summer. Plant seed edgewise as soon as weather is warm. Pkt. 15¢; large pkt. 40¢.

15

Cosmos Planting

COSMOS *For Cutting*

For armloads of cut flowers in late summer and fall plant Cosmos. The more you pick the more they bloom. Sow seeds outdoors as soon as ground can be worked and then thin or transplant to stand 12 to 18 inches apart.

EARLY DOUBLE. Pkt. 25¢.
Carnelia, 2026. Rich rosy crimson.
Peachblossom, 2027. Deep rosy pink.
Whirlwind, 2028. Pure white.
Early Double Mixed, 2030.
COLLECTION, 4806. Buy one pkt. each of the 3 colors for 60¢.
Double Sensation Mixed, 2031. Extra early large, flowering double Cosmos. All colors. Pkt. 25¢.
RADIANCE, The new Cosmos, also Single Cosmos see page V.

Orange and Yellow Cosmos

Early Orange Flare, 2049. Well-branched plants 3 to 4 ft. tall, bloom from July until frost. Brilliant orange flowers, 2 inches across. Marigold-like foliage. Pkt. 15¢.
Early Orange Ruffles, 2050. Like Orange Flare but with an extra row of petals at the center. Brilliant orange. July until frost. Pkt. 15¢.
Early Yellow Ruffles, 2053. Golden yellow, semi-double blooms. Pkt. 15¢.

Clarkia Elegans—Double

Pretty, easily grown annuals with double, rose-like flowers along the stems. Does well in poor soil. 2-2½ ft. Pkt. 10¢.

Alba, 1981. Pure white.
Illumination, 1985. Orange-rose.
Purple Prince, 1987. Deep purple.

Scarlet Queen, 1989. Bright scarlet.
Salmonea, 1988. Rich salmon.
Double Mixed, 1990. Pkt. 10¢.

COLLECTION, 4802. Buy one 10¢ pkt. each of the 5 varieties for 40¢.
CLEMATIS, Mandshurica, 1994. Hardy Bush Clematis 2 to 3 ft. high bearing fragrant, pure white flowers in large clusters. Blooms all summer. Pkt. 25¢.
COLEUS, Dreer's Hybrids, 2010. Beautifully colored leaves, no two plants alike. Red, green and yellow in varying combinations. Use as pot or box plants or for sunny edges. Start seed indoors in March. Annual. 1 ft. Pkt. 25¢.
COLLINSIA, Mixed, 2007. Bushy annual from California that bears pagoda-like flowers in shades of white, rose and blue. Blooms June-July and likes moist location. Pkt. 10¢.

Coreopsis

A hardy perennial that blooms intermittently from June to frost. Full sun or partial shade. A splendid cut flower.
Lanceolata Grandiflora, 2021. Old-fashioned favorite with large showy bright yellow flowers. Pkt. 15¢.
Mayfield Giants, 2023. Considerably larger blooms than Lanceolata but not quite so free blooming. 30 inches. Pkt. 15¢.
Double Sunburst, 2025. Almost full double, brilliant yellow flowers on long stems. 2 ft. Pkt. 15¢.
CUPHEA, Firefly, 2080. (Firecracker Plant.) Bushy annual plants about 1 ft. tall with bright scarlet, tubular flowers. Pkt. 15¢.
CYPRESS VINE, Mixed, 2120. (Ipomoea Quamoclit.) Annual climber with delicate fern-like foliage. Star-shaped scarlet and white flowers from July until frost. 15 ft. Pkt. 15¢.

Chinese Forget-Me-Not
Cynoglossum

Easy to grow. Sow outdoors in May, blooms all summer. Small four-petalled forget-me-not-like flowers on bushy plants.
Firmament, 2103. Compact bushy plants with rich blue flowers, 18 inches tall. Pkt. 15¢; ¼ oz. 40¢.
Amabile Blue, 2107. Heavy sprays of fragrant deep blue flowers. 18 to 24 inches tall. Pkt. 10¢; ¼ oz. 25¢; oz. 75¢.
Pink, 2109. Rich, deep pink blooms. Pkt. 15¢.
Linifolium, 2104. White flowers 1 ft. tall. Pkt. 10¢.
CYCLAMEN, Dreer's Giant Prize, 2100. Prize winning mixture of the best strains from the best growers. Pkt. 50¢; large pkt. (100 seeds) $3.00.

Chinese Forget-Me-Not—Firmament

Coreopsis Grandiflora—Double Sunburst

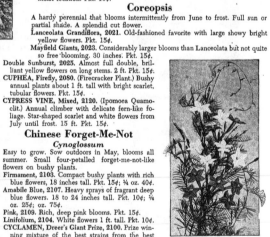

Cypress Vine

16

World's Finest
DELPHINIUMS

From California, Washington, England and Holland come the world's finest Delphiniums to grace your garden. For the largest spikes of large double flowers, grow the Giant Pacific Hybrids. For more spikes (not quite so large) with a full array of color and double and single flowers with "bees," grow Dreer's De Luxe Hybrids. For a continuous supply of cut flowers grow the sky blue Belladonna and deep blue Bellamosum. The Chinese varieties are also good cut flowers. Sow seed in well prepared beds from May until September. Transplant to their permanent position when large enough to handle.

Dreer's Giant Pacific Hybrids

Magnificent flower spikes closely set with 2 to 2½ inch flowers. Blooms are about 90 per cent double. Vigorous, very uniform, from 5 to 7 ft. tall.
Pkt. 50¢; Large Pkt. $1.50.

Black Knight, 2164. The darkest violet blue.
Blue Jay, 2162. Fascinating blue shades from light to dark, all with dark bee.
Blue Bird, 2167. The huge spikes of medium blue flowers with white bees.
Cameliard, 2167. Pure lavender self with white bee.
Galahad, 2161. Clear white blooms, averaging 3 inches.
Guinevere, 2163. Beautiful light pinkish-lavender with white bee.
King Arthur, 2165. Brilliant rich violet with white bee.
Round Table Series, 2170. A superb mixture of all the above varieties.
Summer Skies, 2169. That rare blue of a summer sky with white bee.
Giant Pacific Hybrids Mixed, 2180. All shades, all types collected from specimen plants that are used for crossing. Pkt. 50¢; large pkt. $1.50; ⅛ oz. $2.50.

Giant Pacific Delphiniums

Pacific Mixtures

Dark Blue Shades, 2171.
Light Blue Shades, 2173.
Mid-Blue Shades, 2175.
Lavender Pastel Shades, 2176.
Pure White, 2179.
Pkt. 50¢; large pkt. $1.50; ⅛ oz. $2.50.
COLLECTION, 4816. Buy one pkt. each of the 5 colors, for $2.15.
Dreer's De Luxe Hybrid Delphinium, 2160. Our own strain of Hybrid Delphiniums gives a wider range of colors and types than any other mixture. Base branching with many fine spikes per plant. Pkt. 25¢; large pkt. 75¢.

Various Delphiniums

Belladonna Improved, 2135. (Cliveden Beauty.) Sky blue flowers on long stems. 3 ft. Pkt. 25¢; large pkt. 60¢; ¼ oz. $1.50.

Bellamosum, 2137. Deep rich blue. Pkt. 15¢; large pkt. 50¢.

Chinese Delphinium

Chinese Album, 2141. Pure white flowers. Blooms from July to September. Will bloom the first year. 2 ft. Pkt. 15¢; large pkt. 40¢.
Blue Mirror, 2150. New Chinese Delphinium with bright navy blue, spurless flowers. Flowers face upward on 12-in. stems. Grow this for lovely cut flowers all summer. Pkt. 25¢.
Cambridge Blue, 2143. A rich clear blue. Pkt. 15¢; large pkt. 50¢.
Blue Butterfly Improved, 2147. Rich aquamarine blue flowers on plants 20 inches high. Pkt. 15¢; large pkt. 50¢; ¼ oz. 75¢.

Didiscus Blue Lace Flower

Coeruleus, 2311. Showy Australian annual bearing lacy, light lavender flower heads from July to frost. Excellent for borders and cutting. 18 inches. Pkt. 10¢; large pkt. 30¢.

Blue Lace Flower

Grow Dahlias From Seed

Coltness, Mignon and Unwin Dahlias are as easy to grow from seed as Zinnias and bloom as quickly. Bushy plants 18 inches to 20 inches tall, with brightly colored flowers 3 inches across on good cutting stems. The larger flowered sorts do not bloom the first year but may produce new varieties. Start seed indoors in March or sow outdoors as soon as ground is warm.
Coltness Hybrids, 2122. Dwarf single type which will bloom in 3 months. All bright colors, reds, yellow and crimson. Pkt. 15¢.
Mignon, 2123. Compact plants, covered with showy single flowers. Pkt. 15¢.

Giant Perfection, Mixed, 2124. Single flowers of immense size, measuring 6 inches in diameter. Pkt. 20¢; large pkt. 40¢.
Double Cactus, 2126. Seed saved from the best exhibition varieties, many rich colors, all true Cactus form. Pkt. 25¢; large pkt. 75¢.
Double Decorative, 2128. Seeds from a superb collection of Decorative Dahlias. Pkt. 25¢; large pkt. 75¢.
Unwin's Dwarf Hybrids, 2130. Semi-double flowers in many shades of red, pink, yellow and purple. Pkt. 25¢.

Dahlia—Coltness Hybrid

DIANTHUS *Pinks for Fragrance*

Easily grown free-blooming annuals in bloom from June to frost, and sweet scented, too. For beds, borders and for cutting. 12 to 15 inches.

ANNUAL PINKS

Heddewigi, Single Mixed, 2226. Large, single blooms. All colors. Pkt. 10¢; large pkt. 30¢; ¼ oz. 50¢.

Laciniatus Splendens, 2227. Large single, fringed, crimson flowers with white eyes. Pkt. 10¢; large pkt. 40¢.

Laciniatus, Single Mixed, 2229. Large single flowers more than 2 inches across. All colors with deeply fringed or laciniated flower petals. Pkt. 10¢.

Double Fireball, 2203. Rich fire-red blooms with fringed edges. Pkt. 15¢.

Double Mourning Cloak, 2207. Deep velvety crimson with white edge. Pkt. 15¢.

Double Salmon King, 2211. Fringed salmon-rose blooms. Pkt. 15¢.

Double Snowball, 2213. Fringed pure white. Pkt. 15¢.

Double Gaiety, 2206. New annual Pink with beautifully marked, fringed double blooms in many color combinations. Pkt. 15¢.

Double Chinensis, Giant Mixed, 2200. (China or India Pink.) Extra-double flowers many bright colors. Pkt. 10¢; large pkt. 30¢; ¼ oz. 50¢.

Double Heddewigi Mixed, 2204. Colorful mixture from delicate rose to velvety crimson. Pkt. 10¢; large pkt. 30¢; ¼ oz. 50¢.

COLLECTION, 4826. 1 packet each of the 5 double separate colors for only 30¢.

DIANTHUS hybridus

Sweet Wivelsfield, 2246. Hardy Dianthus, individual blooms as large Dianthus borne in heads like Sweet William, many colors. Will bloom first year if sown early. 1 ft. Pkt. 15¢.

Double Sweet Wivelsfield, 2247. Double-flowering strain of the above. Pkt. 15¢.

DIANTHUS, Heddensis. A new strain combining the large open flowers of Dianthus Heddewigi with the rapid growth of Dianthus Chinensis. 2-inch flowers on plants 16 inches tall and blooms freely all summer.

Westwood Beauty, 2238. Showy crimson and scarlet shades. Pkt. 15¢.

Mixed, 2240. Many splendid colors. Pkt. 15¢.

Dianthus—Plumarius

Dicentra—Eximia

Dianthus—Heddewigi

HARDY PINKS

One of the oldest and most useful of perennial flowers. Perfectly hardy; seldom troubled by insects or diseases. The different varieties are at home anywhere, walls, rock gardens, semishade, in big borders or ribbon beds. Sweet scented and fine for cutting.

Latifolius atroccineus, fl. pl., 2243. (Everblooming Annual Sweet William.) Brilliant velvety, crimson-scarlet double blooms. Blooms first year. 12 inches. Pkt. 15¢.

Allwoodi Alpinus, 2251. Single and semidouble fragrant blooms on 4 to 6 inch plants. Pkt. 25¢.

Caesius, 2253. (Cheddar Pinks.) Dense tufts of grass-like foliage; sweet-scented rosepink blooms. May-June. 6 inches tall. Pkt. 15¢.

Deltoides Brilliant, 2257. (Maiden Pink.) Brilliant carmine flowers in June and July. 6 inches tall. Pkt. 25¢.

Plumarius Spring Beauty, 2261. Large Carnation-like blooms. Fully double and richly fragrant. All colors. Pkt. 20¢.

Plumarius Semperflorens, 2262. (Ever-blooming Hardy Garden Pink.) Single, semi-double, and double blooms in a great diversity of colors. 18 inches tall. Pkt. 15¢; large pkt. 50¢.

Plumarius Single Mixed, 2266. (Grass Pink, Scotch Pink, Pheasant Eye Pink.) The true old-fashioned pink. Beautiful single fringed flowers in various colors. 18 inches. Pkt. 10¢.

Winteri, 2254. New hardy pink with sweet scented, pure white flowers. Blooms first year from seed. 12 inches. Pkt. 25¢.

Rock Garden Species, Mixed, 2300. All the best varieties of dwarf growth. Pkt. 25¢.

DICTAMNUS, Rose, 2305. (Gas Plant.) Hardy perennial with large bushy plants 3 ft. high bearing showy rosy-pink flower spikes during June and July. (On warm days the leaves give off a volatile oil that may be lit with a match, hence the name.) Pkt. 35¢.

DIMORPHOTHECA—African Golden Daisy

Aurantiaca, 2335. Brilliant, orange-gold blooms with dark halo and disc. Blooms continuously from early summer until late fall. Bushy plants 12 to 15 inches tall. Annual. Pkt. 10¢.

Salmon Beauty, 2339. Rosy salmon flowers. Does best in full sun. Pkt. 20¢.

Aurantiaca, New Hybrids, 2340. Shades of yellow, salmon and orange, 15 inches. Pkt. 10¢.

Double Hybrids Mixed, 2344. Large, double, orange, yellow and salmon flowers. Pkt. 25¢.

DOLICHOS, Darkness, 2347. (Hyacinth Bean.) Heart-shaped leaves and purple-violet flowers and pods. A splendid annual climber. Pkt. 20¢.

DICENTRA Eximia, 2302. (Plumy Bleeding Heart.) Nodding rose-pink blooms above a tuft of graceful leaves. Easy to grow in cool moist soil or a sheltered rock corner where the roots are kept moist. Blooms all summer. Pkt. 25¢.

Digitalis

Digitalis — Foxglove

Handsome biennials with stately flower spikes in June. Flowers have spotted throats. 3-5 ft.

Gloxiniaeflora

Purple, 2317. Pkt. 10¢.   White, 2319. Pkt. 10¢

Rose, 2318. Pkt. 10¢. Mixed Colors, 2320. Pkt. 10¢

Giant Shirley Mixed, 2321. Marvelous strain with extra-large bells. Pkt. 15¢; large pkt. 40¢; ¼ oz. 75¢.

Lutea, 2323. Stocky plants 2 ft. high, with white to yellow blooms. Pkt. 15¢.

ECHINOPS, Ritro, 2361. (Globe Thistle.) Tall hardy perennials with thistle-like foliage crowned with showy globular heads of steel blue flowers. July-September. 5 ft. Pkt. 15¢.

ECHIUM, Blue Bedder, 2363. (Viper's Bugloss.) Bushy annuals, covered with masses of showy bell-shaped bright blue flowers. 2 ft. Pkt. 20¢.

Gaillardia Annual

Lovely annuals and perennials that bloom freely right through the hot summer weather. Grow most any place except dense shade. Fine for cutting. Single and double Daisy-shaped flowers. Sow seed outdoors as soon as ground can be worked.

Picta, Indian Chief, 2427. Large, deep coppery red flowers. 18 inches tall. Pkt. 15¢.

Double Mixed, 2432. (Lorenziana.) Showy, fully double blooms. Rich shades of orange, scarlet and crimson. Pkt. 15¢; large pkt. 35¢; ¼ oz. 60¢.

Single Mixed, 2430. Many lovely color combinations. Pkt. 10¢.

Eschscholtzia — California Poppy

Gaillardia Perennial

Burgundy, 2435. Wine-red flowers on long stems. 2½ ft. tall. Pkt. 15¢.

Grandiflora, Dazzler, 2443. Large bright golden yellow blooms with maroon red centers. 1½ ft. Pkt. 15¢.

Grandiflora, Superb Mixed, 2440. Very fine. Pkt. 10¢.

Grandiflora Compacta, Goblin, 2441. Compact plants 12 to 15 inches tall, with large yellow-bordered deep red flowers. Pkt. 25¢.

Portola Giant Hybrids, 2446. Extra-large, well-rounded blooms of bright bronzy red, edged with a border of golden yellow. 3 ft. Pkt. 15¢.

FELICIA (Agathaea) Bergeriana, 2419. (Kingfisher Daisy.) Annual. Brilliant blue Daisy-like ¾-inch flowers on 6-inch stems. Pkt. 25¢.

ERIGERON, Speciosus Grandiflorus, 2367. (Fleabane.) Large, Daisy-like purple blooms. Blooms from May to October. Perennial. 2½ ft. Pkt. 25¢.

ERINUS, Alpinus, 2365. (Jewel Flower.) Low rosettes, 4 inches high with purple flowers in May and June. Perennial. Pkt. 25¢.

ERYNGIUM, Giganteum, 2370. (Sea Holly.) Greenish white, spiny foliage and steel-blue flowers from June to September. Perennial. 3 ft. tall. Pkt. 20¢.

Eschscholtzia — California Poppy

Just broadcast the seed here and there for a show of satiny bright Poppy-like flowers all summer. Likes full sun. 12 inches tall.

Aurantiaca, 2373. Rich golden yellow. Pkt. 10¢.

Mandarin, 2384. Deep yellow with orange-red reverse. Pkt. 10¢.

Red Chief, 2376. Coppery-red. Pkt. 10¢.

Rosy Queen, 2385. Delicate soft pink. Pkt. 10¢.

Mixed, 2400. Pkt. 10¢; ¼ oz. 25¢; oz. 75¢.

PELLETIZED SEED, California Poppy, P2400. Pkt. 20¢.

Euphorbia

Heterophylla, 2415. (Annual Poinsettia, Mexican Fire Plant.) About mid-summer the top leaves become attractively marked with rich orange-scarlet. 2 to 3 ft. Pkt. 15¢; large pkt. 25¢.

Variegata, 2417. (Snow on the Mountain.) Bright green and white variegated foliage, top leaves white. 2 ft. Pkt. 15¢.

GAZANIA, Hybrids, 2448. Annuals 10 inches high with showy large Daisy-like blooms in yellow and deep orange, all black centers. Pkt. 20¢.

GODETIA, Double Azalea-Flowered Mixed, 2490. (Satin Flower.) Annual plants covered with large double Azalea-like blooms. Blooms June to August and likes poor soil. 2 ft. Pkt. 10¢; large pkt. 30¢.

GLOXINIA, Hybrida Grandiflora Mixed, 2480. Open trumpet-shaped blooms in rich velvety colors. White, pinks, reds and purples. Sow in March to bloom 5 months later. Pkt. 50¢. (See page X for Bulbs.)

Gaillardia Grandiflora

Helichrysum—Strawflower

Geranium—*Pelargonium*
Zonale, Mixed, 2450. Grow your own Geraniums from seed, they will flower first year if started early indoors. You may even find a new variety. 15 inches tall. All colors. Pkt. 25¢.
GERBERA, Jamesoni Hybrids, 2454. (Transvaal Daisy.) Daisy-like flowers, 3 to 4 inches in diameter. Many shades of yellow, orange and scarlet. Pkt. 25¢; large pkt. (100 seeds) 75¢.

Geum—*Avens*
Hardy perennials with double Rose-like flowers blooming through the summer. Will stand semi-shade. 18 inches.
Lady Stratheden, 2459. Double, golden yellow flowers. Pkt. 20¢; large pkt. 60¢.
Mrs. Bradshaw, 2461. Large, double, rich scarlet blooms. Pkt. 15¢.
Prince of Orange, 2463. Glistening, golden orange flowers. Pkt. 25¢.
GILIA, Capitata Reselected, 2467. (Queen Anne's Thimble.) All summer-blooming annual with feathery foliage and globular, light lavender-blue flower heads. 2 ft. Pkt. 10¢.
HIBISCUS, Giant Mixed, 2630. (Marshmallow.) Perennials with flowers 10 to 12 inches in diameter. Grows 5 to 8 ft. tall and blooms from early July until late fall. Pkt. 15¢; large pkt. 50¢.

Gypsophila
Baby's Breath
Annual Varieties
Dainty four petalled flowers on thin stems. Indispensable for cut flower arrangements. Buy by the ounce and sow in any bare spot through the summer. Blooms in six weeks.
Alba Grandiflora, 2539. (Paris Market Strain.) Large pure white flowers ¾ inch across on 18 inch plants. Pkt. 10¢; oz. 25¢; ¼ lb. 75¢.
Covent Garden, 2540. Pure white blooms slightly larger than Alba Grandiflora. Pkt. 15¢; oz. 40¢; ¼ lb. $1.25.
Carmine, 2543. Bright carmine-rose. 18 inches. Pkt. 10¢.
Rose Shades, 2545. 18 inches. Pkt. 10¢.

Gomphrena
Globe Amaranth Mixed, 2478. Clover-blossom-like flowers good for cutting and may be dried for winter bouquets. White, pink, purple and orange in mixture. June to August. 2-3 ft. Pkt. 10¢.

Helichrysum—*Strawflower*
Monstrosum, fl. pl. Double Daisy-shaped blooms with stiff straw-like petals. For summer cutting or dry for winter bouquets. 30 inches tall. Sow where you want them to grow in a sunny spot. Pkt. 15¢.
Buttercup, 2592. Yellow. Silvery Pink, 2597.
Fireball, 2593. Red. Violet Queen, 2598.
Salmon, 2596. White, 2599.
Mixed Colors, 2600. Pkt. 15¢; large pkt. 40¢.
COLLECTION, 4842. One packet each of the 6 colors for 75¢.

Heuchera—Sanguinea

Gypsophila—Alba Grandiflora

Perennial Gypsophila
Oldhamiana, 2551. Bright flesh-pink flowers from midsummer until frost. 3 ft. Pkt. 15¢.
Paniculata, 2555. Tiny white flowers on wire-like stems for mixed bouquets. Blooms the first year if seed is sown early. 3 ft. tall. Pkt. 10¢.
Double White, 2556. Lovely little double blooms in much-branched panicles. Easily dried for winter use. Pkt. 20¢.
Repens, 2558. Hardy trailing plants for walls and rock gardens. With small white blooms during July and August. Pkt. 15¢.
Repens Rosea, 2559. Deep rose blooms. Pkt. 15¢.

Gomphrena—Globe Amaranth

HELIOTROPE, Choice Mixed, 2608. (Cherry Pie.) Delightfully fragrant, large blue and white flower heads. Grow in pots, porch boxes or beds. 2 ft. Pkt. 20¢.
HELIOPSIS, Pitcheriana, 2605. (Orange Sunflower.) Brilliant single golden-yellow flowers all summer. 3-4 ft. tall. Pkt. 25¢.
HELENIUM, Hoopesii, 2566. Perennials 2 ft. tall with a mass of bright orange Daisy-like flowers in June. Pkt. 25¢.

Heuchera—*Coral Bells*
Showy plants 30 inches tall with graceful pendent bell-like flowers all summer.
Sanguinea Splendens, 2615. Rich coral red blooms on slender graceful stems. Pkt. 25¢.
Sanguinea Hybrids, 2616. White and several shades of rose, pink and red. Pkt. 25¢.
HEMEROCALLIS, Peerless Hybrids, 2614. (Lemon Day-Lily.) Seed collected from only the newer Hybrids. All the best Day-Lily shades. Perfectly hardy. 3-5 ft. Pkt. 25¢.
HUNNEMANNIA, Fumariaefolia, 2673. (Santa Barbara Poppy.) Large, Buttercup-yellow poppy-like blooms from July until frost. The one Poppy that makes a good cut flower. 2 ft. tall. Pkt. 10¢; large pkt. 40¢; ¼ oz. 60¢.

Ornamental Gourds
Gourds for table decoration sell for 10 to 15¢ each. Grow more than you can use for 20¢. Sow seed in May. Vining 15 ft. Pkts. 20¢.
Apple, 2496. Spoon, 2507.
Pear-Shaped, 2505. Striped.
COLLECTION, 4834. One 20¢ packet each of the 3 varieties for 50¢.
Mixed, 2510. All kinds, small and large. Pkt. 10¢; ½ oz. 25¢; oz. 40¢.
Dreer's Surprise Mixture, 2512. All the interesting small shapes. Pkt. 15¢; ½ oz. 30¢.

Ornamental Gourds

Iberis
Hardy Candytuft

Hardy, bushy plants for edging perennial borders or for Walls and Rock Gardens.

Gibraltarica Hybrida, 2677. Small white flowers shading to lilac. Blooms from early spring to early summer. 12 inches tall. Pkt. 15¢; large pkt. 50¢.

Sempervirens, 2679. Showy white blooms in large heads covering plants during May and June. 1 ft. Pkt. 15¢; large pkt. 60¢.

Jucunda, 2681. (Aethionema.) Compact 6 inch plants with dainty pink flower clusters. Superb for the Rock Garden. May-June. Pkt. 25¢; large pkt. 75¢.

Iberis—Sempervirens

INULA, Golden Beauty, 2696. (Elecampane.) Showy perennial 2 ft. tall with golden yellow Daisy-like flowers 2 to 3 inches across. August. Pkt. 25¢; large pkt. 40¢.

IRIS, Avalon Blend, 2704. (Flags.) A mixture of many different species including rare types. Blooms in 2 years. Pkt. 25¢.

IRIS, JAPANESE, Mixed, 2706. (Iris Kaempferi.) Blooms during June and July. 2½ ft. tall. Pkt. 25¢; large pkt. 75¢.

HONESTY, Lunaria-Biennis Alba, 2665. (Moon-penny.) Hardy biennial, grown for its silvery transparent seedpods which are used for winter bouquets, 3 ft. tall. Pkt. 15¢.

JOB'S TEARS, 2005. (Coix Lachryma.) You may have cut your teeth on these. Vigorous plants, 2 ft. tall, grown for their large smooth, gray bead-like seeds used for teething rings and Rosaries. Pkt. 25¢.

KENILWORTH IVY, 2795. (Linaria Cymbalaria.) Graceful trailing plants for hanging baskets, porch boxes, etc. Bright green foliage and dainty lavender flowers. 4 inches tall. Pkt. 15¢.

LANTANA, Large Flowering Mixed, 2710. Verbena-like flower heads in white, rose, orange and scarlet on compact plants. 1½ ft. tall. Pkt. 15¢.

LAVATERA, Sunset, 2763. (Mallow.) Showy annual with large blooms of satiny rose-carmine. Blooms from July to October. 3 ft. Pkt. 10¢.

LAVENDER, Munstead Strain, 2759. (Lavendula.) True sweet scented flowers of the common English Lavender. 1 ft. Pkt. 25¢.

LEPTOSIPHON, Hybridus Mixed, 2766. (Fairy Trumpet.) Dense cushions studded with dainty star-shaped flowers from cream to deep scarlet. Fine for dwarf beds, borders and Rock Gardens. June to September. Pkt. 15¢; lge. Pkt. 40¢.

Honesty—Moon-penny

Imperial Larkspur

Kochia

KOCHIA, Trichophylla-Childsi, 2709. (Burning Bush.) Bushy plants like small evergreens. Easily grown from seed and makes a fine summer hedge. Foliage turns red in the fall. 3 ft. Pkt. 10¢; ½ oz. 25¢; oz. 40¢.

Hollyhock—Indian Spring

Hollyhock

An old fashioned favorite, in fact any garden is not complete without these stately flowers. In constant bloom from July to September and not choosy as to their location. 5 to 7 ft. tall.

Double Varieties
Pkt. 15¢.

Maroon, 2637.   Salmon-Rose, 2645.
Rose, 2641.   White, 2647.
Red, 2643.   Yellow, 2649.

Extra-Choice Double Mixed, 2650.

COLLECTION, 4848. One packet each of the 6 colors for 75¢.

PELLETIZED SEED, Double Hollyhock Mixed, P2650. Pkt. 20¢.

Newport Pink, 2639. Exquisite, double pure pink blooms. Pkt. 15¢.

Single Mixed, 2660. Many showy colors. Pkt. 10¢.

Indian Spring, 2632. New annual Hollyhock, blooms 5 months after sowing. Showy, semi-double, fringed pink flowers. Pkt. 15¢.

Double Larkspur—*Giant Imperial*

Modern annual Larkspur vie with Delphinium in stately beauty. Base branching plants with 3 to 4 ft. spikes of full double flowers in the most lovely colors, imaginable. Seed is hardy, sow outdoors on prepared ground at any time in the spring. Make another sowing for succession.

Blue Bell, 2721. Deep azure blue.
Blue Spire, 2723. Deep Oxford blue.
Dazzler, 2727. Carmine-scarlet.
Exquisite Pink Improved, 2728. Soft pink, shaded salmon.
Gloria Improved, 2730. Deep rose.
Lilac King, 2731. Rich lilac.
Miss California, 2732. Lovely pink shaded salmon.
Pink Perfection, 2733. Lively pink.
Sweet Lavender, 2735. Lavender.
White King, 2739. Dazzling white.
Dreer's Superior Mixture, 2740. Pkt. 15¢; large pkt. 40¢; ¼ oz. 65¢.
COLLECTION, 4855. One packet each of the 10 varieties for $1.25.
PELLETIZED SEED, Imperial Larkspur Mixed, P2740. Pkt. 20¢.

SURPRISE MIXTURE OF ANNUAL FLOWERS
3020. More than twenty varieties of flowers that will grow with very little care. Dig the ground, fertilize, broadcast the seed and weed once or twice, for a summer of beauty. Pkt. 15¢; oz. 50¢; ¼ lb. $1.25; lb. $4.00.

$\mathcal{D}reer's$ $\mathcal{R}eliable$ FLOWER SEEDS

Liatris

Liatris
Blazing Star Gay Feather

Pycnostachya, 2773. Long spikes densely covered with fuzzy, rosy purple blooms from July to September. Splendid for tall borders and cutting. 4 ft. Pkt. 15¢.

Scariosa, 2775. Showy, deep purple flowers 4 ft. tall. Pkt. 15¢.

September Glory, 2777. Improved strain with large purple flowers during late August and September. 4 ft. Pkt. 20¢.

LEPTOSYNE, Stillmani, 2769. (Yellow Daisy.) Cosmos-like blooms of rich golden yellow. Fine for beds and cutting. 1½ ft. Annual. Pkt. 20¢.

Linaria
Toadflax—Miniature Snapdragon

Maroccana, Excelsior Hybrids, 2797. Small spikes like miniature Snapdragons with flowers in yellow, crimson, pink and purple. June to September. Annual. 12 inches. Pkt. 15¢.

Fairy Bouquet, 2799. Only 8 inches tall. Covered with dainty blooms in shades of pink, rose, cream, yellow and white. Blooms freely all summer. Annual. Pkt. 20¢.

Linum—*Flax*

Grandiflorum Rubrum, 2803. (Scarlet Flax.) Showy, crimson-scarlet, five petalled blooms all summer. 15 inches. Pkt. 10¢.

Perenne, Blue, 2807. Free flowering hardy Flax with large rich blue four petalled blooms all summer. 24 inches. Pkt. 10¢; ¼ oz. 25¢; ½ oz. 40¢.

Flavum, 2805. Showy yellow blooms from June until September on 2 ft. plants. A good perennial for background in Rock Gardens. Pkt. 15¢; large pkt. 60¢; ¼ oz. $1.00.

Lychnis
Rose Champion, Maltese Cross

Chalcedonica, 2875. Broad heads of brilliant star-shaped scarlet blooms. June and July. 2 ft. perennial. Pkt. 10¢.

Arkwrighti, 2873. Bright red flower heads during June. Perennial. Pkt. 20¢.

Haageana Hybrids, 2877. Salmon, orange and scarlet flower heads on 18 inch stems. Blooms in June and July. Perennial. Pkt. 25¢.

Lilies—*from seed*

Sow in the coldframe or a special seedbed where the soil can be kept uniformly moist and shaded.

Canadense, 2780. (Canadian Lily.) Bell-shaped, yellow flowers spotted with black. Grows 2-3 ft. tall. Pkt. 15¢.

Formosanum, 2784. (New Wonder Lily.) Long trumpet shaped, fragrant, white blooms 3 to 4 ft. tall. Pkt. 25¢.

Regale, 2787. (Regal Lily.) Ivory-white, shaded pink on outside, yellow in throat. Blooms in July. 5 ft. Pkt. 15¢.

Special Blend, 2794. Special mixture of more than 50 hardy Lilies. Pkt. 25¢.

Tenuifolium, 2791. (Coral Lily.) Graceful, small, glistening scarlet-red blooms in late May and June. 2 ft. Pkt. 25¢.

Lychnis—Haageana

Lobelia—*Fairy Wings*

Dwarf annuals that bloom all summer. Use for edging and patio boxes. Seed is very fine, start in seed flats. The miniature violet-like flowers nearly hide the foliage. 4 to 6 inches tall.

Blue Gown, 2812. Compact growth with lovely, deep blue flowers. Pkt. 20¢.

Cambridge Blue, 2813. Compact plants with light blue flowers. Pkt. 20¢.

Crystal Palace Compacta, 2815. Rich deep blue flowers; dark foliage. 4 inches. Pkt. 15¢.

Sapphire, 2824. Trailing variety with showy blue flowers each with a white eye. Pkt. 20¢.

HARDY LOBELIA, Cardinalis, 2821. (Cardinal Flower.) Hardy variety bearing fine tall spikes covered with brilliant scarlet blooms, all summer. Grows in the shade. Pkt. 25¢; large pkt. 75¢.

LYTHRUM, Roseum Superbum, 2883. (Rose Loosestrife.) Hardy perennial about 3 feet tall, covered with rosy flowers from July to September. Pkt. 15¢.

Lupinus

Tall spikes of pea-shaped flowers in May-June. Fit companion for Delphinium and Foxglove. 3 ft.

Polyphyllus—*Perennial*

Blue, 2841. Pkt. 15¢.
Rose, 2847. Pkt. 15¢.
White, 2855. Pkt. 15¢.
Yellow Shades, 2856. Pkt. 25¢.
Mixed Colors, 2858. Pkt. 15¢.

Reselected Russell Hybrids, 2866. The world's finest perennial Lupins, tall spikes with closely set flowers in every conceivable Lupin color with many bright pastel shades. Seed in the Originator's Packets. Pkt. (20 seeds) 35¢; large pkt. (65 seeds) 75¢; 3 large pkts. $1.90.

Russell Hybrids, 2865. American grown seed from originator's stock. Pkt. 25¢.

Subcarnosus, 2867. (Texas Blue Bonnet.) Strong plants, 15 inches high with massive flower spikes closely set with large, deep blue blooms. Pkt. 15¢.

Annual Hartwegi Giants

The plants throw 4 to 6 flower spikes with 25 to 50 blooms each. 2 to 4 ft. tall.

King Blue, 2836. Rich oxford-blue.
King White, 2839. Pure white.
King Mixed, All colors. Pkt. 15¢.
Hartwegi Mixed, 2835. All colors. Pkt. 10¢; large pkt. 25¢.

Lupins

22

From the World's Best Growers

Mignonette For delicate fragrance

An old-fashioned favorite annual. Sow in April and again in July for fragrance, for flowers from June until frost. 12 to 16 inch spikes of closely set flowers.

Defiance, 2993. Large individual, greenish-red florets on compact spikes very fragrant. Pkt. 10¢.

Giant Machet, 2995. Pyramidal growth. Large fragrant flower spikes. Pkt. 10¢.

Golden Goliath, 2997. Golden yellow flower spikes. Pkt. 10¢.

Red Goliath, 2998. Strong, compact plants with giant trusses of a bright red color. Pkt. 10¢.

White Goliath, 2999. Greenish-white compact spikes. Pkt. 10¢.

Sweet-Scented, 3006. The old variety with small spikes set with very fragrant white blooms. Pkt. 10¢.

MARVEL OF PERU, Mixed, 2970. (Four o'clocks.) Small trumpet-shaped blooms on bushy plants, 2 ft. tall. Blooms from July to October. All colors and very sweet scented. Pkt. 10¢; ½ oz. 30¢; oz. 50¢.

MATTHIOLA, Bicornis, 2981. (Evening Scented Stock.) Old fashioned annual delightfully fragrant in the evening. Purplish-lilac, single flowers on spikes like stocks. Blooms all summer. 18 inches. Pkt. 10¢.

MECONOPSIS, Baileyi, 2985. (Blue Satin Poppy.) 2 to 3 ft. high with glorious sky blue cup-shaped flowers. Pkt. 25¢.

MATRICARIA, Double White Improved, 2975. (Feverfew.) Loose heads of small, full double, daisy-like flowers on 24 inch stems. Pkt. 15¢; large pkt. 40¢.

MIMOSA, Pudica, 3009. The rare Sensitive Plant. Touch a leaf and it folds up as though afraid of being harmed. Leaves unfold again in a short time. Small, ball-shaped pink flowers. Grow in pots or sunny spots. 8-10 inches. Pkt. 15¢.

Mesembryanthemum

Criniflorum, 2987. (Livingston Daisy.) Easily grown annual of spreading growth, 4 inches high, covered with showy one inch daisy-shaped flowers. Mixed colors. Pkt. 20¢.

Crystallinum, 2988. (Ice Plant.) Spreading 6-inch plants with icy green leaves. Pkt. 20¢.

MIMULUS, Trigrinus Grandiflorus, 3014. (Monkey Flower.) Small trumpet-shaped flowers with spotted throats. Splendid for greenhouse or moist border. 1 ft. Pkt. 20¢.

Mignonette

Myosotis Forget-Me-Not

Only Forget-Me-Nots can be as blue as Forget-Me-Nots. Use in rock gardens and moist half shady spots. Alpestris varieties bloom in May-June and Palustris all summer. Try as ground cover for tulip beds.

Alpestris, Robusta Grandiflora, 3048. Large rich Forget-Me-Not blue flowers on 10-inch plants. Pkt. 15¢; large pkt. 60¢.

Alpestris, Oblongata, Blue Bird, 3063. Deep blue flowers on compact plants. 12 inches tall. Pkt. 15¢; large pkt. 60¢.

Alpestris, Rosea, 3049. Bright rose 6 inches tall. Pkt. 20¢; large pkt. 60¢.

Alpestris, Royal Blue, 3051. Rich indigo blue flowers; 6 inches. Pkt. 15¢; large pkt. 60¢.

Palustris Semperflorens, 3069. (Marsh Forget-Me-Not.) The edge of a small stream is a natural spot for growing these in masses. Blue flowers from May to September. 8 to 12 inches tall. Pkt. 15¢.

Myosotis—Blue Ball

Morning Glories

Superb for covering garden houses, fences and trellis. Do not sow until the soil is warm.

Improved Heavenly Blue, Early Flowering, 3029. The most popular of all. Large sky-blue 4-inch flowers in bloom from midsummer until fall. Will climb 30 ft. Pkt. 15¢; ¼ oz. 40¢; ½ oz. 65¢.

PELLETIZED SEED, Morning Glory, Heavenly Blue, P3029. Pkt. 20¢.

Pearly Gates, 3032. Large white blooms, creamy yellow towards the center. Pkt. 15¢; ¼ oz. 50¢; ½ oz. 85¢.

Cornell, 3030. Large bright rosy red blooms with white edge. Pkt. 15¢.

Scarlett O'Hara, 3039. Magnificent large, bright wine red flowers. Pkt. 15¢; ¼ oz. 50¢; ½ oz. 85¢.

Mixed Imperial, 3036. (Emperor Morning Glories.) Gigantic blooms ranging from snow white to black-purple. Pkt. 10¢.

Dwarf Morning Glories

Tricolor Mixed, 3042. Flowers remain open all day long. Richly colored blooms on compact plants from June to September. Fine for window boxes. 12 inches. Pkt. 10¢.

Moonflower—Ipomoea

Grandiflora, 3026. (White Moonflower.) Large, fragrant, satiny pure white flowers 5 to 6 inches across, from August until frost. The flowers open at sundown and remain open until morning. Rapid grower beautiful on trellis, arbors, etc. For early bloom start indoors in individual pots or, sow outdoors when soil is warm. Pkt. 15¢; ½ oz. 40¢; oz. 75¢.

Morning-Glory—Scarlett O'Hara

Dreer's Marigolds

There is a Marigold to suit any garden purpose from small flowered 8 inch plants to the mammoth Chrysanthemum flowered sorts that grow 3 ft. Sow seed indoors in March or outdoors April-May and thin to 12 inches between plants. For best results feed the African varieties and starve the French. All are annuals and bloom from mid-summer until heavy frost. (See in color page VI.)

Gigantea Sunset Giants

Orange Sunset, 2918. Super giant-sized Marigold, deep orange color. Delightfully sweet scented. Pkt. 15¢; large pkt. 50¢; ¼ oz. $1.00.

Sunset Giants Mixed, 2920. Truly a giant Marigold with blooms measuring 5 to 7½ inches across. Many lovely yellow shades. Pkt. 15¢; large pkt. 50¢; ¼ oz. 85¢.

Pot O'Gold, 2915. This dwarf giant Marigold is only 14 inches high but each plant bears a dozen or more large, deep golden blooms. Pkt. 15¢; large pkt. 50¢.

Carnation-Flowered Marigolds

Guinea Gold, 2891. Pkt. 15¢; large pkt. 40¢; ¼ oz. 75¢. (See page VI.)

Yellow Supreme, 2897. Pkt. 15¢; large pkt. 40¢; ¼ oz. 75¢. (See page VI.)

Real Gold, 2924. 20-25 inches tall, fully double, brilliant gold, mammoth blooms. Pkt. 25¢; large pkt. 75¢; ¼ oz. $1.50.

Canary Bird, 2922. Clear, canary yellow, 2 ft. tall. Pkt. 15¢; large pkt. 40¢; ¼ oz. 75¢.

Gold Improved, 2921. Brilliant gold with orange highlights. 2½ ft. tall. Pkt. 10¢; large pkt. 40¢; ¼ oz. 60¢.

Giant Chrysanthemum-Flowered

Goldsmith, 2901. Tall bushy plants with extra-large, brilliant, golden orange blooms 4 to 5 inches across. Pkt. 15¢; large pkt. 50¢; ¼ oz. $1.00.

Yellowstone, 2905. Double incurved and quilled, 3 inch, golden yellow flowers. 18 inches tall. Pkt. 15¢; large pkt. 50¢; ¼ oz. $1.00.

Limelight, 2907. Incurved Chrysanthemum-like flowers. Soft primrose yellow 2¾ inches across. 20 inches tall. Pkt. 15¢; large pkt. 50¢; ¼ oz. $1.00.

Mammoth Mum, 2912. 30-inch. Light sulphur yellow blooms 3½ inches across. Pkt. 25¢; large pkt. 75¢; ¼ oz. $1.25.

Giant Chrysanthemum-Flowered Mixed, 2910. Pkt. 15¢; large pkt. 40¢; ¼ oz. 75¢.

Dreer's Special Giant Marigold Mixture, 2919. Our own blend of all the finest and largest Marigolds. Pkt. 25¢; 4 pkts. for 75¢.

Marigold—Sunkist

Marigold—Harmony

Marigold—Orange Sunset

Marigold—Mammoth Mum

Double African

The old-fashioned type with lightly quilled petals 3 ft.

Lemon Alldouble, 2887. Large, well-rounded lemon yellow blooms. Pkt. 15¢; large pkt. 50¢; ¼ oz. $1.00.

Orange Alldouble, 2889. Rich orange, fully double blooms. Comes 100 per cent double. Pkt. 15¢; large pkt. 50¢; ¼ oz. $1.00.

Lemon Queen, 2895. Soft lemon yellow. Pkt. 10¢; large pkt. 40¢; ¼ oz. 75¢.

Double African Mixed, 2900. Pkt. 10¢; large pkt. 30¢; ¼ oz. 60¢.

PELLETIZED SEED, Marigold, African Mixed, P2900. Pkt. 20¢.

Double French Marigold

Pkt. 15¢; large pkt. 40¢; ¼ oz. 60¢.

Butterball, 2929. Double, butter-yellow flowers with clustered center and broader guard petals. 12 inches.

Harmony, 2934. Broad, deep mahogany red outer petals surrounding a crested cushion of golden yellow center petals. 15 inches tall.

Mahogany, 2936. Velvety mahogany brown.

Melody, 2937. Double, brilliant orange flowers one inch in diameter. 1 ft.

Scarlet Glow, 2942. The brightest dwarf Marigold with flowers 2 inches in diameter. Brilliant red. 12 inches tall.

Spry, 2943. Extra-double flowers with a light orange center and maroon outer petals. Neat compact plant. 9 inches tall. PELLETIZED SEED, Marigold Spry, P2943. Pkt. 20¢.

Sunkist, 2944. Compact dwarf plants from early summer until frost, with double orange blooms.

Yellow Pygmy, 2926. Extra-dwarf variety only 4 inches tall completely covered with double 1 inch lemon yellow flowers.

COLLECTION, 4866. One packet each of the 8 double French Marigolds for $1.00.

Dwarf Double French Mixed, 2940. Pkt. 10¢; large pkt. 25¢; ¼ oz. 40¢.

PELLETIZED SEED, Marigold, French Mixed, P2940. Pkt. 20¢.

Tall Double French Mixed, 2946. Pkt. 10¢; large pkt. 25¢; ¼ oz. 40¢.

Hybrid Marigolds

Red and Gold Hybrids, 2947. Bushy plants 1½ ft. tall. Full double 2¼ inches. Pkt. 35¢.

Wildfire, 2959. Single-flowered French-African hybrid with flowers of medium size. Combining shades of deep mahogany, orange and yellow. 3 ft. bushy plants. Pkt. 15¢; large pkt. 50¢.

24

Nasturtium—Double Gleam Hybrids

Nierembergia—*Blue Cups*

Coérulea, 3159. (Hippomanica.) Charming 8-inch annual covered with cup-shaped lavender-blue flowers from mid-summer until frost. Splendid for dwarf beds, borders and rock gardens. Pkt. 20¢.

Purple Robe, 3161. Deep violet blooms on compact, free-flowering plants, 6 inches tall. Pkt. 25¢.

NEMOPHILA, Insignis Blue, 3143. (Baby Blue Eyes.) A charming annual with graceful light blue flax-like flowers. Blooms all summer. 8 inches. Pkt. 10¢.

NIGELLA, Miss Jekyll, 3163. (Love in a Mist.) Showy cornflower blue blossoms nestled against slender fern-like leaves. Splendid for cutting and beds. Blooms freely from May to August. 18 inches tall. Pkt. 10¢; ¼ oz. 30¢.

Nicotiana

Sweet Scented Tobacco

Sweet scented, widely flaring trumpet-shaped flowers. You need a few for fragrance.

Affinis, 3151. Pure white, tubular flowers, 3 ft. tall. Pkt. 10¢; large pkt. 25¢; ¼ oz. 40¢.

Affinis, Crimson Bedder, 3153. Covered with brilliant deep crimson flowers. 16 inches tall. Pkt. 25¢; large pkt. 40¢; ¼ oz. 75¢.

Affinis Hybrids Mixed, 3156. White, pink and crimson blooms on plants 3 ft. tall. Pkt. 10¢; large pkt. 25¢; ¼ oz. 40¢.

Sanderae, Crimson King, 3157. Dark velvety crimson-red flowers. 3 ft. Pkt. 10¢.

Suaveolens, 3154. Dwarf in comparison to other Nicotiana. Pure white, sweet scented trumpets. 18 inches. Pkt. 25¢.

Sylvestris, 3158. Sweet-scented, long, pure white flowers. 5 ft. tall. Pkt. 10¢.

OTHAKE, Sphaceolata, 3177. (Rosy Wings.) Annuals with bright rose flowers resembling Sweet Sultan. Grows 18 inches high. Pkt. 25¢.

Oenothera—*Evening Primrose*

Missouriensis, 3175. Large bright yellow flowers on bushy 1 ft. tall plants. Perennial. Pkt. 25¢.

Youngi, 3176. Bright golden yellow cup-shaped blooms on plants 2 ft. tall. Strong and vigorous. Pkt. 20¢.

Sunny NASTURTIUMS

Double Sweet-Scented

Vigorous semi-trailing plants covered with fragrant double blooms from July until frost. Use in porch and window boxes, along fences, or as a border for vegetable gardens. Colorful cut flowers all summer. Add leaves and flowers to your salad bowl! 1½-2 ft.
Pkt. 15¢; oz. 50¢; ¼ lb. $1.50.

Fiesta, 3092. Large golden yellow flowers with scarlet-red blotches.
Golden Gleam, 3093. The first and still the most popular of all double sweet-scented Nasturtiums, gleaming gold.
Indian Chief, 3094. Brilliant scarlet flowers and dark foliage.
Mahogany Gleam, 3095. Bright mahogany.
Moon Gleam, 3097. Light cream.
Salmon Gleam, 3103. Gold with delicate salmon suffusion.
Scarlet Gleam, 3105. Dazzling scarlet.
Glorious Gleam Mixed, 3110. All colors.
Finest Dwarf Single Mixed, 3090. Free-blooming plants a foot high; many rich colors. Pkt. 10¢; oz. 30¢; ¼ lb. $1.00; lb. $3.00.
Finest Single Tall Mixed, 3080. A free-blooming trailing strain, all colors. Pkt. 10¢; oz. 30¢; ¼ lb. $1.00; lb. $3.00.

Dwarf Double Scented

Long stemmed double flowers on bushy compact plants. 18 inches tall.
Pkt.15¢; oz. 45¢; ¼ lb. $1.35.
Golden Globe, 3117. Golden yellow.
Mahogany Gem, 3121. Mahogany-red.
Orange Glory, 3114. Bright orange.
Art Shades, 3115. A fine mixture of lighter pastel shades.
Primrose Globe, 3123. Cheerful shades of yellow.
Scarlet Empress, 3126. Deep scarlet.
Dwarf Double Giants Mixed, 3130.
NEMESIA, Dwarf-Flowering Hybrids Mixed, 3140. Pretty annual, with exquisite small Orchid-like flowers throughout the summer and fall. Pkt. 15¢.
NEPETA, Mussini, 3147. Perennial 2 ft. high with showy rich blue flowers on long racemes. Pkt. 20¢.

Nemophila—Insignis Blue

PHACELIA, Campanularia, 3245. (California Blue Bell.) Beautiful annual with intense Gentian blue flowers. Very effective for edgings, pots, etc. 9 inches. Pkt. 15¢.
PENTSTEMON, Gloxinioides, Sensation, 3256. (Beard 'Tongue.) Spreading well-branched plant with spikes 30 inches tall set with Gloxinia-like flowers of many bright colors from July to September. Generally listed as half-hardy but it is perfectly hardy in Philadelphia. Pkt. 25¢.
PENTSTEMON, Perennial Varieties Mixed, 3262. Many fine botanical types in a superb mixture easy to grow. Pkt. 25¢.

Platycodon—*Balloon Flower*

This splendid perennial should be permitted to remain where planted for many years in order to develop base branching, sturdy plants, with balloon-like buds and open bell-shaped flowers. Blooms in June when good perennials are at a premium.
Grandiflora, Blue, 3473. Vigorous plants with neat bright green foliage and large wide open bells of a clear blue color. Pkt. 15¢.
Mariesi Album, 3478. Plants 1 ft. tall with pure white flowers. Pkt. 25¢

Nicotiana

Dreer's Giant Pansies

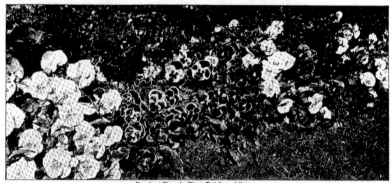

Pansies—Dreer's Giant Rainbow Mixture

Pansies in the spring! Almost as traditional as Tulips and Daffodils. Plant Pansies in your Tulip beds for ground cover, the effect is breath taking.

Plant seed in March indoors for this summer's bloom or sow outdoors in July or August for next year. Where winters are very severe cover plants with straw about the end of November or winter the plants in a cold frame.

Dreer's Royal Exhibition Mixture, 3250. A superb mixture of the finest strains made to our own formula to give the widest possible assortment of colors. Huge blooms, many with attractively waved petal edges. Pkt. 25¢; large pkt. 75¢; ⅛ oz. $2.00.

Giant Trimardeau Mixed, 3200. Smaller flowered dwarf, compact plants covered with flowers. Pkt. 20¢; large pkt. 60¢; ⅛ oz. $1.50.

Super Maple-Leaf Giants Mixed, 3244. Splendid compact plants with rich dark green foliage covered with showy velvety flowers of immense size. Pkt. 25¢; large pkt. 75¢; ⅛ oz. $2.00.

Dreer's American Mixture, 3230. A truly American type that does not include so many dark shades as imported varieties. Bright shades of yellow and blues. Compact plants with long stemmed flowers. Pkt. 25¢; large pkt. 75¢; ⅛ oz. $2.00.

Johnny Jump-Ups

3238. (Miniature Pansies.) The old fashioned kind scarcely bigger than a wild Violet in the charming old shades of blue, yellow and purple. Fine for Rock Gardens or semi-shaded moist spots. Pkt. 25¢. large pkt. 75¢.

Viola Cornuta—Tufted Pansies

Miniature Pansies in delightful shades that bloom and bloom and bloom. They delight in half shaded spots. 6 inches high. Pkt. 25¢; large pkt. 75¢.

Arkwright Ruby, 4409. Bright rosy crimson.
Blue Perfection, 4411. Rich purple-blue.
Chantreyland, 4413. Showy rich apricot.
Lutea Splendens, 4415. Rich golden yellow.
White Perfection, 4419. Pure white.
Blue Gem, 4410. (Jersey Gem.) A fine rich mid-blue.
Cornuta Finest Mixed, 4420. Pkt. 20¢; large pkt. 60¢; ¼ oz. $1.50.
COLLECTION, 4988. One 25¢ pkt. of the 6 colors for $1.25.

Dreer's Giant Rainbow Mixture, 3234. Compact bushy plants with long stemmed flowers that are ideal for cutting. Individual flowers will measure up to 4 inches across. Every conceivable Pansy color is included. Pkt. 50¢; large pkt. $1.25; ⅛ oz. $2.25.

Swiss Giants

From Switzerland, where they grow to perfection, come these fine separate colors of Giant Pansies. Compact plants with extra large long stemmed flowers.

Pkt. 25¢; large pkt. 75¢.

Alpenglow, 3201. Cardinal-red with three dark blotches.
Berna, 3205. Rich purple color with a charming velvety finish.
Coronation Gold, 3179. Canary yellow upper petals, lower ones flushed golden orange.
Lake of Thun, 3209. (Ullswater.) Exquisite rich ultramarine blue with a darker blotch on each petal.
Snow White, 3217. Giant pure white.
Rhinegold, 3219. Bright yellow with deep mahogany blotch in the center.
Swiss Giant Orange, 3218. Mellow orange.
Dreer's DeLuxe Mixture of Swiss Giants, 3228. Hand mixed from named varieties to give the proper color proportions according to intensity of color. Pkt. 50¢; large pkt. $1.25; ⅛ oz. $2.50.
COLLECTION, 4892. One 25¢ pkt. of each of the 7 colors for $1.50.

Viola Cornuta

Phlox—Drummondi

Poppies

Poppies are the brightest of annuals and will grow most anywhere. Odd spots in the perennial border, on banks and terraces and with a little care along the curb. Sow seed thinly and barely cover.

Shirley Poppies

American Legion, 3511. Greatly improved Flanders Field Poppy with large single flowers of a rich, dazzling, orange-scarlet. 2 ft. Pkt. 15¢.

Dreer's Select Shirley Mixed, 3520. Magnificent strain in all the lovely, light pinks, white, and reds. Scatter liberally in any part of the garden. Good cut flower if you scald the stems immediately after cutting. 18 inches. Pkt. 10¢; ¼ oz. 25¢; oz. 75¢.

Double Sweet Briar, 3537. The lovely pink of a Wild Rose. Flowers resemble the double Tuberous Begonia. Pkt. 15¢.

Double Shirley or Begonia-Flowered Mixed, 3540. Showy double blooms in many shades. 30 inches. Pkt. 15¢; ¼ oz. 35¢; oz. $1.00.

California Poppy. See Eschscholtzia.

POPPY, Amurense, 3575. (Yellow Wonder Poppy.) Sensational new Poppy. Buttercup yellow blooms on stems 2 ft. tall. Pkt. 20¢.

Oriental Poppies

Gorgeous flowers 6 inches across, dominating the flower display. The hardiest of hardy perennials, with huge bowl-like flowers from white through the glorious pink shades to brightest scarlet. For sun or semishade. Transplant only in August or September. 2-3 ft.

Orientale, 3631. Magnificent large blooms, bright orange-scarlet with a large black blotch at the base of each petal. Pkt. 15¢.

Princess Victoria Louise, 3645. A clear and luminous salmon-pink. Pkt. 25¢.

Oriental Hybrids Mixed, 3650. Seed saved from a large number of extra-fine named varieties. Can be depended upon to give a wide range of color. Pkt. 15¢; large pkt. 60¢; ¼ oz. $1.50.

Iceland Poppies

Poppy Nudicaule, the hardy Poppy that blooms the first year from seed. Established plants bloom from April through June. Sow seed as early in the spring as ground can be prepared.

Coonara Pink, 3579. Glorious strain with large flowers in pink shades. 18 inches. Pkt. 15¢.

New Hybrids Iceland Mixed, 3590. Grand assortment of charming colors. Pkt. 15¢.

Red Cardinal, 3608. Bright crimson-scarlet. Pkt. 25¢.

Imperial Jewels Mixed, 3606. Superb strong-stemmed blooms in a complete color range that includes many salmon shades. Pkt. 15¢.

Sanford's Giant Strain, 3610. Wonderful petal substance and stems 2 to 3 feet long. Many of the flowers are 5 inches in diameter. Contains a wide range of exquisite colors. Pkt. 25¢.

Brilliant Annual PHLOX

Brilliant annuals for beds, borders or cutting. Flowers are borne in flat heads continuously from midsummer until frost. Sow seed outdoors where plants are to grow as soon as ground is warm.

New Giant-Flowering—*Phlox Drummondi gigantea*

New strain in which individual florets are as big as quarters. All have contrasting eyes. 18 inches.

Pkt. 25¢; large pkt. 60¢; ¼ oz. $1.50.

Gigantea, Red Glory, 3424. Rich red with large white eye.
Gigantea, Rosy Morn, 3426. Rose-pink with a large white eye.
Gigantea, Salmon Glory, 3427. Deep salmon with large cream eye.
Gigantea, Art Shades Mixed, 3430. There are many more colors in this special mixture than those offered as separate sorts.

Select Large-Flowering—*Phlox Drummondi grandiflora*

This is the standard type and provides a great many separate colors remarkably true, to help you carry out definite color schemes. 15 inches.

Brilliant Rose, 3431.		Soft Lilac, 3436.
Fiery Scarlet, 3432.	Pkt. 15¢; large pkt. 50¢;	Snow White, 3437.
Rose, 3433.	¼ oz. $1.25; oz. $4.00.	Splendens, 3438.
Primrose, 3434.		Violet Blue, 3439.
Shell Pink, 3435.		Choicest Mixed, 3440.

COLLECTION: 4916. One 15¢ pkt. each of the 9 varieties for $1.20.
PELLETIZED SEED, Phlox Large Flowering Mixed, P3440. Pkt. 20¢.

Large-Flowering Dwarf
Drummondi grandiflora nana

Delightful, dwarf, compact plants for ribbon beds or even for edging. Individual blooms are large but stems are short. Use also in porch or window boxes.

Large-Flowering Dwarf Phlox, Mixed, 3450. Pkt. 15¢; large pkt. 50¢; ¼ oz. $1.25.

Annual Star Phlox, Cuspidata, 3458. Colorful strain in which the flowers are all of graceful star-shape. Grows 1 ft. tall. Pkt. 15¢.

POLEMONIUM, Coeruleum, 3481. (Jacob's Ladder.) Perennial. Vigorous plants 2 ft. high with graceful, bell-shaped, sky-blue flowers from April till July. Likes moist soil. Pkt. 15¢.

SEED SOER 50¢

Plastic - seeds visible as sown - go twice as far. Saves thinning - for peas to petunias.

Single Shirley Poppies

Oriental Poppy

Primula—Japonica Mixed

Primula—Polyanthus

Vulgaris, 3737. (Primrose.) Bushy plants 4 inches tall, with bright yellow flower heads on 10 inch stems. Splendid for beds, borders and the wild garden. Perennial. Pkt. 25¢; large pkt. 75¢.

Japonica Mixed, 3736. Sturdy plants with masses of bright green foliage close to the ground and flower stems which rise to 2 ft. Flowers in various shades of yellow in tiers along the stems. Pkt. 25¢; large pkt. 75¢.

Polyanthus, Large-Flowered Mixed, 3485. (Primula Veris Elatior.) Popular hardy perennial with showy large flower clusters in a wide range of beautiful yellow, bronze and orange shades. Grows 6-9 inches high. Pkt: 25¢; large pkt. 75¢.

Giant Munstead Strain, 3486. Vigorous plants, 12 inches high, with umbels of large individual cream, yellow and white flowers. Pkt. 25¢.

Tender Primroses

Malacoides, New Hybrids Mixed, 3730. (Baby Primrose.) Greenhouse pot plant and cut flower. Many showy colors. 1 ft. high. Pkt. 25¢; large pkt. $1.25.

Obconica, Gigantea, Wyaston Wonder, 3708. Greenhouse pot plant. Huge individual bright crimson florets. Vigorous and free-flowering. Pkt. 50¢; large pkt. $1.50.

Obconica Gigantea, Mixed Colors, 3710. A showy greenhouse pot plant with extra-large, graceful flowers of heavy texture in showy large trusses. Many colors. Pkt. 40¢; large pkt. $1.25.

PHYSOSTEGIA, Virginica, 3465. Perennial with many spikes of tube-shaped lavender flowers. Plants 30 to 40 inches tall. Pkt. 25¢.

POTENTILLA, Single Hybrids Mixed, 3680. (Cinquefoil.) 1 to 2 ft. high with attractive dark green, divided leaves and showy flowers in a wide range of bright colors. Pkt. 15¢; large pkt. 50¢.

PORTULACA: Listed on page IV in full natural color.

Pyrethrum—*Persian Daisy*

Hybridum Single Mixed, 3760. Splendid hardy long-lived perennial for the garden and cutting. White, rose, and red daisy-like flowers. 2 ft. Pkt. 15¢; large pkt. 60¢.

Extra-Double Choice Mixed, 3750. Double daisy-shaped flowers in shades of pink, red and white. 2 ft. Pkt. 25¢; large pkt. 75¢.

Aureum, 3745. (Golden Feather.) Annuals with bright finely cut, yellow foliage, use for borders or edging. 1 ft. Pkt. 15¢; large pkt. 30¢; ¼ oz. 50¢.

Rudbeckia—*Coneflower*

Cultivated Black-Eyed Susans. Large daisy-like flowers with dark cone shaped centers.

My Joy, 3805. Annual, covered from mid-summer until frost with extra-large golden yellow blooms with dark centers. 2 ft. Pkt. 15¢.

Starlight, 3808. Semi-double flowers, yellow to mahogany. 3 ft. Annual. Pkt. 25¢.

Purpurea, 3809. (Giant Purple Coneflower.) Large, reddish purple flowers 4 inches across with a black-purple cone. Blooms all summer. 3 ft. perennial. Pkt. 15¢.

Saponaria—*Soapwort*

Ocymoides, 3861. 9 inches tall and 18 inches across covered with lovely rose-pink flowers during May and June. Excellent for rock gardens, borders, rock walls, etc. Pkt. 15¢.

Vaccaria, Rose, 3869. Showy satiny pink flowers something like annual Gypsophila. Blooms all summer. Use for conservation work on banks and terraces. Pkt. 10¢.

SANVITALIA, Creeping Zinnia, Procumbens, fl. pl. 3863. Fine for dwarf beds, edges or borders. Double, bright yellow blooms all summer. 6 inches tall. Pkt. 20¢.

Ricinus—*Castor Oil Bean*

Picturesque annual plants with lush tropical appearance, large leaves and brilliantly colored seed pods. Use to cover up unsightly fences or to provide privacy.

Ricinus—Castor-Oil Bean

Physostegia—Virginica

Sanguineus, 3781. Rich blood-red stalks and flower clusters. Very vigorous. 7 ft. tall. Pkt. 15¢; ½ oz. 50¢.

Zanzibarensis Mixed, 3786. A gorgeous species with leaves up to 3 feet across. Includes light green, dark green and bronze leaved plants. 8 ft. tall. Pkt. 10¢; oz. 25¢; ¼ lb. 75¢.

All Varieties Mixed, 3790. Pkt. 10¢; oz. 25¢; ¼ lb. 75¢.

Salpiglossis
Painted Tongue

Charming annual growing 24 to 30 inches tall. Trumpet-shaped velvety blooms delicately veined with gold. Blooms from mid-summer until frost. Sow seed where plants are to grow. Hot, dry soil is best.

Improved
Large-Flowering

Pkt. 15¢; large pkt. 40¢; ¼ oz. 60¢.
Crimson and Gold, 3821.
Violet and Gold, 3824.
Purple and Gold, 3825.
Rose and Gold, 3827.
Scarlet and Gold, 3828.
White and Gold, 3829.
Finest Mixed Colors, 3830.
COLLECTION, 4940. One pkt. each of the 6 colors for 75¢.

Salpiglossis

Salvia—Scarlet Sage

Bushy hedge-like plants with bright scarlet flowers on spikes covering the whole plant. Traditional to plant in front of country porches. Start seed indoors. Blooms from July until frost.

Dreer's America, 3853. The earliest and most uniform strain with scarlet flowers. 20 inches tall. Pkt. 25¢; large pkt. 75¢; ¼ oz. $1.75.

St. John's Fire, 3856. Compact plants 10 inches high covered with brilliant scarlet blooms. Pkt. 35¢; large pkt. $1.00.

Splendens, 3851. (Scarlet Sage.) Beautiful, bright scarlet flower spikes. 3 ft. Pkt. 20¢; large pkt. 60¢; ¼ oz. $1.25.

Bonfire, 3855. (Clara Bedman.) Lovely well-rounded bushes 2 ft. tall and as wide. Brilliant scarlet spikes. Pkt. 25¢; large pkt. 75¢; ¼ oz. $1.75.

Blue Salvia

Azurea Grandiflora Pitcheri, 3841. Stately perennial plants 3½ to 4 ft. tall bearing long racemes set with beautiful, deep clear blue flowers from July until late September. Easy to grow and perfectly hardy. Pkt. 25¢.

Farinacea, 3843. Half-hardy perennial grown as an annual because it blooms so quickly. Has showy light blue flowers. Requires thorough winter protection. Pkt. 20¢.

Farinacea, Blue Bedder, 3845. More compact form with flowers of a deeper blue color. Hardy with protection. Blooms from August till October. 2½ ft. Pkt. 25¢; large pkt. 60¢.

Patens, 3849. Gorgeous large blooms of deep indigo blue. Half-hardy perennial. 2½ ft. tall. Pkt. 25¢.

Salvia—Farinacea

Scabiosa Annual

See page V in full natural color among the "Tall Stuff" for Cutting.

Scabiosa—*Perennial*

The hardy Scabiosa are long lived, free blooming perennials excellent for border planting or for cutting.

Caucasica Perfecta, 3893. (Blue Bonnet.) Large, well-rounded, soft lavender-blue flowers from June to September. 3 ft. Pkt. 15¢.

Caucasica, Giant Hybrids, 3895. (Isaac House Strain.) Vigorous plants with giant blooms ranging from light to darkest blue. June to September; 2½ ft. Pkt. 25¢; large pkt. 60¢.

Caucasica, Alba, 3894. Showy white flowers, 2½ ft. tall. Pkt. 15¢.

Columbaria, Pink, 3897. Soft pink. 2 ft. Pkt. 15¢.

Columbaria, Lavender, 3896. 2 ft. Pkt. 15¢.

Sidalcea

Schizanthus

Butterfly or Fringe Flower

One of the airiest and daintiest annuals. Grows 2 to 3 ft. tall and is practically covered with blooms throughout the season.

Excelsior, Compactus Mixed, 3906. Very large flowers with handsome markings on white, buff, brilliant rose, blue and purple ground. Pkt. 25¢.

Giant-Flowering Hybrids, 3907. Magnificent blooms the size of a silver dollar in a perfect blend of colors. Remarkably free-flowering. Pkt. 20¢.

Mixed, 3910. (Wisetonensis.) A splendid mixture which forms pretty plants about 18 inches tall. Pkt. 15¢.

SIDALCEA, Stark's Hybrids, 3920. (Prairie Mallow.) A splendid perennial containing many beautiful shades. Five petalled flowers borne on spikes above the foliage. Grows 3 ft. tall and blooms all summer. Pkt. 20¢.

SHASTA DAISY, Alaska, 1949. Magnificent white, daisies averaging 5 inches across. Blooms all summer. 3 ft. Perennial. Pkt. 15¢.

Diener's Giant Double White, 1952. Pure white and quite double resembling a giant Aster with their long, loosely arranged flower petals. 3 ft. Perennial. Pkt. 25¢; large pkt. 75¢.

SILENE, Armeria, 3927. (Catchfly.) Lovely, slender annual, blooms all summer, showy bright rose blooms on plants 1 ft. tall. Pkt. 20¢.

STRAWBERRY, Baron Solemacher, 4038. Runnerless, everbearing Strawberry of compact growth which may be included in the flower or vegetable garden. Bear small, long pointed fruits of delightful flavor and sweetness. Pkt. 25¢; large pkt. 75¢.

Sunflower—*Helianthus*

Cucumerifolius Stella, 2577. (Helianthus.) Annual. Well-branched plants with large yellow ray petals encircling a small dark brown center. Excellent for cutting. 3 ft. Pkt. 10¢.

Double Sun Gold, 2582. Annual. Large, densely double, brilliant golden yellow flowers like giant Chrysanthemums 6 to 8 inches across. 3 to 5 ft. Pkt. 10¢; ¼ oz. 25¢.

Red Hybrids, 2585. Reddish maroon flowers 4 to 5 inches across. Grows 4 to 6 ft. Pkt. 10¢.

Red Sunflower

29

Annual STATICE

Statice—Sinuata

Showy flower clusters of strawy texture used in winter bouquets but equally as useful as a garden flower. Blooms all summer long. 2-2½ ft. tall. Pkts. 10¢.

Bonduelli, 3943. Yellow.
Lavender Queen, 3946.
Snowwitch, 3949. Best pure white.

Rosea Superba, 3947. Rose.
Blue Perfection, 3948.

Suworowi, 3951. (Russian Cat-tail Statice.) Long slender spikes closely set with beautiful, small, rose-colored blooms. Pkt. 15¢.

Sinuata Mixed, 3950. All colors. Pkt. 10¢.

COLLECTION, 4954. One pkt. each of the 6 colors for 50¢.

Perennial Statice

Latifolia, 3957. (Sea Lavender.) Blooms all summer, showy sprays densely covered with minute purplish blue flowers which can be used for winter bouquets. 2 ft. Pkt. 15¢.

Caspia, 3955. Vigorous plants 3 ft. tall, lilac flowers. The most beautiful of all Sea Lavenders. Pkt. 15¢.

STAR OF THE DESERT, Muricata, 3940. (Amberboa.) Lacy stars of bright tyrian purple with lighter center. Easy to grow. 2 ft. tall. Will grow in the driest and hottest spot in the garden. Annual. Pkt. 25¢.

Statice—Latifolia

SCARLET RUNNER BEAN, 3903. (Phaseolus Coccineus.) A splendid climbing bean with large sprays of bright scarlet pea-shaped blossoms followed by edible beans of good flavor. Oz. 15¢.

SOLANUM, Cleveland Red, 3937. (Christmas Cherry.) Christmas Pot Plant, greatly improved form with small oval leaves and globular bright scarlet berries. 1 ft. Pkt. 25¢.

STAR OF ARGENTINE, 3178. (Oxypetalum Caeruleum.) Bushy annual plants with graceful sprays of light, peacock blue flowers. Blooms from July to frost. For beds, borders, rock gardens or cutting. Pkt. 25¢.

Stocks—*Sweet Scented*

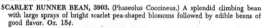

One of the most sweet scented of annuals. Tall spikes of full double flowers. Particularly fine where summers are cool.

CUT-AND-COME-AGAIN. Sow in March or April for July to frost bloom. Well-branched free-blooming plants 2 ft. tall. Pkt. 15¢.

Brilliant, 3991. Red.
Creole, 3992. Cream.
La France, 3993. Rose.
Finest Mixed Colors, 4000. Pkt. 15¢; large pkt. 50¢.

Princess Alice, 3997. White.
Silvery Lilac, 3998.
Sapphire, 3999. Blue.

COLLECTION, 4960. One pkt. each of the 6 colors for 75¢.

10-WEEK STOCKS. Stocky branching plants, bloom in 10 weeks from seed. 12 to 15 inches tall. Pkt. 15¢.

Blood Red, 3971.
Canary Yellow, 3972.
Lavender, 3973.

Bright Rose, 3975.
Purple, 3977.
Pure White, 3979.

Stock—Giant Imperial

Finest Mixed, 3980. Pkt. 15¢; large pkt. 40¢; ¼ oz. $1.00.

COLLECTION, 4958. One pkt. each of the 6 colors for 75¢.

GIANT IMPERIAL. Base branching, with extra long spikes for cutting. Pkt. 20¢.

Buttercup, 4005. A pleasing yellow.
Chamois, 4007. Pink and cream.
Elk's Pride, 4009. Rich royal purple.
Fiery Red, 4011. Striking.

Golden Rose, 4012. Golden rose.
Lavender, 4013. A charming shade.
Rose-Pink, 4017. Has special appeal.
Shasta, 4019. Glistening white.

Finest Mixed, 4020. Pkt. 15¢; large pkt. 50¢.

COLLECTION, 4962. One pkt. each of the 8 varieties for $1.40.

STOKESIA, Cyanea Blue, 4033. (Cornflower Aster.) Vigorous plants 2 ft. tall each with 20 to 30 large lavender-blue Cornflower-like blooms. July to September. Pkt. 20¢.

STREPTOCARPUS Hybrids, 4040. (Cape Primrose.) Tender perennial 6 inches tall. Velvety leaves with masses of tubular flowers in many attractive colors. Pkt. 50¢; large pkt. $1.25.

SWEET ROCKET, Matronalis, 4220. (Hesperis.) Old fashioned hardy perennial growing 3 ft. tall. Bears its flowers in showy heads of white, lilac and purple. Excellent for naturalizing on banks and terraces. Delightfully fragrant. Pkt. 10¢.

Stokesia—Cyanea

Dreer's Superb SWEET PEAS

Sweet Peas

The loveliest of summer flowers and one of the few that can boast a National Society. Charming, graceful flowers, sweet-scented and delightful shades. Plant seed as early in the spring as ground can be worked in drills 3 inches deep. Provide support as soon as 6 inches high. Use TRAIN-ETTS, Rot-resistant Twine Netting.

No. 1 60 x 72 in. $ .75 each
No. 2 60 x 96 in. .95 each
No. 3 69 x 180 in. 1.40 each
Postpaid

Summer Flowering

The regular or standard Summer-Flowering Sweet Peas. Recommended for planting from Philadelphia, north, particularly in the cooler districts.

Pkt. 15¢; ½ oz. 35¢; oz. 60¢.

Chieftain, 4119. Satiny mauve.
Chinese Blue, 4121. Rich deep blue.
Cream-Gigantic, 4122. Very large.

Ecstacy, 4120. Blush pink.
Gigantic, 4125. Black-seeded white.
Highlander, 4127. Pure lavender.
Patricia Unwin, 4144. Salmon-pink.
Pinkie, 4147. Large rose-pink.
Rubicund, 4159. Crimson-scarlet.
Salmon-Gigantic, 4160. Salmon-pink.
The Admiral, 4169. Navy blue.

Welcome, 4173. Dazzling scarlet.
Summer-flowering Mixed, 4180. Splendid mixture of all colors. Pkt. 15¢; ½ oz. 30¢; oz. 50¢; ¼ lb. $1.25; lb. $4.00.
PELLETIZED SEED, Sweet Peas Mixed, P4180. Pkt. 20¢.
COLLECTION, 4972. One pkt. each of the 12 varieties for $1.50.

Ruffled Orchid-Flowered

Ruffled petals that make the flowers look larger than they are. Usually 4 blooms to a stem. The most perfect and loveliest of all.

Pkt. 20¢; ½ oz. 40¢; oz. 75¢.

Bonnie Ruffles, 4184. Salmon-pink.
Burpee Blue, 4188. Deep blue.
Crimson Ruffled, 4192. Very brilliant.
Exquisite, 4194. Salmon-cerise.

Heyday, 4196. Amber rose-pink.
Ruffled Rose, 4197. A beauty.
Ruffled White, 4198. Snow white.
Ruffled Mixed, 4200. All colors. Pkt. 20¢; ½ oz. 40¢; oz. 75¢; ¼ lb. $2.00; lb. $6.00.

COLLECTION, 4975. One pkt. each of the 7 varieties for $1.20.
COLLECTION, 4977. ½ oz. each of the 7 varieties for $2.50.

Early-Flowered Orchid Sweet Peas

For the Greenhouse and Early Outdoor Blooming.

Pkt. 15¢; ½ oz. 45¢; oz. 75¢.

American Beauty, 4054. Crimson rose.
Bridesmaid, 4047. Silvery pink.
Daphne, 4048. Soft salmon-pink.
Grenadier, 4056. Dazzling scarlet.
Harmony, 4053. Lovely lavender.
Hope, 4055. Black-seed white.
Mrs. Herbert Hoover, 4069. Rich blue.

Shirley Temple, 4081. Soft rose-pink.
Princess Blue, 4073. Early bright blue.
Tops, 4085. Deep blood-red crimson.
Triumph, 4086. Lilac-mauve.
Valencia, 4087. Sunproof orange.
Dreer's Early-Flowering Mixture, 4100. Pkt. 15¢; ½ oz. 35¢; oz. 60¢; ¼ lb. $2.00.
COLLECTION, 4964. One pkt. of the 12 varieties for $1.50.

Hot Weather Sweet Peas

Spring Flowering Cuthbertson

Now! Sweet Peas that you can grow all summer! A special strain to withstand summer heat, start to bloom early and bloom for months.

Pkt. 20¢; ½ oz. 60¢; oz. $1.00.

Coline, 4101. Bright scarlet.
Evelyn, 4102. Salmon cream pink.
Frank G., 4103. Clear lavender.
Janet, 4104. Pure white.

Lois, 4105. Clear rose pink.
Tommy, 4106. Clear marine blue.
Mixed, 4110. A delightful blend of many colors.
COLLECTION, 4979. One pkt. each of the 6 colors for $1.00.

Dwarf Sweet Peas

Charming dwarf plants covered with large flowers. Good for flower boxes or borders. 8 in.

Cupid Mixed, 4210. Pkt. 10¢; ½ oz. 30¢; oz. 50¢.
Bo-Peep, 4212. New dwarf Sweet Pea with extra-large salmon-pink flowers. Makes a wonderful spring and summer display in solid beds or borders. Pkt. 15¢; ¼ oz. 45¢.

Lathyrus—*Hardy Sweet Pea*

Free-flowering, hardy Sweet Pea for covering old stumps, fences and banks. Blooms continuously from mid-summer until frost. 5-6 ft. Pkt. 20¢.

Latifolius, Pink Beauty, 2751. Rose-pink.
Red, 2753. Crimson red.

White Pearl, 2755. Pure white.
Mixed Colors, 2756.

Hardy Sweet Peas—Lathyrus

31

Dianthus Barbatus
(Double Sweet William)

Sweet William—*Dianthus Barbatus*

Who doesn't know the charm of these old fashioned favorites. Showy flowerheads on 18 inch stems. Perfectly hardy and last for years. Pkt. 15¢; large pkt. 50¢.

Dark Crimson, 4222. Deep crimson, no eye.
Scarlet Beauty, 4223. Rich scarlet.
Newport Pink, 4225. Salmon-rose.
Purple Beauty, 4226. Deep purple.
Giant Pure White, 4229. Single white.
COLLECTION, 4978. One pkt. each of the 5 varieties for 60¢.

Single Mixed, 4230. Pkt. 10¢; large pkt. 30¢; ¼ oz. 50¢; oz. $1.50.
Holborn Glory, Mixed, 4236. Impressive single flowers with large eyes. Pkt. 15¢; large pkt. 50¢; ¼ oz. 85¢.
Double Mixed, 4240. Pkt. 15¢; large pkt. 50¢; ¼ oz. 85¢.
Midget Double Mixed, 4246. A splendid double-flowered, dwarf compact variety. 10 inches. Pkt. 20¢; large pkt. 60¢.
Midget Single Mixed, 4250. Very showy dwarf, compact plants 6 inches tall completely covered with flowers. Pkt. 25¢; large pkt. 75¢.
Annual Sweet William Mixed, 4252. Well-branched plants, 15 inches high, bearing large flower trusses in many beautiful colors. Blooms first year if sown early. Pkt. 15¢.

THUNBERGIA, Mixed Colors, 4280. (Black-Eyed Susan Vine.) Rapid growing annual climber splendid for baskets, vases, ground cover, etc. Buff, white or orange blooms, many with black eye. Pkt. 10¢.

Thalictrum
Meadow Rue

Showy tall perennials with attractive foliage not unlike the Maiden Hair Fern but larger, the flowers are borne freely all summer.

Adiantifolium, 4264. Robust plants 18 inches tall, splendid for cutting, with attractive fern-like foliage. Dainty greenish yellow flowers in airy panicles. Pkt. 15¢; large pkt. 40¢.

Dipterocarpum, 4269. Airy panicles of delightful mauve blooms. 3 ft. Pkt. 15¢.

SEED SOER 50¢
Plastic · seeds visible as sown · go twice as far. Saves thinning · for peas to petunias.

Tithonia

Tithonia—*Speciosa*

Avalon Earliest Hybrids Mixed, 4288. (Golden Flower of the Incas.) Stately plants 6 ft. tall with showy long-stemmed blooms ranging from orange to flame scarlet. Flowers resemble single Dahlias. Pkt. 25¢.
Early-Flowering, 4289. Brilliant, golden-orange flowers borne on 6 ft. plants from July until frost. Pkt. 15¢.
TORENIA, Fournieri, 4293. (Wishbone Flower.) Showy compact 10 inch plants. Flowers are like trumpet-shaped Pansies, sky blue and purple with a yellow wishbone at the throat. Free-blooming all summer and will stand some shade. Pkt. 15¢; large pkt. 60¢.

Surprise Garden Mixture, 3020. Don't know what to plant? Want the most flowers with the least care and attention. Try this surprise Garden mixture over twenty varieties of easily grown Annuals to sow as you would grass seed in a bed or border. One weeding is generally all the care they need. Pkt. 15¢; oz. 50¢; ¼ lb. $1.25; lb. $4.00.

THERMOPSIS, Caroliniana, 4273. (Carolina Lupine.) Tall showy hardy perennial with long spikes of Lupine-like yellow blooms. 3 ft. June and July. Pkt. 15¢.
TROLLIUS, Europaeus, 4304. (Globeflower.) Large flowers the color of green gold. Grows 15 inches tall and blooms all summer. Perennial. Pkt. 15¢.
TUNICA, Saxifraga, 4307. (Tunic-flower.) Slender-stemmed creeping plants covered with small star-shaped pink flowers during spring and early summer. Pkt. 25¢.
TRITOMA, Hybrids Mixed, 4300. (Red Hot Poker.) Hardy perennial. New continuous flowering Tritoma easy to grow from seed. Many of the plants will bloom in the first year. Contains splendid yellow, orange and scarlet shades. May to October. 3 ft. Pkt. 15¢; large pkt. 50¢.
URSINIA, New Hybrids, 4312. (Jewel of the Veldt.) Showy bushes covered from midsummer until late fall with rich yellow to orange daisy-like flowers, jet black at the base. 15 inches. Pkt. 15¢.
VALERIANA, Officinalis Mixed, 4320. (Garden Heliotrope.) Upright 4 ft. plants with satiny fragrant flower heads in pinkish-lavender shades. Perennial. Pkt. 10¢.
VERBASCUM, Hybrids Mixed, 4331. (Mullein.) Vigorous plants, 5 ft. tall, with wooly leaves and showy flower spikes in many colors. Perennial. Pkt. 15¢.

Torenia—Fournieri

Giant Flowering VERBENA

For beds, for borders, for boxes, Verbenas are ideal. They are colorful, fragrant and bloom all summer. Flowers are borne in flat heads on stems long enough for cutting. 12 to 15 inches tall. **Pkt. 15¢;** large pkt. 60¢.

Annapolis Blue, 4354. Very brilliant.
Cerise Queen, 4355. Salmon-cerise.
Floradale Beauty, 4358. Rose-pink.
Lavender Glory, 4361. Fragrant.
Royale, 4365. Royal blue.
Salmon-Pink, 4367. Large trusses.
Spectrum Red, 4368. Sparkling color.
White, 4369. Pure white.

Dreer's Giant Flowering Mixed, 4370. Pkt. 15¢; large pkt. 60¢; ¼ oz. $1.00.
PELLETIZED SEED, Verbena Giant Flowering Mixed, P4370. Pkt. 20¢.
COLLECTION, 4982. One pkt. each of the 8 varieties for $1.00.

Dwarf Compact Verbena

Dwarf compact form growing into cushion-like plants 6 inches tall and 1 foot wide. Fine for borders for larger beds.
Salmon Pink, 4346. Lovely, clear salmon pink. Pkt. 15¢.
Dwarf Compact Mixed, 4350. All colors. Pkt. 15¢; large pkt. 60¢.

Perennial Verbena

Venosa, 4375. Spreading plants with large showy bright purplish heliotrope flowerheads during June and July. 16 inches tall. Pkt. 15¢.
Venosa, Lilacina, 4377. Bright lilac-blue flowers. Pkt. 15¢.
Bonariensis, 4334. Imposing plants 4 ft. tall bearing rosy violet flowers through the summer. Pkt. 25¢.

Giant Flowering Verbena

Viscaria

Rainbow Drops

Hardy annuals about 1 ft. high. Five-petalled flat flowers on graceful stems. Blooms all summer.
Blue Pearl, 4445. Large showy, clear light blue. Pkt. 20¢.
Mixed Colors, 4450. Many beautiful shades all with a contrasting darker eye in the center. Pkt. 15¢.
VENIDIUM, Fastuosum Hybrids, Mixed, 4330. (Monarch of the Veldt.) Beautiful, tall bushy annuals with Daisy-like flowers in pastel shades of cream, lemon, buff, light orange, each with a black circle around the center. Blooms throughout the summer. Prefers cool weather. 30 inches tall. Pkt. 25¢.

Veronica — Longifolia

VIRGINIAN STOCKS, Mixed, 4444. (Malcomia Maritima.) Old-fashioned hardy annual that blooms in June and July. Grows about 1 foot tall and bears lovely, richly fragrant blooms in white, red, rose, and lilac shades. Pkt. 10¢; ¼ oz. 25¢; ½ oz. 40¢.
VERONICA, Longifolia, 4380. (Speedwell.) Beautiful deep lavender-blue flowers on long racemes all summer on bushy plants 2 ft. tall. Perennials. Pkt. 15¢.

Vinca rosea

Ornamental free-blooming annual with bright green, shiny foliage. One of the most satisfactory bedding plants. Blooms from July to October. 12 to 18 inches tall. Pkt. 15¢.
Rosea, 4393. Rose with dark eye.
Pure White, 4397. White.
Crimson, 4398. White with rose eye.
Mixed Colors, 4400.

Wallflower

Old country favorite with colorful spikes of stock-like flowers. Requires protection where winters are severe. 18 to 24 inches tall.
Extra-Early Mixed, 4456. Beautiful single-flowered variety. Blooms first year if sown early. Pkt. 10¢.
PELLETIZED SEED, Wallflower, Extra Early Mixed, P4456. Pkt. 20¢.
Early Wonder Double Mixed, 4466. Large double fragrant blooms. Pkt. 15¢.

Venidium — Fastuosum

Soil Test Kits

It is easy and inexpensive to test your own soil with Sudbury Soil Test Kits. You can quickly test for nitrogen, phosphorus, potash, and acidity, and adjust your soil to the crops you want to grow. Home garden size (20 tests) $2.50, Jr. Professional (50 tests) $4.75, Horticultural Model (100 tests) $12.50, De Luxe Model (200 tests) $22.50.

Zinnia—California Giant

World's Finest

Alphabetically Zinnias are last, but for range of size (from 6 inch plants with button-like blooms, to 4 ft. plants with flowers big as Dahlias); variety of color, ease of growth and free-blooming qualities they easily rank as "First" among the annual flowers.

Zinnias love warm, even hot, weather, don't sow seed too early; 10th of May is soon enough and they may be planted up to the end of June. Give them plenty of room to develop; half their full grown height apart is a good rule to follow. For continuous bloom, keep faded flowers picked.

California Giant Zinnias

Big, big, big! flat, full double flowers up to 6 inches across. Plants 3 to 4 ft. Bloom freely up to heavy frost. Illustration in full color on page VI, gives an idea of the size of these beauties. Pkt. 15¢; large pkt. 40¢; ¼ oz. 60¢; oz. $1.75.
Daffodil Improved, 4545. Canary yellow.
Golden Queen, 4546. Bright lemon yellow.
Lavender Queen, 4548. Bright lavender.
Miss Willmott, 4549. Bright rose-pink.
Orange King, 4551. Rich golden orange.
Purity, 4553. Large white flowers.
Rose Queen, 4555. Deep rose.
Salmon-Rose, 4557. A lovely shade.
Scarlet Queen, 4558. Deep scarlet.
Violet Queen, 4559. Deep purple.
California Giant Mixed, 4560.
COLLECTION, 4994. One 15¢ packet each of the ten colors for $1.25.

Dahlia-Flowered Zinnias

Huge flowers 6 inches across and 3 to 4 inches deep like a decorative Dahlia. Plants 3 to 4 ft. tall. Bloom all summer, up to heavy frost.
Pkt. 15¢; large pkt. 40¢; ¼ oz. 60¢.
Canary Bird, 4521. Canary yellow.
Crimson-Monarch, 4523. Crimson-scarlet.
Dream, 4525. Deep lavender.
Exquisite, 4527. Luminous rose-pink.
Golden State, 4529. Golden yellow.
Illumination, 4530. Deep rose.
Oriole, 4531. Orange and gold.
Polar Bear, 4533. White.
Purple Prince, 4535. Deep purple.
Scarlet Flame, 4537. Fiery Scarlet.
Finest Mixed, 4540. Pkt. 15¢; large pkt. 40¢; ¼ oz. 60¢; oz. $1.75.
COLLECTION, 4993. One 15¢ packet each of the ten varieties for $1.25.

Dahlia-Flowered Zinnia

Four Unique Zinnias

New Super Giant Mixed, 4542. The largest of all Zinnias, with flowers measuring 5½ to 6½ inches across. An entirely new range of colors is presented, pastels, picotees and many two and three toned effects. Pkt. 25¢; large pkt. 60¢; ¼ oz. 85¢; ½ oz. $1.50.
Super Crown of Gold Pastel Tints, 4510. Pastels! The Decorators' and Flower Arrangers' delight. This lovely Zinnia has all the pastel shades, all blending but still with scarcely any two alike. Extra large flowers on 3 ft. plants. Pkt. 15¢; large pkt. 50¢; ¼ oz. 75¢.
Giant Crested Howard, 4486. Mindful of gigantic Scabiosa with broad outer guard petals framing a crested center of smaller quilled petals. Flowers are 4 to 5 inches across. All the really good Zinnia colors are included. Pkt. 20¢; large pkt. 60¢; ¼ oz. 85¢.
Cactus-Flowered Giants, 4586. Large flowers with long pointed, twisted, petals in an outstanding array of color. Distinct from the Fantasy type. 3 ft. plants. Pkt. 15¢; large pkt. 50¢; ¼ oz. 75¢.

Zinnia, Luther Burbank Mixture

4543. Named for the Dean of American Horticulturists. Immense blooms on 3 to 4 ft. bushy plants and almost every conceivable color. Pkt. 25¢; 2 pkts. 45¢.

Zinnia—Giant Crested Howard

ZINNIAS

Cut-and-Come-Again Zinnias

The most popular type of Zinnia for cutting. Produces neat compact plants, 2-2½ ft. tall, bearing great quantities of double perfectly shaped flowers, about 3 inches in diameter.

Buff Beauty, 4512.   White, 4519.   Pinkie, 4515.
Canary, 4513.   Orange, 4516.
Crimson, 4514.   Salmon-Rose, 4517.
Pkt. 10¢; large pkt. 25¢; ¼ oz. 50¢.

Finest Mixed, 4520. Pkt. 10¢; large pkt. 25¢; ¼ oz. 40¢; oz. $1.25.
PELLETIZED SEED, Zinnia Cut-and-Come-Again Mixed, P4520. Pkt. 20¢.
COLLECTION, 4990. One 10¢ packet each of the 7 colors for 60¢.
Pastel Sunshine Tints, 4511. All the best pastel shades in a glorious mixture. Pkt. 25¢; large pkt. 60¢; ¼ oz. 85¢.

Fantasy Zinnias

A new type of Zinnia widely different from all others. The large well-rounded flowers are a mass of shaggy curled petals not unlike the shaggy Chrysanthemums. Pkt. 15¢; large pkt. 40¢; ¼ oz. 75¢.

Orange Lady, 4491. Bright orange.   Rosalie, 4493. Deep rose.
Stardust, 4495. Golden yellow.

White Light, 4497.
Wildfire, 4498. Bright red.
Fantasy Mixed, 4500. Pkt. 15¢; large pkt. 40¢; ¼ oz. 65¢.
COLLECTION, 4999. One 15¢ pkt. each of the 5 varieties for 60¢.
Super Fantasy Giant Mixture, 4635. All the charm of the regular Fantasy-type but flowers are nearly twice as large. All shades in a magnificent mixture. Pkt. 25¢; large pkt. 60¢; ¼ oz. 85¢; ½ oz. $1.50.
Scabiosa-Flowered Autumn Tints, 4632. Scabiosa-Flowered Zinnias ranging in color through the gorgeous tints of autumn foliage. Pkt. 15¢; large pkt. 40¢; ¼ oz. 75¢.

Zinnia, Linnearis

4595. 10 inches tall and forms a dense cushion 1 ft. in diameter. Completely covered with single golden-orange blooms with lemon-yellow stripe through the center of each petal. Pkt. 15¢; large pkt. 40¢; ¼ oz. 75¢.

Cut-and-Come-Again Zinnia

Dreer's Double Lilliput or Pompon

Pretty, full double, rounded, almost ball-shaped blooms on compact plants 18 inches tall. Splendid for beds, borders and cutting. Pkt. 10¢; large pkt. 25¢; ¼ oz. 50¢; oz. $1.50.

Black Ruby, 4562.   Golden Orange, 4569.
Maroon.   Purple Gem, 4572.
Canary Yellow, 4563.   Salmon-Rose, 4575.
Crimson Gem, 4565.   Scarlet Gem, 4577.
Flesh Pink, 4567.   White Gem, 4579.

COLLECTION, 4996. One 10¢ packet each of the 9 colors for 80¢.
Lilliput Finest Mixed, 4580. Pkt. 10¢; large pkt. 25¢; ¼ oz. 40¢.
Lilliput Pastel Mixture, 4582. Only the most attractive pastel shades.
Pkt. 15¢; large pkt. 30¢; ¼ oz. 50¢; oz. $1.50.
Red-Riding Hood, 4603. Graceful, small button-like, scarlet blooms. One ft. tall. Pkt. 10¢; large pkt. 25¢; ¼ oz. 50¢.

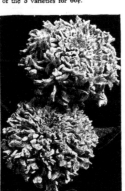

Zinnia—Fantasy—Star Dust

Mexicana—Perfection Mixed, 4610. Lovely small-flowered Zinnias in a profusion of odd shades tipped with contrasting colors. Use an old fashioned bean pot for a vase and win a prize at your garden club. Pkt. 15¢; large pkt. 35¢; ¼ oz. 60¢.
Tom Thumb Miniature Mixed, 4590. 6 to 10 inches tall covered with perfectly double blooms of miniature size. All shades. Pkt. 15¢; large pkt. 40¢; ¼ oz. 75¢.
Gaillardia-Flowered Mixed, 4592. The blooms are fully double and resemble double Gaillardias. About 2 inches across and come in a wide range of colors. 2 ft. tall. Pkt. 10¢; large pkt. 35¢; ¼ oz. 60¢.

The Book of Annuals. (A. C. Hottes.) A splendid book on growing all the annuals. 180 pages and 122 illustrations. $2.00. Postpaid.

Mexicana Zinnias

Lilliput Zinnias

GROW *Your Own Flowers* FROM SEED

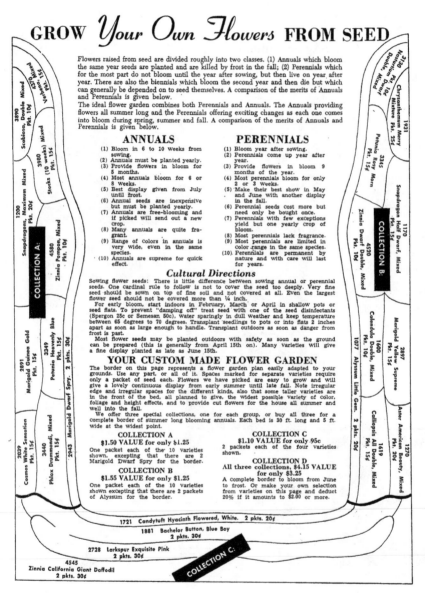

Flowers raised from seed are divided roughly into two classes. (1) Annuals which bloom the same year seeds are planted and are killed by frost in the fall; (2) Perennials which for the most part do not bloom until the year after sowing, but then live on year after year. There are also the biennials which bloom the second year and then die but which can generally be depended on to seed themselves. A comparison of the merits of Annuals and Perennials is given below.

The ideal flower garden combines both Perennials and Annuals. The Annuals providing flowers all summer long and the Perennials offering exciting changes as each one comes into bloom during spring, summer and fall. A comparison of the merits of Annuals and Perennials is given below.

ANNUALS

(1) Bloom in 6 to 10 weeks from sowing.
(2) Annuals must be planted yearly.
(3) Provide flowers in bloom for 5 months.
(4) Most annuals bloom for 6 or 8 weeks.
(5) Best display given from July until frost.
(6) Annual seeds are inexpensive but must be planted yearly.
(7) Annuals are free-blooming and if picked will send out a new crop.
(8) Many annuals are quite fragrant.
(9) Range of colors in annuals is very wide, even in the same species.
(10) Annuals are supreme for quick effect.

PERENNIALS

(1) Bloom year after sowing.
(2) Perennials come up year after year.
(3) Provide flowers in bloom 9 months of the year.
(4) Most perennials bloom for only 2 or 3 weeks.
(5) Make their best show in May and June with another display in the fall.
(6) Perennial seeds cost more but need only be bought once.
(7) Perennials with few exceptions yield but one yearly crop of bloom.
(8) Most perennials lack fragrance.
(9) Most perennials are limited in color range in the same species.
(10) Perennials are permanent by nature and with care will last for years.

Cultural Directions

Sowing flower seeds: There is little difference between sowing annual or perennial seeds. One cardinal rule to follow is not to cover the seed too deeply. Very fine seed should be sown on top of fine soil and not covered at all. Even the largest flower seed should not be covered more than ¼ inch.

For early bloom, start indoors in February, March or April in shallow pots or seed flats. To prevent "damping off" treat seed with one of the seed disinfectants (Spergon 25c or Semesan 50c). Water sparingly in dull weather and keep temperature between 65 degrees to 70 degrees. Transplant seedlings to pots or into flats 2 inches apart as soon as large enough to handle. Transplant outdoors as soon as danger from frost is past.

Most flower seeds may be planted outdoors with safety as soon as the ground can be prepared (this is generally from April 15th on). Many varieties will give a fine display planted as late as June 15th.

YOUR CUSTOM MADE FLOWER GARDEN

The border on this page represents a flower garden plan easily adapted to your grounds. Use any part, or all of it. Spaces marked for separate varieties require only a packet of seed each. Flowers we have picked are easy to grow and will give a lovely continuous display from early summer until late fall. Note irregular edge and irregular spaces for the different kinds, also that some taller varieties are in the front of the bed, all planned to give, the widest possible variety of color, foliage and height effects, and to provide cut flowers for the house all summer and well into the fall.

We offer three special collections, one for each group, or buy all three for a complete border of summer long blooming annuals. Each bed is 30 ft. long and 5 ft. wide at the widest point.

COLLECTION A
$1.50 VALUE for only $1.25

One packet each of the 10 varieties shown, excepting that there are 2 Marigold Dwarf Spry for the border.

COLLECTION B
$1.55 VALUE for only $1.25

One packet each of the 10 varieties shown excepting that there are 2 packets of Alyssum for the border.

COLLECTION C
$1.10 VALUE for only 95c

2 packets each of the four varieties shown.

COLLECTION D
All three collections, $4.15 VALUE for only $3.25

A complete border to bloom from June to frost. Or make your own selection from varieties on this page and deduct 20% if it amounts to $2.00 or more.

COLLECTION A:

3890 Scabiosa, Double Mixed Pkt. 10¢
4370 Mixed Verbena, Pkt. 15¢
3980 Stocks (10 weeks) Mixed Pkt. 15¢
1200 Snapdragons, Maximum Mixed Pkt. 20¢
4580 Zinnia Pompon, Mixed Pkt. 10¢
2891 Marigold Guinea Gold Pkt. 15¢
3349 Petunia Heavenly Blue Pkt. 15¢
2943 Marigold Dwarf Spry. 2 pkts. 30¢
2039 Cosmos White Sensation Pkt. 15¢
3440 Phlox Drummondi, Mixed Pkt. 15¢

COLLECTION B:

3130 Nasturtium Double, Dwarf Mixed Pkt. 10¢
1931 Chrysanthemum Merry Mixture Pkt. 25¢
3345 Petunia Rosy Morn Pkt. 15¢
1170 Snapdragon Half Dwarf, Mixed Pkt. 15¢
4520 Zinnia Dwarf Double, Mixed Pkt. 10¢
2897 Marigold Yellow Supreme Pkt. 15¢
1600 Calendula Double, Mixed Pkt. 10¢
1077 Alyssum Little Gem. 2 pkts. 20¢
1270 Aster American Beauty, Mixed Pkt. 20¢
1619 Calliopsis All Double, Mixed Pkt. 15¢

COLLECTION C:

1721 Candytuft Hyacinth Flowered, White. 2 pkts. 20¢
1881 Bachelor Button, Blue Boy 2 pkts. 30¢
2728 Larkspur Exquisite Pink 2 pkts. 30¢
4545 Zinnia California Giant Daffodil 2 pkts. 30¢

DAHLIAS

SELECTED; for size (1½ to 2 inch Pompons to 12 to 14 inch Giant Exhibition); for type (Honey Comb to shaggy "Mumlike" petals); color (all the good true colors); ease of culture (the kind you can plant and just "let grow like Topsy"). FD: Formal Decorative; ID: Informal Decorative; C: Cactus; SC: Semi-Cactus.

Four Recent Introductions

Amos Kirby, 45-260. (ID). Gigantic, deep purple 12 inch blooms on extra long stems. Twice Winner of largest bloom in show. $5.00 each; 3 for $12.50.

Autumn Blaze, 45-259. (ID). Fiery-red tinged with gold, flowers up to 14 inches across. Has won medals for the largest and most nearly perfect Dahlia. $3.50 each; 3 for $9.75.

Fashion, 45-307. (SC). Soft purple veined white blooms, measuring 10 inches across. 4 ft. high. $2.00 each; 3 for $5.50.

Noble Glory, 45-308. (SC). Primrose yellow shaded amaranth with heavier shading on reverse of petals. The center is a beautiful tyrian rose. Strong plants 5 ft. high, blooms measure 15 inches across. $2.00 each; 3 for $5.50.

BUY all 4 for $10.95. SAVE $1.55. 2 of each of the four for $19.95.

Decorative Dahlia

Popular Varieties For Cutting

California Idol, 45-267. (ID). More than a foot across. Clear bright yellow. $1.00 each; 3 for $2.75.

Carl G. Dahl, 45-217. (ID). Bright apricot-buff, shaded old-rose on the reverse. $1.00 each; 3 for $2.75.

Gallant Fox, 45-274. (FD). Luminous dark claret-red flowers measuring 6 inches across. 50¢ each; 3 for $1.35.

Jane Cowl, 45-278. (ID). Giant flowers of buff blended with gold and shading to apricot and rose. 50¢ each; 3 for $1.35.

Jersey Beauty, 45-282. (FD). The most popular of all pink Dahlias. 50¢ each; 3 for $1.35.

Mrs. George Le Boutillier, 45-288. (ID). Exquisite carmine-red Dahlia grows 14½ inches across. 60¢ each; 3 for $1.50.

Pink Giant, 45-293. (ID). Gorgeous, mammoth blooms of bright Tyrian pink. 5½ ft. tall. 75¢ each; 3 for $2.00.

Prince of Persia, 45-292. (ID). Iridescent cardinal red. A vigorous grower and free bloomer. 75¢ each; 3 for $2.00.

Sherwood's Peach, 45-297. (ID). A newer giant Dahlia of delightful orange-apricot color. $1.00 each; 3 for $2.75.

Thomas A. Edison, 45-302. (FD). Rich royal purple or Petuniaviolet color. Does best in rich soil. 60¢ each; 3 for $1.50.

Volcano, 45-303. (FD). Large well-formed blooms of a flaming orange-red. $1.00 each; 3 for $2.75.

Blue Moon, 45-273. (ID). Overlapping petals like a pleated skirt. Distinct blueish hue. $1.00 each; 3 for $2.50.

Dahliamum, 45-279. The twisted petals and delightful colorings of an orange and gold Chrysanthemum. $1.00 each; 3 for $2.50.

Six Top Exhibition Dahlias

Daylight, 45-263. (ID). Six foot plants with heavy dark green foliage. The biggest white Dahlia you have ever seen, flowers up to 12 inches across. $1.50 each; 3 for $4.25.

Kemps Red Pilot, 45-281. (ID). Short, stocky growth with large dark red flowers nice for cutting. $1.00 each; 3 for $2.75.

Maffie, 45-285. (SC). One of the largest and most spectacular Exhibition Dahlias. Immense sparkling rose-red blooms. $1.50 each; 3 for $4.25.

Mme. Chiang Kai-shek, 45-289. (ID). Large blooms with beautiful wavy petals, lemon yellow tipped peach pink. Also pink on reverse. $1.50 each; 3 for $4.25.

Ogden Reid, 45-284. (ID). Bright rose with golden highlights. $1.50 each; 3 for $4.25.

Salem Sunshine, 45-309. (ID). Large, light lemon yellow blooms. An excellent grower 4 ft. high. $1.50 each; 3 for $4.25.

BUY all 6 for $6.95. SAVE $1.55. 2 each of the 6 colors $12.75.

Pompon Dahlias

Delightful, perfectly formed flowers for cutting. Blooms about 2 inches in diameter, plants 2 to 3 ft. tall.

Amber Queen, 45-406. Amber shaded with bright apricot.

Bobby, 45-410. Deep plum purple.

Indian Chief, 45-426. Bright red, tipped white.

Joe Fette, 45-428. Pure white.

Mary Munns, 45-430. Fuchsia red, shaded orchid.

Morning Mist, 45-434. Pure white, tipped pink.

Sherry, 45-435. Bright Petunia-purple.

White Fawn, 45-407. Pure white a little more open than the other "Poms'."

Yellow Gem, 45-438. Creamy yellow.

POSTPAID: 50¢ each; 3 for $1.35; 9 for $2.97.

Collection Ball Dahlias

Easiest culture, extremely free-flowering and perfect blooms 3 to 4 inches in diameter.

Red Chief, bright red; A. D. Livoni, lavender pink; Storm King, pure white; Yellow Duke, golden yellow.

COLLECTION: One each of the 4, $1.00; 2 collections $1.75. Not sold separately.

Decorative Collection

Four of the best time tested informal decorative varieties at a price within the reach of all.

Kemp's White Wonder, mammoth white; King Alfred, huge red; Jane Cowl, extra large bronze; Zant's Purple, best purple.

COLLECTION: One each of the 4, $2.00; 2 collections, $3.75. Not sold separately.

Glorious Gladiolus

Dreer's Top Size Guaranteed-to-Bloom Bulbs

Few flowers can compare with the stateliness and beauty of Gladiolus. Make plantings every two weeks from May first to July first for a summer of beauty. Plant bulbs (corms) no closer than 12 inches apart and cover 5 inches deep. Easy to grow from our simple planting instructions.

EXHIBITION GROUP

Postpaid: 25¢ each; 3 for 60¢; 12 for $2.10; 100 for $15.00.

Abu Hassan, 46-102. Deep velvety, violet-blue flowers, well arranged.
Elizabeth the Queen, 46-248. Lavender-mauve blooms with darker lines in the throat.
Leading Lady, 46-391. A sport of Picardy with pearly, cream-white blooms.
Majuba, 46-418. Massive spikes with huge orange-scarlet flowers.
Oregon Gold, 46-527. Light creamy-yellow with 9 or 10 charming florets open at one time.
Red Charm, 46-629. Charming shade of red. Large well-formed blooms.
Yellow Herald, 46-744. Extra large ruffled flowers of clear amber yellow.
COLLECTION: 6 each of the 7 Exhibition "Glads" (42 Bulbs) for $6.95.
COLLECTION: 12 each of the 7 Exhibition "Glads" (84 Bulbs) for $12.95.

HOME GARDEN GROUP

Postpaid: 3 for 45¢; 12 for $1.50; 100 for $9.95.

Algonquin, 46-126. Splendid straight spikes with brilliant scarlet blooms.
Blue Beauty, 46-187. Medium blue, darker at the edges.
Black Opal, 46-177. Dark glistening red.
Corona, 46-229. Creamy-white, edged with rosy lavender.
Dr. F. E. Bennett, 46-255. Bright scarlet with white spearhead markings.
Ethel Cave Cole, 46-253. Magnificent light pink.
Golden Chimes, 46-327. Large, slightly ruffled blooms of rich yellow.
Jeanie, 46-361. Rich clear pink; white midrib; creamy throat.
King Lear, 46-384. Deep clear purple, edged with silver.
Maid of Orleans, 46-399. Milky-white with cream throat.
Margaret Beaton, 46-417. Pure snow white with orange-red blotch.
Minuet, 46-459. Light pinkish lavender.
Pelegrina, 46-542. Beautiful, deep rich violet blooms.
Rewi Fallu, 46-642. Superb dark blood-red.
Vredenburg, 46-729. Immense pure white blooms.
COLLECTION: 6 each of any 6 varieties (your choice) for $4.25.
COLLECTION: 12 each of any 6 varieties (your choice) for $7.50.

CUTTING GROUP

Postpaid: 3 for 35¢; 12 for $1.15; 100 for $7.50.

Aladdin, 46-121. Bright salmon with cream blotch.
Bagdad, 46-147. Pleasing smoky old-rose.
Beacon, 46-159. Bright rose-scarlet with large creamy blotch.
Betty Nuthall, 46-171. Rich coral-pink, shaded yellow.
Bit O'Heaven, 46-174. Pretty orange with yellow throat.
Golden Dream, 46-330. Clear brilliant golden-yellow.
King Arthur, 46-381. Heavily ruffled, rosy-lavender blooms.
Morocco, 46-479. Deep rich red with a velvety sheen.
Peggy Lou, 46-535. Splendid tall spikes with large light red florets.
Picardy, 46-578. Giant shrimp-pink blooms arranged in glorious spikes.
Vagabond Prince, 46-714. Garnet-brown with scarlet on lower petals.
Red Lightning, 46-632. Bright, scarlet red with cream blotch on throat.
COLLECTION: 6 each of any 6 varieties (your choice) for $2.95.
COLLECTION: 12 each of any 6 varieties (your choice) for $5.75.

JUMBO MIXED GLADIOLUS

100 Big! Big! Bulbs, for $7.00.

This mixture is made up of innumerable giant-flowering varieties of all colors. These large size bulbs will quite naturally produce larger spikes. There are few gardens where 100 of these bulbs could not be used to great advantage and add their stately appearance and brilliant colors during the summer and fall.
46-805. 3 for 35¢; 12 for $1.00; 25 for $1.90; 100 for $7.00; 250 for $16.00, postpaid.

GLADIOLUS DUST

Combines Spergon (fungicide), for storage rot and corm decay, and DDT to control thrips. Dust bulbs before planting and before storing for winter.
1 lb. $1.50; Postpaid $1.65.

38

The Garden Book Corner

Begonias and How to Grow Them. (V. R. Buxton. 128 pages. All you want to know about growing Begonias. $2.25.
Better Lawns. (Howard B. Sprague.) We believe this is the best book on this subject. $2.00.
The Book of Bulbs. (F. F. Rockwell.) 284 pages; 31 full page halftones and numerous sketches. $4.00.
Climbers and Ground Covers. (A. C. Hottes.) A most complete book on vines. 250 pages, 80 illustrations. $3.00.
Favorite Flowers in Color. 640 pages, 800 natural color photographs. $4.95.
Garden Guide. A real help to every gardener. 576 pages and 300 illustrations. $3.50.
Garden in Your Window. (Jean Hersey.) Filled with facts and instructions to make your window "bloom." $3.00.
Garden Magic. (R. E. Biles.) 324 pages, 8 color plates, and numerous helpful sketches. $3.50.
How to Landscape Your Ground. (L. R. Johnson.) 232 pages and 147 illustrations. $3.50.
All About House Plants. (Montague Free.) 250 pages with many illustrations. Really an excellent volume. $3.50.
Plants and Flowers in the Home. (K. Post.) 200 pages of up-to-date information, $2.50.
How to Increase House Plants. (A. C. Hottes.) A highly interesting book full of valuable information, 236 pages. $3.00.
The Book of Annuals. (A. C. Hottes.) A splendid volume. 180 pages and 122 illustrations. $2.00.
Soils and Fertilizers for Greenhouse and Garden. (Laurie and Kiplinger.) A book every gardner should have. 119 pages. $2.50.
The Gardener's Bug Book. (Cynthia Westcott.) 590 pages giving the information every home gardener needs. $4.95.
The Book of Perennials. (A. C. Hottes.) Full information about hardy plants. 280 pages. $2.75.
The Book of Shrubs. (A. C. Hottes.) 446 pages; covers the most popular as well as many rare shrubs. 184 illustrations. $4.00.
The Book of Trees. (A. C. Hottes.) A splendid companion volume to the preceding. 448 pages. $4.00.
Pruning Trees and Shrubs. (E. P. Felt.) An important guide. 237 pages and 94 illustrations. $2.50.
How to Grow Roses. (MacFarland and Pyle.) 192 pages covering all subjects thoroughly. $2.50.
The Vegetable Encyclopedia. (V. A. Tiedjens.) To the point, up-to-date information on growing all kinds of vegetables; 307 pages. Many line drawings; for only $1.00.
Encyclopedia of Trees, Shrubs, Vines, and Lawns. (Albert E. Wilkinson.) A splendid book economically priced. $1.50.
Weeds of Lawn and Gardens. (J. M. Fogg.) The 175 illustrations enable you to identify all important weeds. 211 pages. $2.50.
1001 Garden Questions Answered. (A. C. Hottes.) 386 pages with 214 interesting illustrations. $3.00.

The prices quoted are postpaid but subject to changes by the publishers.

RELIABLE FOR TOP QUALITY AND FAIR PRICES SINCE 1838

ORDER SHEET

DREER'S

202 North 21st St.
Philadelphia 3, Pa.

Henry A. Dreer, Inc., warrants to the extent of the purchase price that
seeds or bulbs sold are as described on the container within recognized
tolerances. Seller gives no other or further warranty, expressed or implied.

Please don't write in this space

SPECIAL INSTRUCTIONS

Date.............Ship by Mail ☐;　Express ☐;　Freight ☐

Name　Mr.　..
　　　　Mrs.
　　　　Miss　　　　　　Please Print

Street　R.D.　..
　　　　Box No.

City........................, Zone........ State.........

Amount　　　　　　　　(Cash—M. O.—Check—Stamps—)　Charge
Enclosed $.............　(Paym'nt in full—on Budget Plan—)　My Account $............

F...... | B...... | V...... | L...... | R...... | P...... | S......

Quantity	Catalog Number	NAME OF ARTICLE	PRICE $	¢
......	......	..Your Lawn Comes First!...................	......	....
......	..6100..	..The Dreer Lawn Grass...................	......	....
......	......	......	......	......
......	......	......	......	......
......	......	......	......	......
......	......	......	......	......
......	......	......	......	......
......	......	......	......	......
......	......	......	......	......
......	......	......	......	......
......	......	......	......	......
......	......	......	......	......
......	......	......	......	......
......	......	......	......	......
......	......	......	......	......
......	......	......	......	......
......	......	......	......	......
......	......	......	......	......
......	......	......	......	......
......	......	......	......	......
......	......	Total Amount Forward	......	......

We Should Appreciate the Names of Gardening Friends

Name................. St............. City............., State.............

Name................. St............. City............. State.............

Thank You!

SAVE 5%—ORDER EARLY—BEAT THE RUSH

YOU MAY DEDUCT 5% FROM YOUR ORDER IF POSTMARKED ON OR BEFORE MARCH 10, 1950

Quantity	Catalog Number	NAME OF ARTICLE	PRICE $	¢
		Brought Forward		
			TOTAL	

If ordering on DREER'S BUDGET PLAN, please be sure to fill in and sign

References:

Bank .... Address ....

Store .... Address ....

Employer or Personal .... Address ....

Signature ....

We Should Appreciate the Names of Gardening Friends

Name...................... St................ City.............. State............

Name...................... St................ City.............. State............

Thank You!

RELIABLE FOR TOP QUALITY AND FAIR PRICES SINCE 1838

ORDER SHEET

DREER'S

202 North 21st St.
Philadelphia 3, Pa.

Henry A. Dreer, Inc., warrants to the extent of the purchase price that seeds or bulbs sold are as described on the container within recognized tolerances. Seller gives no other or further warranty, expressed or implied.

Please don't write in this space

SPECIAL INSTRUCTIONS

Date............Ship by Mail ☐;   Express ☐;   Freight ☐

Name Mr.
      Mrs. ....
      Miss   Please Print

Street R. D.
        Box No. ....

City........................ Zone........ State..........

Amount   (Cash—M. O.—Check—Stamps—)   Charge
Enclosed $............   (Paym'nt in full—on Budget Plan—)   My Account $..........

F......   B......   V......   L......   R......   P......   S......

Quantity	Catalog Number	NAME OF ARTICLE	PRICE $	¢
		How About The Dreer Dozen Roses?..........		
			Total Amount Forward		

We Should Appreciate the Names of Gardening Friends

Name..................... St............. City............. State...........

Name..................... St............. City............. State...........

Thank You!

Quantity	Catalog Number	NAME OF ARTICLE	PRICE $ ¢
		Brought Forward	
		TOTAL	

If ordering on DREER'S BUDGET PLAN, please be sure to fill in and sign
References:

Bank .... Address ....

Store .... Address ....

Employer or Personal .... Address ....

Signature ....

We Should Appreciate the Names of Gardening Friends

Name....................... St................ City................ State............

Name....................... St................ City................ State............

Thank You!

For Your
Window Garden

39—1   39—4

WALL BRACKET PLANT HOLDER
Decorative, hand wrought, coppered Wall
Brackets. Holds 3-inch coppered plastic pot.
Use them with Ivy or Philodendron to "set
off" pictures or mirrors.
Four Scroll No. 39-4. 10 in. high; 9 in. wide.
Postpaid 95c; 2 for $1.75.
Musical Clef No. 39-1. 10½ in. high; 4¼ in.
wide. Postpaid 95c; 2 for $1.75.

Plant Box (Self-Irrigating). Plants are watered
through ends of box. Water reaches plant
roots through reservoir in bottom. 15 x 4 x
4½ in. can be had in the following colors:
Red, Green, Blue or White. $2.00 each. Large
size, 27 x 5¼ x 6 in., Nile Green only, $3.75.
Add 25c postage.

Wik-Fed Flower Pot. Especially designed for
African violets or any plant that should be
watered from the bottom. The base is a
reservoir for water, which is carried directly
to the roots by a special wick. Made of non-
warping, unbreakable plastic; will last for
years. Colors: Ivory, Yellow, Red and Pink.
$1.15 each; 2 for $2.00, postpaid.

Plant Fountain Sprinkler. Most practical for
watering plants in the home. Correct amount
of water where you want it. No spilling.
Gardeners also say it's ideal for watering
seeds. $1.00 each, postpaid $1.15.

Garden In Your Window (Jean Hersey).
Reading this fine book is almost as
much fun as watching your Window
Garden burst into bloom. $3.00 postpaid.

Lilies
From June Through September

Extend the blooming season
by planting Lilies both spring
and fall. Spring planted Lilies
grow just as luxuriantly as
those planted in the fall, and
bloom a little later.

All varieties listed are
stem, as well as base rooting
and bulbs should be covered
8 to 10 inches. Plant bulbs
as soon as ground can be
dug. We shall ship bulbs on
receipt of your order unless
instructed differently. Severe
frost after planting will not
harm them. Full cultural directions with every order.
Lilies are listed in the order
in which they bloom. All best
quality bulbs, guaranteed to
bloom.

Lily—Regale

Croceum, 40-563. June; 3 ft. Orange-yellow spotted black. 55¢ each; $5.50 per
doz.; $42.00 per 100.
Umbellatum Erectum, 40-565. (Candlestick Lily.) June; 3 ft. Rich crimson spotted
black. 50¢ each; $5.00 per doz.; $38.00 per 100.

Umbellatum, Golden Fleece, 40-621. June; 3 ft.
Orange-yellow flowers tipped scarlet. 75¢ each;
$7.50 per doz.; $58.00 per 100.
Umbellatum, Orange Triumph, 40-623. June; 4
ft. Bright orange. 50¢ each; $5.00 per doz.;
$38.00 per 100.
Centifolium, Olympic Hybrids, 40-560. July; 8
ft. Large, fragrant, ivory-white blooms. 60¢
each; $6.00 per doz.; $45.00 per 100.
Henryi, 40-580. July; 3 ft. Apricot-yellow with
chocolate spots. 60¢ each; $6.00 per doz.;
$45.00 per 100.
Pardalinum Giganteum, 40-595. (Sunset Lily.)
July; 6 ft. Scarlet blooms spotted crimson. 50¢
each; $5.00 per doz.; $38.00 per 100.
Princeps, George C. Creelman, 40-598. July; 6 ft.
Pure white inside, brown outside. 60¢ each;
$6.00 per doz.; $45.00 per 100.
Regale, Mammoth Bulbs, 40-600. July; 5 ft.
White, shaded pink on the outside. 45¢ each;
$4.00 per doz.; $27.00 per 100.
Regale, Extra Large Bulbs, 40-599. 35¢ each;
$3.25 per doz.; $22.00 per 100.

Lily—Willmottiae

Regale, Pure White, 40-601. July; 5 ft. A magnificent white strain. 75¢ each $7.50
per doz. $58.00 per 100.
Speciosum Album, 40-602. (White Showy Lily.)
August; 4 ft. White with a green band. $1.00
each; $10.00 per doz.
Tigrinum Splendens, 40-615. (Tiger Lily.) August;
5 ft. Orange-red with black spots. 40¢ each;
$3.50 per doz.; $26.00 per 100.
Willmottiae, 40-620. August; 6 ft. Showy orange-
red blooms. 60¢ each; $6.00 per doz.; $45.00
per 100.
Speciosum Rubrum, Mammoth Bulbs, 40-606.
(Pink Showy Lily.) September; 4 ft. Rosy white
flowers heavily spotted crimson. 90¢ each;
$9.00 per doz.; $70.00 per 100.
Speciosum Rubrum, Extra Large Bulbs, 40-605.
75¢ each; $7.50 per doz.; $58.00 per 100.
Formosanum, 40-570. September; 4 ft. Large
white blooms, tinted rose on the outside. 40¢
each; $4.00 per doz.; $30.00 per 100.

Lily—Rubrum

Summer Bulbs for Summer Flowers

Some of our most beautiful summer flowers can only be grown from bulbs. The bulbs will increase and last for years if stored over winter in a frost-proof cellar. Easy to grow; full directions with each order.

Dreer's Large-Flowering Cannas

Cannas bloom from early summer until frost in all sections of the country. They succeed best in a sunny position and in practically any kind of soil. For best results, prepare the bed about a foot deep and include a generous supply of pulverized manure. All varieties have green foliage unless otherwise noted.

DORMANT ROOTS. Postpaid, 30¢ each; 3 of one variety 75¢; 12 of one variety $2.25; 25 of one variety $4.00.

City of Portland, 45-222. Huge glowing, bright pink flowers. 3½ ft.

Copper Giant, 45-223. Immense madder red flowers suffused with coppery rose. 4 ft.

Hungaria, 45-226. Large trusses of clear rose flowers, extraordinary size and brilliance. 3½ ft.

King Humbert, 45-228. Enormous rich orange-scarlet flower trusses and dark coppery-bronze foliage. 5 ft.

The President, 45-233. Brilliant fiery scarlet. The most spectacular of all Cannas. 5 ft.

Yellow King Humbert, 45-238. (Orchid-Flowered.) Bright yellow, spotted red. A grand old favorite. 4½ ft.

The Beautiful Hardy Amaryllis

Halli, 45-025. (Lycoris Squamigera.) Perfectly hardy in well-drained soil. They start in spring with heavy foliage growth which dies down in mid-summer. Towards the end of August the roots send up 3 to 4 ft. stems each bearing 4 to 8 large, fragrant, pink lily-like blooms. $1.00 each; 3 for $2.75; 12 for $10.00; 25 for $18.00.

Lycoris radiata
September Spider Lily

40-630. Order now for July delivery and plant upon receipt to secure flowers this year. A splendid plant with showy carmine-rose flowers carried on graceful strong stems. Blooms between early September and November. Often called Nerine or Guernsey Lily. Mammoth Bulbs: 3 for 40¢; 12 for $1.40; 25 for $2.50; 100 for $9.00.

Cannas

Ismene—Peruvian Daffodil

Hyacinthus Candicans

Anemones

Gaily colored, velvety textured Poppies. Grow best in cool climates but can be grown in latitude of Philadelphia, if planted on a northern exposure. Fine for greenhouse forcing.

Giant French Mixed, 40-025. (DeCaen.) Includes all colors. 3 for 25¢; 12 for 80¢; 25 for $1.40.

St. Brigid, 40-027. (Creagh Castle Strain.) Semi-double blooms in many colors. 3 for 30¢; 12 for 90¢; 25 for $1.65.

Summer Blooming Oxalis

Lasiandra, 47-091. Clusters of rosy crimson blossoms on 18-inch stems, bloom for months. 3 for 25¢; 12 for 75¢; 100 for $5.00.

Dieppi Alba, 47-092. Pretty rock garden or edging Oxalis. Little white flowers on 9-inch plants. 3 for 25¢; 12 for 75¢; 100 for $5.00.

Tetraphylla, 47-094. Old rose flowers over brown-banded leaves. 10 inches. 3 for 25¢; 12 for 75¢; 100 for $5.00.

Summer Hyacinth—*Cape Hyacinth-Galtonia*

Hyacinthus Candicans, 47-060. Stately strong flower spikes, 3 to 5 ft. tall, with 20 to 30 pure white bell-shape pendant flowers. Bloom late summer and early fall. 25¢ each; 3 for 60¢; 12 for $2.00; 25 for $3.75.

Ismene—*Peruvian Daffodil*

Calathina, 47-082. Large, fragrant, Amaryllis-like white blooms with apple-green markings in the throat. Very easy to grow in well-drained sunny spots. May also be forced indoors like Amaryllis. 18 inches. 40 each; 3 for $1.00; 12 for $3.75.

Summer Bulbs for Summer Flowers

Montbretias

Tigridia—Shell Flower

Montbretia

Giant-Flowered Mixed, 47-220. Exquisite Gladiolus-like flowers on wiry branching stems. Plant in April or May to bloom in summer or fall. 2 ft. 3 for 40¢; 12 for $1.10; 25 for $2.00.

Earlham Hybrids, 47-221. Wonderful color range and magnificent spikes set with extra large, well-formed blooms. 3 for 45¢; 12 for $1.40; 25 for $2.50.

Ranunculus

Tecolote Strain, 40-851. Double Buttercups in a riot of colors. Plant bulbs in a moist shady location for mid-summer bloom. Plant in pots in the house for blooms in 12 weeks. 3 for 25¢; 12 for 75¢; 25 for $1.35; 100 for $5.00.

Tigridia—*Shell Flower*

Hybrids Mixed, 47-269. (Pavonia Grandiflora.) Orchid-like blooms on Gladiolus-like spikes. Delightful shades of yellow and orange with spotted central cups. Flowers open on successive days. 2 ft. 20¢ each; 3 for 50¢; 12 for $1.75; 25 for $3.25.

Crocus
Fall-Flowering
Order now for delivery in August for September bloom. Perfectly hardy. 12 for 75¢; 25 for $1.35; 100 for $5.00.

Tuberoses

Richly fragrant, summer flowering bulbs. Plant outdoors the middle of May for August-September bloom.

Mexican Everblooming, 47-286. Fragrant, single, pure white blooms from July onward. 3 for 35¢; 12 for $1.10; 25 for $2.00; 100 for $7.50.

Double Pearl, 47-283. Showy, pearly white, double blooms on strong stems. Excellent for cutting. 3 for 50¢; 12 for $1.75; 25 for $3.25; 100 for $12.00.

Tuberose—Double Pearl

Colchicum
Meadow Saffron
40-073. The Wonder Bulb! Blooms without soil or water. Just set in a sunny window for bloom in 4 weeks. Large, crocus-like, lavender flowers, bloom in September outdoors. Perfectly hardy. August shipment. 3 for $1.65; 12 for $6.00.

Sternbergia
Autumn Daffodil
Lutea, 40-885. Very pretty, dwarf autumn-flowering bulbs with blooms like a glorified yellow Crocus. Should have a rather dry, sunny position and well-drained lime soil. Cover 4 inches deep. Provide a layer of leaves for winter protection. July Delivery. 3 for $1.00; 12 for $3.00; 25 for $6.50.

Zephyranthes
Zephyr Flower-Fairy Lilies
Showy lily-shaped blooms during the summer months. Easy to grow. Postpaid: 3 for 35¢; 12 for $1.25; 25 for $2.25.

Ajax, 47-308. Large clear yellow flowers. Bloom profusely.

Alba, 47-311. Pure white.

Rosea, 47-315. Large rose-colored.

Zephyranthes—Fairy Lily

Anemone Japonica

We have endeavored to cover a wide range of varieties to give you flowers for cutting, general garden effect and for permanent beds and borders. If the variety you desire is not listed, please inquire as we have many other varieties.

SHIPPING

All plants listed will be sent prepaid at the proper time for planting. However, due to cost of packing small orders we cannot accept orders for plants for less than a $1.00 value, nor will we ship plants C.O.D.

ACONITUM, Fischeri. Loose heads of dark blue flowers for shady gardens of rich, moist soil. 2 to 3 ft. September. 75¢ each; 3 for $1.75.

ANTHEMIS, Moonlight. These rampant-growing perennials produce an abundance of Daisy-like yellow flowers. 18 to 24 inches. 65¢ each; 3 for $1.50.

ALYSSUM, Saxatile Compactum. Masses of golden yellow flowers on spreading plants that combine with any plant in the rock or wall garden. 65¢ each; 3 for $1.50.

Campanula—Medium

Plants for *Perennial Gardens*

See page IX for a complete Perennial Garden in full natural color.

Anemone Japonica

Beautiful, fall-blooming, flat poppy-shaped flowers from September until freezing weather. Plant in rich, moist soil, partial shade or full sun. 2 to 3 ft.

Marie Manchard. Semi-double blooms of clear white. 3 ft. 65¢ each; 3 for $1.50.

September Charm. Lovely, single silvery-rose flowers 2 to 2½ ft. tall. 65¢ each; 3 for $1.50.

September Queen. Semi-double, rose-red flowers, very productive. 65¢ each; 3 for $1.50.

AQUILEGIA, Mrs. Scott Elliott's Strain. Columbines are a "must" for every garden however small. Graceful in form and fine for cutting with a wide range of colors. 65¢ each; 3 for $1.50.

ARMERIA, Bee's Ruby. Large heads of ruby-red flowers on stiff, wiry stems. 18 inches. 65¢ each; 3 for $1.50.

COREOPSIS, Baden-Gold. Large, golden yellow Cosmos-like flowers 3 to 4 inches across. 2 to 3 ft. 65¢ each; 3 for $1.50.

Geum—Princess Juliana

Campanula—*Bellflower*

Use Campanulas in your rock garden or perennial planting, or in the foreground of your shrub border. Good for cutting, too.

Carpatica, Blue Carpet. Unusually compact and free-flowering. 6 inches. 65¢ each; 3 for $1.50.

Medium, Canterbury Bells. Single bell-shaped flowers on long spikes. Mixed or separate colors. White, pink or blue. 2 ft. 65¢ each; 3 for $1.50.

Medium, Calycanthema. Cup-and-saucer shaped blooms. White, pink or blue or mixed colors. 65¢ each; 3 for $1.50.

Delphinium

Three different types of these universal favorites.

Belladonna. Sky blue blooms nearly all summer. 3 to 4 ft. 65¢ each; 3 for $1.50.

Chinensis, Tom Thumb. Dwarf plants resembling a giant Lobelia. Fine for cutting. 15 inches. 65¢ each; 3 for $1.50.

DELPHINIUM, Giant Pacific Hybrids. Many fine shades, massive spikes 6 to 8 ft. tall. 75¢ each; 3 for $1.75.

DICENTRA, Spectabilis. Old-fashioned Bleeding Heart that everybody loves. Heart-shaped, pink flowers in long racemes in June. 85¢ each; 3 for $2.00.

DIGITALIS, Giant Shirley. Stately spikes of pink, white and lavender-purple, glove-finger blooms. Mixed only. 5 to 6 ft. 65¢ each; 3 for $1.50.

GEUM, Princess Juliana. These bright orange, semi-double rose-like flowers bloom freely in June and July. Prefer rich soil and a sunny location. 18 to 24 inches. 75¢ each; 3 for $2.00.

Gypsophila

Bristol Fairy. A cloud of tiny white flowers in huge panicles. July and August. May be dried for winter bouquets. 4 ft. 65¢ each; 3 for $1.50.

Repens, Rosy Veil. Delightful dwarf form. Fine for rock or wall gardens. 65¢ each; 3 for $1.50.

IBERIS, Sempervirens. (Hardy Candytuft.) Pure white flowers in flat mounds in early spring and evergreen foliage the year round. Fine for rock gardens. 10 to 12 inches. 65¢ each; 3 for $1.50.

Linum, Alpinum. (Flax.) Dwarf, brilliant sky-blue flowers in mid-summer. 15 inches. 65¢ each; 3 for $1.50.

LINUM, Flavum. (Golden Flax.) Beautiful clumps of golden yellow flowers from May to July. 12 inches. 65¢ each; 3 for $1.50.

LIATRIS, Pycnostachya. (Kansas Gay Feather.) Stately 4 ft. spikes of rich purple tuft-like flowers that bloom through July and August. 65¢ each; 3 for $1.50.

LUPINS, Russell. Yellow, pink, blue and white pea-shaped blooms on spikes 3½ ft. tall. Upper 2 ft. a mass of bloom. 65¢ each; 3 for $1.50.

PRIMULA, Munstead Strain Mixed. (Hardy Primrose.) A large-flowered strain of the old-fashioned Cowslip in white, cream and deep orange. Prefer a damp shaded spot. 65¢ each; 3 for $1.50.

Dicentra Spectabilis—Bleeding-Heart

For Perennial Beauty
Hardy Phlox

The backbone of the garden, commencing to bloom when most perennials are through. We offer a list of early midseason and late varieties. 70¢ each; 3 of one variety $1.65; 12 of one variety $5.50.

Adonia. Dark red. (Midseason.)
Appleblossom. Soft pink. (Midseason.)
Border Queen. Watermelon pink. (Early.)
Carolina Vanderberg. Lavender blue. (Midseason.)
Mary Louise. Pure white. (Late.)
Miss Lingard. Finest white Phlox. (Very early.)
Progress. Light blue with purple eye. (Midseason.)
Red Bird. New fiery red. (Early.)
Rosalinda. A pink Miss Lingard. (Early.)
Salmon Beauty. Salmon-pink with white eye. (Midseason.)
San Antonio. Dark blood red. (Late.)
Silvertone. Clear lavender. (Midseason.)
COLLECTION: One plant of the 12 varieties $7.00.
COLLECTION: Three plants of each of the 12 varieties $18.00.
PHLOX Subulata. Dwarf, creeping plants covered with white, blue and red flowers in May. "The Rock Garden Plant Supreme." 65¢ each; 3 for $1.50; 12 for $5.50.

Perennial Phlox

SALVIA, Pitcheri. Lovely lavender-blue flowers loosely arranged on tall branching spikes. Blooms in late summer and fall. 4 ft. 65¢ each; 3 for $1.50.
SHASTA DAISY, Majestic. Huge, white daisy-like flowers with a small yellow center on stiff stems. Fine for cutting. 18 to 20 inches. 85¢ each; 3 for $2.00.

Tamed Wild Flowers For Moist Shady Spots

Cypripedium Acuale

CYPRIPEDIUM. (Lady Slipper.) These natives can be made a part of a woodland garden or some shady corner.
Acaule. Pink.   Pubescens. Yellow.
Spectabilis. Charming pink species.
DODECATHEON, Media. (Shooting-Star.) Deep purple-pink. Fine for rock gardens or shade. 6 to 8 inches.
GENTIANA, Andrewsi. (Bottle Gentian.) Dark, violet-blue, pale fringes. Prefers moist, moderately acid soil. 1 to 1½ ft.
HEPATICA. (Anemone.) Ground cover for moist shaded places.
SANGUINARIA, Canadensis. (Bloodroot.) Deciduous. Large white flowers.
TRILLIUM, Grandiflorum. These early spring, white blooms are indispensable in a shady garden.
Sessile, Luteum. Long blooming lemon-yellow flowers with broad ovate leaves of dark mottled green. Likes shade and fairly loose, woods soil.
Stylosum. Large, nodding rose-pink flowers, a rare mountain species. Plant in semi-shade in woodland, border or rock garden.
The above varieties are 65¢ each; 3 for $1.50; 12 for $5.00.

Trillium Grandiflora

Portable Plant Pool

Koroseal Portable Plant Pool
$19.95

A practical, portable, plant pool wherever you want it; in the yard, on your porch or patio. No foundation necessary. Pool is made of Goodrich Koroseal. When filled (75 gallon capacity) pool is a generous 55 inches in diameter. Easily emptied for changing location or storing over winter. Will last for years.

Pool complete with: 1 beautiful Water Lily, 5 floating plants, 4 shallow water plants, 3 Bog plants, 2 Oxygenating plants and 8 snails (to keep it clean). Just add water for a summer's enjoyment. $19.95, Postpaid. West of the Mississippi add 50¢ for postage. Pool only (no plants) $9.95, (postpaid $10.45).

47

—and enjoy the fresh-from-the-garden tastiness of truly home grown vegetables—your own. A small plot (20' x 50')—a minimum of time (only 15 to 30 minutes a day) and you will have the finest of vitamin-packed food for your family table from early May until late November.

Asparagus

If you own your own home an Asparagus bed is a must. It will last for years. 100 roots (plants) for a family of five. 1 ounce of seed will produce 200 roots. Full cultural directions with each order (or free on request).

WASHINGTON, 012. Large thick stalks with compact tips of rich purplish green. Very tender and tasty. Rust-resistant. Pkt. 10¢; oz. 25¢; ¼ lb. 70¢.

Paradise, 017. A new Asparagus, earlier and heavier yielder but not fully rust-resistant. Pkt. 15¢; oz. 65¢; ¼ lb. $2.30.

Washington Roots, 17-701. One-year-old. 12 for 75¢; 25 for $1.15; 50 for $1.90; 100 for $3.50, prepaid. 1000 for $21.60, not prepaid.

Bush (Dwarf) "String" Beans

Grow more food per square foot with Bush Beans either green or yellow. Plant as soon as soil is warm in rows 2 to 2½ feet apart spacing the seeds 3 to 4 inches apart. Sow every two weeks, until six weeks before frost, for continuous supply. A packet for 25 feet of row; a pound for 150 feet.

Asparagus — Washington

Green Beans

POSTPAID: Pkt. 15¢; ½ lb. 35¢; lb. 60¢; 2 lbs. $1.10; 5 lbs. $2.55.

Stringless Black Valentine, 021. 53 days. Early, hardy and productive. Pods are oval in cross section, hold their rich green color in cooking and canning.

Bountiful, 023. 48 days. The earliest and most productive variety. Flat, long green pods, excellent quality.

Stringless Green Pod, 057. 53 days. Fleshy, long, round, stringless pods. Produces an enormous crop of rich green tender pods.

Giant Stringless Green Pod, 059. 53 days. Medium green, 6 inch pods. A heavy yielder, fine for canning.

TENDERGREEN, 061. 53 days. The best round-podded variety, light green, excellent for freezing.

Longreen, 035. 54 days. Extra long, dark green pods with never a trace of string or fibre. Round and meaty, an excellent producer.

Pole "String" Beans

One packet for 15 poles; one pound for 100 poles.

POSTPAID: Pkt. 15¢; ½ lb. 35¢; lb. 60¢; 2 lbs. $1.10; 5 lbs. $2.55.

KENTUCKY WONDER OR OLD HOMESTEAD, 128. 65 days. Pods are borne in clusters of 2 to 4, each pod measuring 7 to 8 inches long.

Horticultural (Speckled Cranberry or Wren's Egg), 127. 70 days. For Snap or Shell Beans. Attractive, thick, straight, stringless pods 6 inches long. Use as Snap Beans when young.

Kentucky Wonder Wax, 137. 70 days. The best of all wax-podded pole beans. They are fleshy, brittle, tender and practically stringless.

Green Bean — Longreen

> TOP CROP, 030, 1950 All American Selection, Gold Medal Winner. Latest development by the United States Department of Agriculture. Long, round tender pods, not a trace of string or fibre. Fine for freezing. Pkt. 25¢; ½ lb. 60¢; lb. $1.00.

Yellow Beans

POSTPAID: Pkt. 15¢; ½ lb. 35¢; lb. 60¢; 2 lbs. $1.10; 5 lbs. $2.55.

PENCIL-POD BLACK WAX, 065. 54 days. The pods are 6 to 7 inches long, round, nearly straight, stringless and clear yellow. Rust-resistant.

Improved Golden Wax (Top Notch), 071. 51 days. The pods average 5 inches long, fleshy, straight, broad, flat, rich golden yellow and stringless.

Brittle Wax (Round-Podded Kidney Wax), 079. 58 days. Pods 6 inches long, thick, perfectly round and clear yellow.

IMPROVED KIDNEY WAX, 081. 62 days. Almost straight, oval pods, 6 inches long. The favorite flat-podded wax variety.

Sure-Crop Stringless Wax (Bountiful Wax), 084. 53 days. The handsome, rich yellow pods average 6 to 7 inches long, are very meaty, flat but thick.

Wax Bean — Improved Golden Wax

48

With a Vegetable Garden

Bush Lima Beans

One pkt. for 25 ft. of row; one pound for 150 ft.

Lima Bean seeds should be planted when ground has become thoroughly warm. Sow in rows 2½ feet apart, placing the beans 4 inches apart in a row, eye down. Cover about one inch deep.

POSTPAID: Pkt. 15¢; ½ lb. 40¢; lb. 75¢; 2 lbs. $1.40; 5 lbs. $3.10.

Fordhook Bush, 107. 75 days. Vigorous, upright plant holding the pods well above the ground.

FORDHOOK 242, 108. 75 days. 1945 Bronze Medal Winner. Produces a heavy crop of slightly curved pods each with 4 large thick beans of an exceptionally fine flavor.

Early Market, 106. 68 days. A tasty large flat-seeded variety. Has 3 or 4 rich green beans per pod.

Baby Fordhook, 113. 70 days. Light green, with 3 or 4 small thick beans.

Burpee Improved Bush, 103. 75 days. Thick beans packed close together 4 or 5 to a pod.

BUTTER BEANS, HENDERSON'S BUSH, 109. 85 days. Bushes 20 inches tall bearing a heavy crop of pods 3 inches long, each containing 3 or 4 white beans.

Pole Lima Beans

More productive, later than Bush Limas. Set poles 4 feet apart each way and plant 6 to 8 beans, eye down, around each. When plants are up, thin to 3 per pole. One packet for 15 poles; one pound for 100 poles.

POSTPAID: Pkt. 15¢; ½ lb. 35¢; lb. 65¢; 2 lbs. $1.20; 5 lbs. $2.85.

CHALLENGER (DREER'S IMPROVED), 118. 90 days. Vigorous climbing plants. Pods containing 4 or 5 attractive, thick, light green beans.

Early Leviathan, 122. 79 days. The earliest large-podded Pole Lima. The pods are 5 to 6 inches long and contain 5 or 6 beans.

King of the Garden, 121. 88 days. Large, dark green pods containing 4 to 5 light green beans.

Beans—Fordhook Bush Lima

Broccoli

1 oz. for 1500 plants.

A few plants will yield a continuous supply of tasty, wholesome Broccoli for your table from mid-summer until heavy frost. Sow indoors March-April for early. Sow outdoors May-June for late. Cover ¼ inch and transplant to 2 feet apart.

Sprouting Calabrese, 179. 70 days. Vigorous, early, forming a large center head followed by a number of smaller side heads. Pkt. 10¢; ½ oz. 25¢; oz. 45¢; ¼ lb. $1.50.

Pelletized Seed (P179, Pkt. 20¢).

Broccoli—Calabrese

SOY BEANS, Bansei, Edible, 101. 95 days. Strong upright bushes bearing small pods; each containing 2 or 3 delicious light green beans of nut-like flavor. Included in special diets. Pkt. 15¢; ½ lb. 30¢; lb. 55¢; 2 lbs. $1.00; 5 lbs. $2.00.

DWARF SHELL BEANS, Dwarf Horticultural, 028. 65 days. Generally grown for shell beans. When young, the thick, flat green pods are stringless and used as snap beans. Pkt. 10¢; ½ lb. 30¢; lb. 60¢; 2 lbs. $1.10; 5 lbs. $2.55.

ENGLISH BROAD BEANS, Broad Windsor, 138. Genuine English Broad Beans or Fava Beans. Strong plants bearing a heavy crop. Beans are shelled and eaten as Limas. A new flavor treat. Pkt. 15¢; ½ lb. 40¢; lb. 75¢.

Chicory

1 Pkt. for 50 ft., 1 oz. for 200 ft.

French Endive (Witloof Chicory), 300. 150 days. Have this delicious salad fresh all winter. Grow the roots in the garden, sowing the seed ¼ inch deep in rows 2 ft. apart. Dig roots before severe freezing weather and grow in your cellar in boxes of loose soil. Pkt. 15¢; ½ oz. 35¢; oz. 65¢; ¼ lb. $2.50.

Asparagus or Radichetta, 301. 65 days. A rapid-growing annual with Dandelion-like leaves of pleasant flavor. Gives that Continental tang to mixed salads. Pkt. 10¢; ½ oz. 30¢; oz. 50¢; ¼ lb. $1.65.

Brussels Sprouts

DELICIOUS! A really tasty green vegetable for your table. Have them garden fresh from September to December by sowing outdoors in June. Transplant to 2 feet apart.

Long Island Improved, 182. 90 days. Very productive. Pkt. 15¢; ½ oz. 40¢; oz. 75¢.

Or use Pelletized Seed (P182, Pkt. 20¢) and plant where you want them to grow. See page 7.

Brussels Sprouts

Nitragin	

Nitragin Inoculation for Beans, Pkg. 25¢

Beets—Detroit Dark Red

Table Beets

The tender sweetness of Beets the size of walnuts is a treat reserved for those who grow their own, try them, tops and all, when they're as big as marbles. For a continuous supply through the season, make the first sowing outdoors about the first of April and every two weeks up to July 15. Sow seed ½ inch deep in rows 18 inches to 2 feet apart. Or—plant Pelletized Seed 2 inches apart and avoid thinning. One packet for 30 feet; one ounce for 100 feet; 6 pounds per acre.

POSTPAID: Pkt. 10¢; oz. 25¢; ¼ lb. 75¢; ½ lb. $1.35.

DETROIT DARK RED, 149. 60 days. Uniformly globe-shaped, with small neck and tap-root. Deep red flesh.

Pelletized Seed, Detroit Dark Red (P149, Pkt. 20¢). See page 7.

Perfected Detroit, 159. 58 days. Globular 2½ to 3 inches across with dark red flesh. Grow these for canning and winter storing.

Crosby's Egyptian Special, 145. 58 days. Bright red skin and vermilion-red flesh. Fine grained, sweet and tender.

WHITE BEET, LENTZ, 157. 55 days. Almost white flesh showing thin red zones which disappear in cooking. The sweetest of all the early beets. "Once tried always buyed."

Early Wonder, 164. 58 days. Smooth skin and beautiful, deep blood-red flesh that cooks sweet and tender.

Winter Keeper, 166. 80 days. A remarkable beet that grows to largest size but remains tender and sweet. Dark red skin and appetizing, rich red flesh.

Sugar and Mangel Beets

Grow them for poultry and stock feeding.

Klein Wanzleben, 170. 150 days. Solid white fleshed roots of medium size, high in sugar content. Pkt. 10¢; oz. 25¢; ¼ lbs. 70¢; lb. $2.10.

Mammoth Long Red, 177. 150 days. Produces enormous crops of extra-large fine, solid roots. Pkt. 10¢; oz. 25¢; ¼ lbs. 45¢; lb. $1.50.

Cabbage

Garden-fresh young Cabbage is as mouth-watering and tasty as Cauliflower. Even our largest heads cook tender (you supply the Corned Beef!) and give you crisp cole slaw and salads, too.

For early Cabbage, start seed indoors in February-March, for late crop, sow outdoors April-May. Rows 2½ to 3 ft. apart; cover seeds ¼ inch; transplant or thin to 1½-2 ft. apart. Now—with Pelletized Cabbage Seed, you can plant seed outdoors in March where plants are to stand.

Early and Midseason Cabbage

Early Jersey Wakefield, 206. 95 days. Extra-early, with solid pointed heads of uniform size and shape. Pkt. 10¢; ½ oz. 30¢; oz. 50¢; ¼ lb. $1.60.

COPENHAGEN MARKET, 193. 97 days. A favorite early round Cabbage forming firm heads measuring 6 to 7 inches across. Pkt. 15¢; ½ oz. 35¢; oz. 65¢; ¼ lb. $2.35. Try Pelletized Seed "you sow where they grow." P193. Pkt. 20¢.

Early Flat Dutch, 199. 110 days. Solid heads, flat shape weighing 5 to 6 pounds each. Heat-resistant and a sure header. Pkt. 10¢; ½ oz. 30¢; oz. 50¢; ¼ lb. $1.65.

Glory of Enkhuizen, 202. 108 days. A large globe-shaped, second-early. The hard heads weigh 6 to 8 pounds. Pkt. 10¢; ½ oz. 30¢; oz. 50¢ ¼ lb. $1.65.

Golden Acre, 204. 93 days. Extra-early, perfectly round, firm and fine texture. Weighs about 3 pounds. Pkt. 15¢; ½ oz. 40¢; oz. 70¢; ¼ lb. $2.40.

Late and Winter Cabbage

Danish Ballhead, 195. 150 days. Heads average 10 to 12 pounds each. They are round, solid, and fine winter keepers. Pkt. 15¢; ½ oz. 35¢; oz. 65¢; ¼ lb. $2.35.

Pelletized Danish Ballhead, P195. Pkt. 20¢.

PENN STATE BALLHEAD, 197. 140 days. Late, short-stemmed, round-headed Cabbage. It is sure headed and produces a heavy crop. Pkt. 15¢; ½ oz. 40¢; oz. 70¢; ¼ lb. $2.40.

Late Flat Dutch, Premium, 200. 140 days. The favorite kraut cabbage. Flat heads weighing 10 pounds or more. Pkt. 10¢; ½ oz. 30¢; oz. 50¢; ¼ lb. $1.65.

Perfection Drumhead Savoy, 210. 120 days. The plants are vigorous, deep green, heavily crumpled, curled leaves. Pkt. 15¢; ½ oz. 35¢; oz. 60¢; ¼ lb. $2.10.

Yellows-Resistant Cabbage

POSTPAID: Pkt. 15¢; oz. 35¢; oz. 60¢; ¼ lb. $2.10.

Resistant Golden Acre, 224. 94 days.

Jersey Queen, 207. 96 days. Resistant Early Jersey Wakefield.

Marion Market, 226. 105 days. Resistant Copenhagen Market.

Allhead Select, 225. 110 days. Early, round solid heads, 9 inches broad and 7 inches deep.

Wisconsin All Season, 227. 122 days. Large heads measuring 10 to 12 inches across, and 8 inches deep, weighing 9 to 10 lbs. each.

Wisconsin Hollander, No. 8, 228. 135 days. A yellows-resistant selection from Danish Ballhead.

Red Cabbage

Pkt. 20¢; ½ oz. 40¢; oz. 75¢.

Early Red Copenhagen, 218. 100 days. An early round head variety, attractive deep red color.

Mammoth Rock Red, 219. 130 days. Late, deep blood-red color. Measures 7 to 8 inches across and almost 7 inches deep.

Cauliflower

You have heard it called "Cabbage with a College education." Same culture as for cabbage and just as easy to grow.

POSTPAID: Pkt. 25¢; ¼ oz. $1.65; ½ oz. $2.90; oz. $5.00; ¼ lb. $16.00.

Early Snowball "X," 254. 85 days. Compact plants with short outer leaves. Makes a fine snow-white head.

EARLY SNOWBALL "A," 260. 85 days. Very compact, even fine-grained heads. Try Pelletized Seed, P260. Pkt. 20¢.

Veitch's Autumn Giant, 262. 130 days. Large, late variety producing immense compact white heads.

Cauliflower—Snowball

Golden Health Carrots

Enjoy their Garden-Fresh Crispness, eat them raw, whole, sliced in salads or as a side dish. For an early supply, sow seeds of early varieties ½ inch deep as soon as the soil can be dug, and then every 3 weeks until July 1, spacing rows 18 to 24 inches apart and thin seedlings to stand 2 to 3 inches apart. One packet for 30 ft.; 1 oz. for 200 ft. Now, with Pelletized Carrot seed, you can space plant them one by one! See Chantenay and Danvers.

POSTPAID: Pkt. 10¢; ½ oz. 25¢; oz. 45¢; ¼ lb. $1.50.

CHANTENAY RED-CORED, 232. 70 days. Large, thick stump-rooted carrot, 6 to 8 inches long. Smooth, orange skin and crisp, tender flesh.

Pelletized Seed, Chantenay Red-Cored (P232) Pkt. 20¢. See page 7.

Danver's, 234. 75 days. Rich orange-red color, smooth and handsome. The roots are 6 to 7 inches long and taper to a blunt point.

Pelletized Seed, Danver's (P234) Pkt. 20¢. See page 7.

Amsterdam Forcing, 240. 65 days. Extra early and fine quality. 6 inches long and 1 inch thick.

MORSE'S BUNCHING, 239. 77 days. Attractive deep orange carrots 7 to 8 inches long, 1¼ inch thick. Cylindrical, tender, brittle, and sweet.

Nantes Half-Long, 241. 68 days. Stump-rooted cylindrical roots of excellent quality.

Imperator, 237. 77 days. 7 to 8 inches long, tapering gradually toward the tip. Fine-grained, deep orange flesh.

Early Scarlet Horn, 244. 63 days. Rich reddish-orange roots, 3½ inches long and 1½ inches in diameter.

Carrot—Morse's Bunching

Crisp Cool Cucumbers

"Garden-Fresh" Cucumbers are more digestible. Sow ½ to 1 inch in deep in rows or hills 4 to 6 feet apart after the weather has become settled. One pkt. for 20 ft.; one ounce for 100 ft.

POSTPAID: Pkt. 10¢; oz. 40¢; ¼ lb. $1.30.

Black Diamond, 367. 60 days. Handsome, fruits 6 inches long, symmetrical form with square ends and non-fading dark green color. Extra early.

CLARK'S SPECIAL, 365. 62 days. Dark green fruit, 9 to 10 inches long, slightly tapering at both ends. Beautiful clear white, crisp flesh.

Davis Perfect, 369. 68 days. Dark green fruits with tender, brittle, fine flavored flesh. Often 12 inches long.

Early Fortune, 372. 65 days. Tapering fruit 8 to 9 inches long and almost 2¼ inches thick. Dark green skin. Good for pickles too.

LONGFELLOW, 385. 72 days. A fancy extra-long (12 to 14 inch) cucumber with deep green skin.

Improved Long Green, 384. 75 days. Hardy and disease-resistant, good for both pickles and slicing. 12 to 14 inches long.

Straight "8", 391. 66 days. Attractive cylindrical fruits about 1½ inches in diameter. Thin, deep green skin.

White Spine, 392. 70 days. The old favorite, always reliable.

Pelletized Seed, White Spine, P392. 70 days. Pkt. 20¢.

Pickling Cucumbers

Small pickles, pick when small—Large pickles, let them grow.

National Pickling, 389. 70 days. Makes attractive, dark green cylindrical pickles. 6½ inches by 2½ inches when mature. Pkt. 10¢; oz. 30¢; ¼ lb. 90¢.

Snow's Perfected Pickle, 390. 56 days. Very fine, uniform, square-ended fruits. Pkt. 10¢; oz. 30¢; ¼ lb. 90¢.

Small Gherkin, 375. 60 days. Small, oval, pale green fruits covered with soft fleshy spines. These are true Gherkins, do not confuse with very small pickles.

Cucumber—Longfellow

Celery—Golden Plume

Celery

At a quarter a stalk, 100 feet of celery is $25.00 saved. The flavor is free! One ounce produces about 5000 plants. The maturity dates for celery are from setting plants; add 55 days for plant production. For an early crop, start the seeds indoors in February and for a late crop, April 1. Set plants 12 inches apart in the row.

UTAH OR GOLDEN CRISP, 288. 125 days. Full-hearted plants with crisp, solid, flavorful stalks. Pkt. 15¢; ½ oz. 55¢; oz. 95¢.

Winter Queen, 290. 120 days. Vigorous plants large, thick stalks of attractive light green color, tender, creamy-white heart. Pkt. 10¢; ½ oz. 45¢; oz. 85¢.

Golden Plume, 274. 110 days. Heavy, full golden yellow solid-hearts. Easy to blanch, a good cropper and always crisp. Pkt. 15¢; ¼ oz. 40¢; ½ oz. 70¢; oz. $1.25.

Easy Blanching, 270. 125 days. Fine early large thick, pure white, tender and brittle stalks. Pkt. 15¢; ½ oz. 50¢; oz. 90¢.

Giant Pascal, 282. 140 days. Round, thick, solid leaf stalks which blanch to a beautiful light green. Pkt. 15¢; ½ oz. 50¢; oz. 90¢.

GOLDEN SELF-BLANCHING, 276. 115 days. Stocky plants with thick, solid, crisp stalks and a compact golden yellow heart. Pkt. 20¢; ½ oz. 75¢; oz. $1.40.

CELERIAC, Giant Smooth Prague, 294. 120 days. Grown for the thick roots which are either served hot or cold with French dressing. Delicious in soups and stews. Start indoors. Pkt. 10¢; ½ oz. 50¢; oz. 90¢.

51

SWEET CORN—*Truly American*

Erie Sweet Corn—Ready to Eat

Win the race with flavor! Know how toothsome Sweet Corn can be, when it's 30 minutes from garden to table. As soon as corn is picked the sugars start to turn to starch, killing flavor. When soil is warm plant in hills 3 feet apart each way, covering 8 to 10 seeds, ½ inch deep; thin out to three plants to a hill, or plant in rows 3 feet apart, and thin out plants to 12 inches apart. For a supply all summer, plant every two weeks up to July 15. One pkt. for 40 ft.; one pound for 100 hills or 250-foot row.

Yellow Sweet Corn

POSTPAID: Pkt. 15¢; ½ lb. 30¢; lb. 45¢; 2 lbs. 85¢; 5 lbs. $1.95.

GOLDEN BANTAM, 318. 80 days. The original, the famous, the one and only Golden Bantam. The corn that brought yellow Sweet Corn to the American table. Ears are uniformly 8 rowed, 6 inches long. Look delicious, taste delicious, surpass all in quality.

Golden Sunshine, 322. 74 days. Extra-early variety, with 7 to 8 inch, 12 rowed ears. Bright yellow and excellent quality.

Golden Giant, 324. 85 days. Ears 8 inches long. Each cob tightly set with 16 to 18 rows of sugary, creamy yellow kernels.

Yellow Hybrid Sweet Corn

Among the myriad of varieties of Hybrid Sweet Corn, we have found these most adaptable to home gardens. All are tops in productivity, quality and resistance to disease.

Goldengrain, 342. 89 days. Twenty rows of sweet, deep yellow kernels. The plants are drought-resistant and practically free from suckers. Pkt. 20¢; ½ lb. 40¢; lb. 70¢; 2 lbs. $1.30; 5 lbs. $2.95.

Aristogold Bantam Evergreen, 344. 87 days. Vigorous, tall variety with ears 9 to 10 inches long set with 16 to 18 rows of sweet, yellow kernels. Pkt. 20¢; ½ lb. 40¢; lb, 75¢; 2 lbs. $1.40; 5 lbs. $3.15.

ERIE, 346. 87 days. Long, cylindrical, slightly tapering ears with 12 or 14 rows of deep, thin-skinned creamy-yellow kernels. Consistently out-yields the well known Golden Cross Bantam, but later. Pkt. 20¢; ½ lb. 45¢; lb. 85¢; 2 lbs. $1.60; 5 lbs. $4.00.

GOLDEN CROSS BANTAM, 335. 84 days. The ears are 8 inches long, with 14 rows of light yellow grains of delicious flavor. Pkt. 15¢; ½ lb. 40¢; lb. 70¢; 2 lbs. $1.30; 5 lbs. $2.95.

Golden Rocket, 349. 85 days. New yellow Hybrid Sweet Corn. Strong stalks, disease-resistant and usually bears 2 ears. Light yellow kernels of finest quality. Pkt. 20¢; ½ lb. 45¢; lb. 85¢; 2 lbs. $1.60; 5 lbs. $4.00.

Ioana, 340. 87 days. A trifle later than Golden Cross Bantam. Plants 6½ to 7 ft. tall, bearing 8-inch ears with 12 to 14 rows of light yellow kernels. Pkt. 15¢; ½ lb. 40¢; lb. 70¢; 2 lbs. $1.30; 5 lbs. $2.95. .

Marcross, 336. 72 days. Two months and two weeks from seed to table. The best early variety. Ears 12 to 14 rowed and 6 to 7 inches long. Pkt. 15¢; ½ lb. 40¢; lb. 70¢; 2 lbs. $1.30; 5 lbs. $2.95.

Tendergold, 339. 81 days. 7- to 8-inch ears set with 12 rows of sweet creamy-yellow kernels. Pkt. 15¢; ½ lb. 40¢; lb. 70¢; 2 lbs. $1.30; 5 lbs. $2.95.

White Sweet Corn

Country Gentleman Hybrid, 306. (Replaces the old Country Gentleman.) 98 days. Sturdy plants 6½ to 7½ ft. tall, bearing 8-inch ears with zig-zag pattern of deep, very narrow, ivory white kernels. Pkt. 20¢; ½ lb. 40¢; lb. 75¢; 2 lbs. $1.40; 5 lbs. $3.15.

Stowell's Evergreen Hybrid, 338. (Replaces Stowell's and White Evergreen.) 90 days. The plants grow 8 to 10 ft. high and bear extra-large ears 9 inches long. Ears have 14 to 18 rows of deep, narrow white kernels. Pkt. 15¢; ½ lb. 40¢; lb. 75¢; 2 lbs. $1.40; 5 lbs. $3.15.

Vanguard (Improved Howing Mob), 348. 79 days. Appetizing 8-inch ears with 12 rows of pearly white grains. Highly disease-resistant. Pkt. 15¢; ½ lb. 25¢; lb. 45¢; 2 lbs. 85¢; 5 lbs. $1.95.

BLACK MEXICAN, 310. 85 days. Exceptionally sweet with pure white kernels when ready for the table. Blue-black seeds. For something new in quality and taste, mix Black Mexican and Golden Bantam. Pkt. 15¢; ½ lb. 25¢; lb. 45¢; 2 lbs. 85¢; 5 lbs. $1.95.

Pop Corn

The confection that grows. A short row will supply corn for popping all winter. Suggestion: An ideal Cub Scout project, keeps 'em busy all summer, and in the fall they can pop and sell it. Pkt. for 40 ft., one pound for 300 ft. of row.

POSTPAID: Pkt. 15¢; ½ lb. 25¢; lb. 45¢; 2 lbs. 80¢; 5 lbs. $1.85.

White Rice, 353. Early maturing, for late planting or for northern sections.

Queens Golden, 351. Small yellow ears, 2 or 3 to a stalk.

South American, 352. Yellow grains that pop to largest size without hard centers.

Purdue No. 32, 350. The new Hybrid heavy yielding Pop Corn. Outbears all others. Finest quality. Pkt. 15¢; ½ lb. 55¢; lb. 95¢; 2 lbs. $1.80; 5 lbs. $4.35.

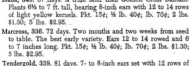

Sweet Corn—Golden Cross Bantam

Grow "Greens" for "Vitameens"

Collards—"Greens"

Collards, unlike Cauliflower, "never had no education," just an "emerald in the rough," for flavor.

POSTPAID: Pkt. 10¢; oz. 20¢; ¼ lb. 55¢; lb. $1.75.

Creole or Southern, 302. 80 days. 2 to 3 feet tall, form thick bunches of delicate tender leaves slightly curled at the edges.

Special **Heading, 303.** 90 days. More compact than Southern, with the leaf clusters inclined to curl inward forming a loose head.

Cress

Extra Curled, or Peppergrass, 357. (Dry ground "Water Cress.") Small finely curled leaves with that snappy Water Cress flavor. Ready for use in 4 to 5 weeks. Sow ¼ inch deep, in April and at two-week intervals through the summer. Use in salads or sandwiches and for garnishing. Pkt. 10¢; ½ oz. 25¢; oz. 50.

Upland or Broad-Leaved, 358. 50 days. Large-leaved strain. Has the flavor of Water Cress and will grow in any good moist soil. Pkt. 10¢; ½ oz. 25¢; oz. 50¢.

Water Cress, 359. 60 days. Easily grown along a stream of running water, a ditch or pond. Broadcast seed at the water's edge. Needs no further care. Pkt. 25¢; ¼ oz. 95¢; ½ oz. $1.70; oz. $3.00.

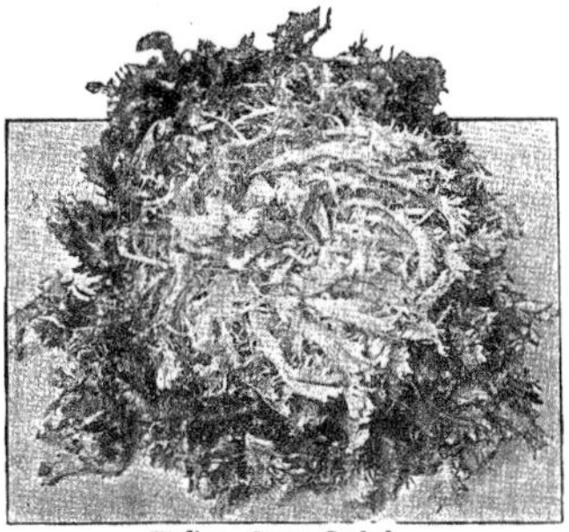

Endive—Green Curled

Leek

Giant Musselbrugh, 434. 150 days. Long white stems and medium green leaves. Very mild and tender. A new onion flavor for soups, stews, and mixed salads. Same culture as for onions. Pkt. 15¢; ½ oz. 35¢; oz. 65.

Egg Plant

Start in hotbed early in March. When 3 inches high pot up. Set the plants outdoors in May or June spacing them 3 feet apart. One pkt. for 50 plants; 1 oz. for 1000 plants. **You can plant Pelletized Egg Plant Seed outdoors in May.**

POSTPAID: Pkt. 15¢; ½ oz. 55¢; oz. 95¢; ¼ lb. $3.50.

BLACK BEAUTY, 404. 150 days. Beautiful, rich purplish black fruits of best quality. Vigorous and productive.

Pelletized, Black Beauty, P404. Pkt. 20¢.

New York Improved Spineless, 406. 145 days. Broad, oval, deep glossy purple fruits. The flesh is firm and of choice quality.

New Hampshire Hybrid. 407. 140 days. Very early with dark purple, blocky, egg-shaped fruits which are smooth, glossy and uniform.

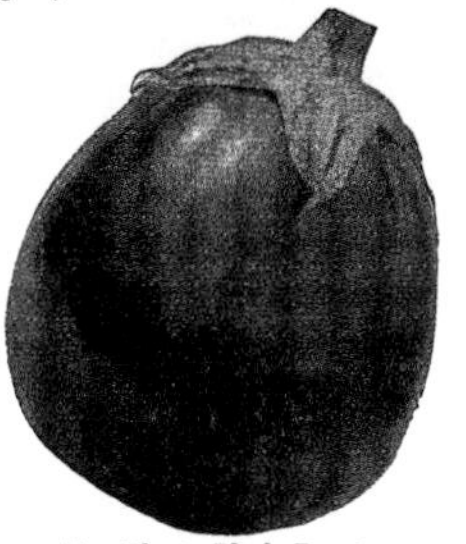

Egg Plant—Black Beauty

Corn Salad

Large-Seeded, 355. Oval light green leaves, a spring tonic in the salad bowl. Sow either in spring or early fall in rows 1-ft. apart and cover ½-inch deep. One ounce for 25 ft. or row. Pkt. 15¢; oz. 50¢; ¼ lb. $1.75; lb. $5.90.

Dandelion

Improved Thick-Leaved, 401. 95 days. Large bushy plants with succulent leaves. Pkt. 15¢; ½ oz. 45¢; oz. 80¢; ¼ lb. $3.00.

Endive for Salads

The salad bowl is a bowl of health. Eat at least one green or yellow vegetable every day. Sow in shallow drills in April, or for late use, in June or July. Thin to a foot apart. When nearly full-grown, tie leaves together to blanch. However, we like it green. One pkt. for 50 ft.; 1 oz. for 400 ft.

POSTPAID: Pkt. 10¢; oz. 35¢; ¼ lb. $1.00.

Deep Heart Fringed, 409. 90 days. Broad leaves, curly at the edges. The outer leaves turn upward enclosing the extra-deep, well-filled creamy yellow heart.

FULL HEART BATAVIAN, 411. 88 days. Broad leaves with extra heavy heart. Easily blanched by tying. Mild and pleasantly bitter flavor.

Green Curled, 414. 95 days. Beautifully curled and finely cut leaves as fine for garnishing as for salads. Will survive light frost without protection.

Finnochio—Florence Fennel

418. 110 days. Splendid as a salad, or served boiled with cream dressing. Leaves thicken at the base and form an Artichoke-like bulb. A taste treat for jaded appetites. Sow seed ½-inch deep and thin to 12 inches apart. Pkt. 10¢; oz. 40¢; ¼ lb. $1.45.

Kale-Borecole

Good in the summer but dug from under the snow it's delicious! Sow May-June ½-inch deep in drills 1½ ft. apart and cultivate like Cabbage. One ounce produces 2000 plants.

DWARF BLUE CURLED SCOTCH, 423. 55 days. Hardy, strong, finely curled foliage with a distinct blue tinge. Pkt. 10¢; oz. 40¢; ¼ lb. $1.20.

Dwarf Siberian, 426. 60 days. Large flat leaves with finely curled edges. Hardy and productive. Pkt. 10¢; oz. 35¢; ¼ lb. $1.00.

Kohl-Rabi

As tasty as Cauliflower, best when the size of a golfball. As easy to grow as Beets. Sow outdoors about the first of April and for succession every two weeks up to July 15th. One pkt. for 30 ft.; one ounce for 100 ft.

POSTPAID: Pkt. 10¢; ½ oz. 40¢; oz. 75¢; ¼ lb. $2.25.

Early Purple Vienna, 430. 55 days. Purple skin, with white flesh.

Early White or Green Vienna, 431. 55 days. White skin and flesh.

Chinese or Celery Cabbage

A new flavor for your salad bowl. Serve raw as a salad or cole slaw, or cooked like Cabbage. Where summers are hot, it is best to sow in June for a fall crop. Sow ¼-inch deep and thin to 12 inches.

POSTPAID: Pkt. 10¢; oz. 50¢; ¼ lb. $1.65.

Chihili, 220. 70 days. Early, sure-heading, 18 to 20 inches tall and 4 inches thick. Firm, crisp, and tender.

Horse-radish

Maliner Kren or Bohemian, 17-702. Grow your own—grind your own—get "he man" flavor. Roots planted in April are ready for use in October. Six roots for 45¢; 12 for 85¢; 25 for $1.65; 100 for $4.50.

LETTUCE *for Healthful Salads*

Lettuce — Oakleaf

"A bed of Lettuce at your kitchen-door will save many trips to the grocery store" and you can have it (Lettuce) there for 6 months of the year. Always ready, always tender and fresh for lunches, sandwiches and to complete a dinner. Sow seeds as early in the spring as possible and follow with successive sowings through the summer. Sow ¼ inch deep and thin plants to 4 or 6 inches apart. 1 Pkt. for 50 ft.; 1 oz. for 500 ft. Try the New Pelletized Lettuce seed. You sow them where they grow; no thinning, no transplanting.

"Butterhead" Lettuce For late Spring

Salamander, 454. 70 days. The few outer leaves enclose a head that is one large solid heart. Best for spring sowing. Light green color and very tasty. Pkt. 10¢; oz. 30¢; ¼ lb. 90¢.

WHITE BOSTON, 458. 76 days. Similar to Big Boston but of a uniform light green color. Creamy heart which is tender and sweet. Withstands hot weather. Pkt. 10¢; oz. 30¢; ¼ lb. 90¢.

Pelletized Seed, White Boston, P458. Pkt. 20¢.

May King, 468. 63 days. Forms firm, round head of light green with brown tinge and crisp, buttery golden yellow, compact heart. Pkt. 10¢; oz. 35¢; ¼ lb. $1.00.

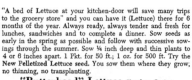

"Loose Leaf" Lettuce

For very early and very late

BLACK-SEEDED SIMPSON, 442. 45 days. A compact bunch of broad, much crumpled, light yellowish green leaves of choice quality. Pkt. 10¢; oz. 25¢; ¼ lb. 85¢.

Pelletized Black-Seed Simpson, P442. Pkt. 20¢.

Grand Rapids, 460. 42 days. The crisp, tender leaves are bright green and crimped at the edges. Pkt. 10¢; oz. 30¢; ¼ lb. 90¢.

OAK-LEAF, 472. 40 days. Lettuce all summer! It is easy! Simply keep planting Oak-Leaf from April to mid-August. Deeply lobed, bright green leaves, heat resistant but crisp and tender. We like it. Pkt. 15¢; oz. 40¢; ¼ lb. $1.35.

Bronze Beauty, 471. 45 days. Bronze Medal Winner. Beautiful to look at, delightful to eat. Bronzy green, deeply lobed leaves. Pkt. 20¢; ½ oz. 65¢; oz. $1.15; ¼ lb. $4.25.

Slobolt, 445. 45 days. Fine, new loose leaf lettuce developed by U.S.D.A. Deeply fringed and curled leaves, crisp and tender, very slow to shoot to seed. Pkt. 15¢; ½ oz. 40¢; oz. 75¢; ¼ lb. $2.80.

Matchless (Deer Tongue), 469. 60 days. As unusual in appearance as in quality. A cross between Cos and Butterhead lettuce producing a thick bunch of pointed, rich green leaves and a delicious white heart. Pkt. 15¢; ½ oz. 30¢; oz. 50¢; ¼ lb. $1.85.

Lettuce — White Boston

"Crisp-Head" Lettuce

For late Spring and Summer

BIBB, 444. 78 days. Do you like your lettuce green? Try this famous old variety forming a solid heart of rich green. Grows best in cool weather. Delightful flavor, you hardly need dressing. Heads are individual serving size! Pkt. 15¢; oz. 40¢; ¼ lb. $1.20.

Imperial "No. 847," 465. 84 days. Medium large, solid round heads of bright green color and tender, icy-crisp greenish white hearts. Pkt. 15¢; oz. 50¢; ¼ lb. $1.85.

Great Lakes, 457. 82 days. Heat and tip-burn resistant, crisphead Lettuce. Pkt. 15¢; ½ oz. 40¢; oz. 75¢; ¼ lb. $2.80.

Pelletized Seed, Great Lakes, P457. Pkt. 20¢.

New York or Wonderful, 483. 80 days. Withstands heat and forms remarkably solid heads which have large, tender light green hearts. Pkt. 10¢; oz. 40¢; ¼ lb. $1.35.

Iceberg, 464. 84 days. Large, broad, well-folded light green heads having a very sweet, crisp, light icy-green heart. Pkt. 15¢; oz. 40¢; ¼ lb. $1.20.

Romaine or Cos Lettuce

Dark Green Cos, 473. 70 days. Forms medium-sized, elongated heads tightly folded to the well-blanched heart. Pkt. 10¢; oz. 30¢; ¼ lb. 90¢.

Trianon Cos, 479. 70 days. The plants are medium large, of upright growth with medium light green heads, 8 to 9 inches tall. Pkt. 10¢; oz. 30¢; ¼ lb. 90¢.

Lettuce — New York

Lettuce — Trianon Cos

Muskmelon—Pride of Wisconsin

Mustard Greens

It is such dishes as Mustard greens and bacon that make Southern cooking so intriguing.
POSTPAID: Pkt. 10¢; oz. 25¢; ¼ lb. 65¢; lb. $2.00.

Fordhook Fancy, 556. 40 days. Rich green, fringed and curled leaves of mild flavor.

SOUTHERN GIANT CURLED, 557. 40 days. Strong and upright plants, with large crumpled and frilled leaves.

White London, 558. 12 days. Dark green, small smooth leaves. Splendid for salad and garnishing. Sow every 10 days and pick when 3 inches tall.

Mustard Spinach, Tendergreen, 559. 35 days. Recommended to be grown in place of Spinach during the summer. Quick growth, leaves ready for use when 5 to 6 inches tall.

HOT KAPS

Use Hot Kaps for earlier Muskmelons. 25 Hot Kaps and Setter 70¢, postpaid 85¢.

Parsnip—Hollow Crown

Muskmelons or Cantaloupes

Grow your own and enjoy the finer quality of vine ripened fruit. Sow when the ground is thoroughly warm in well fertilized hills 5 to 6 feet apart each way. Scatter 10 to 15 seeds on the top of each hill and cover about ¼ inch deep. Thin out to 3 or 4 strongest plants per hill. 1 pkt. for 10 hills; 1 oz. for 50 hills; 6 to 8 pounds in hills per acre.
POSTPAID: Pkt. 10¢; oz. 40¢; ¼ lb. $1.00.

Bender's Surprise, 488. 95 days. Delicious and attractive melon. Greenish-yellow with coarse netting and bright-salmon flesh.

Hale's Best, 510. 86 days. An attractive, well-ribbed melon with netted skin. The salmon flesh is extremely thick with a sweet tangy taste.

Hearts of Gold, Special, 506. 95 days. Well-ribbed fruits with fine gray netting and very juicy, honey-sweet salmon-orange flesh.

Honey Rock or Sugar Rock, 509. 85 days. Salmon fleshed variety of delicious flavor. Fruits of medium size with remarkably thick flesh and small seed cavity.

Gold-Lined Rocky Ford, 523. 90 days. A green fleshed melon with an unusually sweet and spicy taste. The fruits are nearly round, have no ribs, and are covered with a thick gray netting.

PRIDE OF WISCONSIN, 519. 86 days. Beautiful, heavy, coarsely netted fruits of slightly oval form with very thick and very sweet, salmon pink flesh.

Watermelons

They taste good and are good for you. Plant seed the middle of May in hills 6 to 8 feet apart. Sow 6 to 8 seeds in each hill and cover ½ inch deep. Thin to 2 plants per hill. 1 pkt. for 8 hills; 1 oz. for 30 hills.

Early Canada, 537. 80 days. Extra-early, round fruits, icebox size, with bright red sweet flesh. Pkt. 15¢; oz. 50¢; ¼ lb. $1.50.

Golden Honey, 545. 85 days. Extra-early with honey sweet, cream yellow flesh. Pkt. 10¢; oz. 45¢; ¼ lb. $1.65; lb. $5.45.

Improved Kleckley Sweets, 548. (Wilt-Resistant.) 90 days. Large cylindrical fruits 30 to 40 lbs. each. Thin rind, bright scarlet, sweet flesh free from fibre. Pkt. 25¢; oz. 75¢.

Hawksbury, 531. 85 days. A wilt-resistant, large, oblong melon. 18 inches long 10 inches thick. Very sweet flesh. Fine for Home gardens. Pkt. 10¢; oz. 40¢; ¼ lb. $1.35; lb. $4.50.

DIXIE QUEEN 538. 85 days. Large, nearly round fruits weighing 30 to 35 lbs. each. Light green skin with dark green stripes. Sweet bright red flesh. Pkt. 10¢; oz. 45¢; ¼ lb. $1.65; lb. $5.45.

Tom Watson, 550. 95 days. Fruits are long and cylindrical and frequently weigh 40 or more pounds. Deep green skin, bright red flesh. Pkt. 10¢; oz. 30¢; ¼ lb. 90¢; lb. $3.00.
SAVE THE SEEDS TO FEED THE RED BIRDS.

Watermelon—Dixie Queen

Parsnip

Freezing does not harm Parsnips but actually improves their flavor, leave them in the ground all winter. Sow in the spring, spacing the rows 2 feet apart and cover seeds ½ inch deep. 1 pkt. for 20 ft.; 1 oz. for 150 ft.
POSTPAID: Pkt. 10¢; oz. 35¢; ¼ lb. $1.00; lb. $3.00.

All American, 609. 150 days. An improved, Hollow crown with sweet tender, clean white roots free from fibre.

Short Thick, 611. 85 days. Short, thick, sweet, tender roots.

Mushroom Spawn

You can grow Mushrooms all winter long in almost any building, cellar, or shed which can be darkened. Ask for our FREE leaflet on "How to Grow Mushrooms."

Pure Sterilized Spawn, 6321. Shipped with full cultural directions. One carton will spawn about 40 sq. ft. of bed. Per carton $1.35; 5 cartons $6.50; 10 cartons $12.50, prepaid.

American Pure Culture Brick Spawn, 6323. Produces mushrooms of excellent quality. One brick will spawn about 8 sq. ft. of bed. Per brick 50¢; 5 bricks $2.25; 10 bricks $4.00; 25 bricks $9.00, prepaid.

Book, Manual of Mushroom Culture (Rettew). $2.50, postpaid.

ONION *Seed*

Onions have been under cultivation so long that their true origin was lost, not centuries but thousands of years ago! The original measure of quality was how many tears they would bring. (Believe it or not!) Today, you may have them almost as mild and sweet as an apple, but the distinctive flavor remains. Sow early in rows 18 inches apart, cover seeds ½ inch. Thin when 3 to 4 inches tall to stand 3 to 4 inches apart. Try the New Pelletized Seed, space plant seed and avoid thinning. 1 pkt. for 25 ft.; 1 oz. for 100 ft.

Red Onions

POSTPAID: Pkt. 15¢; ½ oz. 35¢; oz. 65¢; ¼ lb. $2.00.
Large Red Wethersfield, 580. 110 days. Large, thick flat onions with bright purplish-red skin. Solid flesh, white shaded pink.
Southport Red Globe, 582. 120 days. Perfectly round with attractive red skin and white flesh.

White Onions

POSTPAID: Pkt. 15¢; ½ oz. 35¢; oz. 65¢; ¼ lb. $2.00.
Southport White Globe, 584. 120 days. Medium size, perfect globe shape, with pure white skin. White, fine-grained flesh.
Pelletized, Southport White Globe, P584. Pkt. 20¢.
White Portugal or Silver Skin, 590. 100 days. Large, flat pure white onions. Sow thickly for pickling onions. Fine-grained flesh of mild and pleasant flavor.
"SANDWICH ONION" White Sweet Spanish, 594. 110 days. The largest of the globe-shaped white varieties. Pure white skin almost transparent white flesh, sweet and mild.
White Bunching, 588. Does not form bulbs, grown exclusively for green onions or scallions. Sow the seed thickly in rows.

Okra or Gumbo

A Southern favorite that is winning the taste palate of the North. You know its delicate flavor from chicken Gumbo soup. Sow when soil is warm in rows 24 inches apart; cover the seed ½ inch deep. Thin the plants to stand 12 inches apart in the row. Bear all summer. 1 pkt. for 15 ft.; 1 oz. for 100 ft. of drill.
POSTPAID: Pkt. 10¢; oz. 25¢; ¼ lb. 75¢; lb. $2.40.
DWARF GREEN LONG POD, 561. 50 days. Dwarf stocky growth, very productive. The long, dark green pods are thick, heavy and solid.
Perkin's Long Pod, 563. 56 days. Deep green, slender, meaty, tapered and ribbed pods 7 to 8 inches long. Very productive.
White Velvet or Creole, 565. 62 days. The white, tender pods are smooth and free from ridges.

Onion—Sweet Spanish

Yellow Onions

POSTPAID: Pkt. 15¢; ½ oz. 30¢; oz. 65¢; ¼ lb. $2.00.
Prizetaker, 578. 105 days. Globe-shaped, pale yellow skin, and pure white flesh. Very mild and delicate flavor.
Sweet Spanish (Utah Strain), 579. 115 days. Well-formed, large, deep amber-orange globe shaped onions with small necks. Mild white flesh.
DANVER'S YELLOW GLOBE, 568. 110 days. The medium-large, round bulbs have a dark yellow skin, and mild firm white flesh.
Pelletized Danver's yellow Globe, P568. Pkt. 20¢.
Early Yellow Globe, 569. 95 days. Medium large, globular onions, with deep yellow skin and thick cream colored flesh which is sweet and tender.
Ebenezer, 571. 120 days. Flattened, dark yellow bulbs with crisp, firm pure white flesh.

Choice Onion Sets

The quickest and easiest way to grow green onions (scallions) and larger onions for summer use. Plant 1 inch deep in rows 12 inches apart, and 2 inches apart in the row. 1 pound will plant a 50-ft. row.

	Prepaid	¼ lb.	Lb.	5 lbs.	10 lbs.
6302	White Onion Sets	$0.30	$0.50	$2.15	$4.20
6304	Yellow Onion Sets	.25	.40	1.85	3.60
6300	Red Onion Sets	.30	.50	2.15	4.20
6311	Garlic	.45	.80	3.65	7.20

Prices subject to change.

Parsley

The finest chefs always have parsley within reach. Sow early in April-May in rows 18 to 24 inches apart and ¼ inch deep. A board placed on top of the row will hasten germination. Thin out plants to stand 3 inches apart in the row or use Pelletized Seeds and space plant and avoid thinning. 1 pkt. for 40 ft.; 1 oz. for 300 ft.
POSTPAID: Pkt. 10¢; oz. 25¢; ¼ lb. 75¢.
Plain or Single, 605. 70 days. If you want true Parsley flavor, grow this dark green variety.
Hamburg or Parsnip Rooted, 606. 90 days. Parsnip-like roots. Adds flavor to soups and stews.
Dwarf Perfection (Paramount), 600. 85 days. Finely curled leaves, rich, dark pea green.
Extra Triple Curled (Champion Moss Curled), 607. 75 days. Dense growth of curled and crimped leaves, deep emerald green.
Pelletized Seed, Extra Tripled Curled, P607. Pkt. 20¢.

Okra—White Velvet

Scallions—From Seed or Sets

Tender Garden PEAS

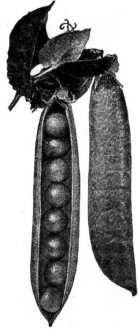

Peas in the pod, canned, or frozen are now a year 'round staple food but wait, if you can, until you pick that first mess of Peas fresh from your own garden in June. New fresh peas and bread and butter! "food for the Gods." Sow the smooth seeded varieties as early as the ground can be worked, in single rows 3 feet apart. Cover seed 2 or 3 inches deep. Wrinkled Peas may rot in cold wet ground and should be sown later. Make sowings at 2-week intervals until May 20th for succession. Pkt. for 20 ft.; 1 pound for 100 ft. of row.

Smooth-Seeded Extra-Early Peas

POSTPAID: Pkt. 15¢; ½ lb. 30¢; lb. 50¢; 2 lbs. 90¢; 5 lbs. $2.00.

Alaska, 618. 54 days. Smooth-seeded, 2 ft. tall, light green pods, 2½ inches long. Wilt-resistant.

PEDIGREE EXTRA-EARLY, 629. 58 days. Very early, prolific and fine quality, vines 24 inches tall, 2½ inch pods. Wilt-resistant.

Mammoth Pod Extra-Early, 667. 58 days. The earliest large-podded Pea, vines grow about 4 ft. tall. Bear a heavy crop of dark green, square-ended pods.

Early—Wrinkled-Seeded Peas

POSTPAID: Pkt. 15¢; ½ lb. 30¢; lb. 50¢; 2 lbs. 95¢; 5 lbs. $2.25.

Freezonian, 644. 63 days. Bronze Medal 1948. Developed for freezing. Vines 30 inches tall, bear attractive, dark green pods 3½ inches long. Exceptionally fine flavored.

American Wonder, 620. 59 days. Dwarf early variety about 12 inches tall. Very productive, fine flavor and quality.

LAXTONIAN (HUNDREDFOLD), 648. 60 days. Bears an enormous crop of 5 inch pods filled with 7 or 8 very large, rich green peas. 18 inches tall.

Laxton's Progress, 650. 60 days. Vines 18 inches tall, bearing 4 inch pods packed with 8 large dark green peas. Fine for freezing.

Little Marvel, 654. 64 days. Grows-18 inches tall, 3 inch pods of large, dark green, sweet peas. Productive and disease resistant.

Thomas Laxton, 705. 57 days. 30 inch vines, loaded with 3½ inch pods. Finest quality and one of the best for freezing.

Peas—Thomas Laxton

It's Easy to Shell Peas with a PEA SHELLER and BEAN SLICER

This amazing device hulls and slices vegetables so easily and quickly that it is wanted by housewives everywhere. Featuring the new base that sits tightly on all non-porous flat surfaces such as table tops, stoves, sinks, etc. without clamps. Five gay colors: white, red, green, yellow and blue. $3.98, postpaid.

Pea Sheller

Late—Wrinkled-Seeded Peas

POSTPAID: Pkt. 15¢; ½ lb. 30¢; lb. 50¢; 2 lbs. 95¢; 5 lbs. $2.25.

Carter's Daisy or Dwarf Telephone, 622. 75 days. Dwarf vines, 24 inches tall, 5 inch pods, 8 to 10 peas to a pod.

Telephone, Dark-Podded, 700. 73 days. Vigorous vines 5 feet tall bearing 5 inch pods filled with 8 to 10 peas of delicious flavor.

Edible—Podded Sugar Peas

You don't shell these, you eat them pod and all. Delicious!

POSTPAID: Pkt. 15¢; ½ lb. 30¢; lb. 50¢; 2 lbs. 90¢; 5 lbs. $2.10.

Dwarf Grey Sugar, 640. 65 days. Grows 2 feet tall, and bears a great abundance of delicious, tender 3 inch pods.

Mammoth Melting Sugar, 662. 72 days. An excellent, large, flat-podded, wilt-resistant variety with tender, fleshy, stringless pods.

Sugar Peas—Don't Shell

Sweet Peppers

The "stuff and bake" Peppers

Sow seed in flats indoors, transplant when 2 to 3 inches tall into other flats, 4 inches apart each way, or into individual pots. When ground is thoroughly warm, transplant to open ground in rows 3 feet apart, with plants 2 feet apart in rows. One ounce of seed will produce about 1000 plants. Pelletized pepper seed may be planted outdoors in May, right where plants are to grow.

CALIFORNIA WONDER, 711. 112 days. Sturdy, upright plants bearing 6, 7, or 8 smooth, blocky, thick-walled crimson fruits, about 4½ inches in length and 4 inches across. Pkt. 15¢; ½ oz. 55¢; oz. $1.00; ¼ lb. $3.65.

Chinese Giant, 722. 120 days. The largest of all Sweet Peppers, with blocky fruits 4½ to 5 inches long and equally as broad. Deep green color ripening to brilliant scarlet red. Pkt. 15¢; ½ oz. 60¢; oz. $1.10; ¼ lb. $4.00.

Large Bell or Bull Nose, 709. 95 days. A popular, large, early scarlet pepper. Pkt. 15¢; ½ oz. 40¢; oz. 75¢; ¼ lb. $2.80.

Ruby Giant or Worldbeater, 738. 115 days. Very large and has a nice flavor. Pkt. 10¢; ½ oz. 50¢; oz. 90¢; ¼ lb. $2.85.

Ruby King, 740. 108 days. Large tapering fruits with thick sweet flesh. Pkt. 15¢; ½ oz. 50¢; oz. 90¢; ¼ lb. $2.85.

Pelletized, Ruby King, P740. Pkt. 20¢.

Small-Fruited Hot Peppers

Hungarian Wax, 733. 115 days. Long, bright yellow fruits turning scarlet. Pkt. 15¢; ½ oz. 60¢; oz. $1.00; ¼ lb. $3.50.

Long Red Cayenne, 712. 115 days. Long slender, bright red, and very pungent. Pkt. 15¢; ½ oz. 50¢; oz. 90¢; ¼ lb. $2.85.

Large Cherry, 735. Pkt. 15¢; ½ oz. 50¢; oz. 90¢; ¼ lb. $2.85.

Small Chili, 718. Pkt. 15¢; ½ oz. 45¢; oz. 85¢; ¼ lb. $2.60.

Tabasco, 744. Pkt. 15¢; ½ oz. 55¢; oz. $1.00; ¼ lb. $3.50.

Pepper—Ruby King

Pumpkins for Pies and Hallowe'en

Sow the seed in rich soil in May. Often sown in every fourth hill of corn which spaces them about 10 feet apart. 1 pkt. for 6 hills; 1 oz. for 25 hills.

Kentucky Field or Large Cheese, 750. 120 days. Light orange yellow fruits weighing from 10 to 25 lbs. Has a hard shell and bright yellow flesh. Pkt. 10¢; oz. 25¢; ¼ lb. 75¢; lb. $2.50.

Connecticut Field (Big Tom), 752. 120 days. Thick, bright orange yellow flesh which is dry and sweet. Bright orange fruits 10 to 14 inches deep and 12 to 15 inches in diameter. Pkt. 10¢; oz. 25¢; ¼ lb. 75¢; lb. $2.50.

KING OF THE MAMMOTH (POTIRON), 756. 120 days. The largest of all pumpkins. Globular, slightly ribbed, flattened fruits weighing 60 to 90 lbs. Light yellow skin mottled with orange, and solid orange yellow flesh. Pkt. 10¢; oz. 35¢; ¼ lb. 95¢; lb. $3.25.

Sugar or New England Pie, 760. 115 days. The best variety for pies with slightly flattened, furrowed fruits 8 to 9 inches in diameter. Reddish orange skin and rich orange yellow flesh. Pkt. 10¢; oz. 30¢; ¼ lb. 90¢; lb. $3.00.

Winter Luxury, 764. 100 days. Resembles Small Sugar but of more rounded form. Has smooth, light orange skin and thick yellow flesh of choice flavor. Pkt. 10¢; oz. 25¢; ¼ lb. 80¢; lb. $2.75.

Pumpkin—Small Sugar

Healthful Spinach

If you have never eaten spinach fresh from your own garden, you don't know how tender and delicious it can be.

For spring and summer picking, sow in drills 1 foot apart and ½ inch deep as early as the ground can be worked and every two weeks up to May 15. 1 pkt. for 25 ft.; 1 oz. for 100 ft.

POSTPAID: Pkt. 10¢; oz. 25¢; ¼ lb. 70¢; lb. $2.00.

Princess Juliana, 843. 48 days. Compact, dense growth close to the ground with rounded, thick, heavily crumpled, very dark green leaves.

Bloomsdale Long-Standing Savoy, 849. 45 days. Dark glossy green leaves heavily crumpled and savoyed. Remarkably long standing.

Bloomsdale Reselected Dark Green, 851. 40 days. Large, broad, glossy dark green leaves which are heavily crimped and curled.

Virginia Blight-Resistant Savoy, 855. 35 days. Resistant to spinach blight. Recommended only for late summer and fall sowing.

New Zealand, Hot Weather Spinach, 847. 65 days. (Tetragonia expansa.) Not a true spinach but provides a great quantity of small dark tender leaves throughout the hot summer and fall season. Grows continuously if only the young tender tips are gathered. Pkt. 15¢; oz. 35¢; ¼ lb. $1.00; lb. $3.00.

Spinach—Bloomsdale Long Standing

58

Radish—Scarlet Globe

Crisp Delicious Radishes

Crisp, appetizing radishes in a matter of days, and you can have them all summer long, garden fresh and oh! so different from "boughten" produce. Sow thinly, in drills ¼ inch deep as soon as the ground is workable and make successive sowings every ten days. For quickest, finest crop use Pelletized Radish Seed and space plant 1 inch apart. See Scarlet Globe and Icicle.

Early Radishes

POSTPAID: Pkt. 10¢; oz. 25¢; ¼ lb. 75¢; lb. $2.00.

EARLY SCARLET GLOBE, 813. Bright cardinal-red globe shaped roots, ready for the table in 20 to 25 days. Remain crisp and tender even in hot weather. Pelletized Early Scarlet Globe, P813. Pkt. 20¢.

Cavalier, 771. 25 days. The firm roots are oblong-globe shaped, slightly longer than broad, and bright scarlet color. A splendid forcing variety.

Cincinnati Market, 773. 29 days. Produces clear bright red roots 6 to 7 inches long.

Crimson Giant, 779. 29 days. Attractive rich crimson red round to oval roots, with pure white mild, and tender flesh. Grows to larger size than any other round radish.

French Breakfast, 783. 25 days. Attractive oblong roots with bright pink skin and the lower portion shaded white. Icy white crisp flesh of excellent quality.

Sparkler, 809. 25 days. Grows quickly and is good for under glass or in the open. Bright scarlet with lower half pure white. Most attractive.

White Icicle, 786. 30 days, Icy white roots 5 inches long and ¾ inch across. Tender white flesh with a pleasant snappy flavor.

Pelletized White Icicle, P786. Pkt. 20¢.

Radish—French Breakfast

Radish—Sparkler

Winter Radishes

Sow July first for use in late fall and winter. The Chinese type develops more rapidly than the Black Spanish sorts. Store in sand.

POSTPAID: Pkt. 10¢; oz. 30¢; ¼ lb. 90¢; lb. $3.00.

Round Black Spanish, 807. 60 days. Crisp hard white flesh. Black skin.

Scarlet China (China Rose Winter), 810. 50 days. Oblong roots 4 to 5 inches long and 2 inches thick. Crisp white flesh.

White Chinese (Celestial), 812. 55 days. Solid crisp white flesh of delightfully mild flavor. Pure white skin. Grows 6 to 7 inches long.

Hint: Slice and cream the large radishes for a rare taste treat with steaks or chops; try this on small ones—boil, drain, cook in saucepan with butter and grated cheese.

Summer Radishes

White Strausburg, 822. 40 days. Tapering, smooth roots 5 inches long and 1½ inches at the shoulder. Crisp, white, snappy flavor.

Rhubarb

From Seed or from Roots

Grows—with little care, year after year. A delicious spring tonic in pie, baked, stewed, or in sherbet.

Victoria, 832. Has large thick stalks of most delicious flavor. Sow seeds outdoors in shallow drills one foot apart and transplant to stand 4 feet apart in the fall. Pkt. 15¢; oz. 50¢; ¼ lb. $1.80.

Victoria Roots, 17-703. We offer strong seedlings 1-1½ inches in diameter, of this splendid variety. Pick sparingly first year. 3 for 55¢; 6 for $1.00; 12 for $1.75; 25 for $3.25; 100 for $12.00, postpaid.

MacDonald Roots, 17-704. MacDonald Rhubarb has a tender thin skin of brilliant red color and no peeling is required. Cooks to an attractive rich red. 75¢ each; 2 for $1.40; 12 for $8.00, postpaid.

Salsify-Oyster Plant

Mammoth Sandwich Island, 837. 135 days. Tapering roots, 7 to 8 inches long, with almost white smooth skin, and very mild, delicately flavored flesh. Sow early in the spring. Parboil, dip in bread crumbs and fry as oysters. 1 pkt. for 20 ft.; 1 oz. for 100 ft. Pkt. 15¢; ½ oz. 40¢; oz. 75¢.

Garden Sorrel

Narrow-Leaved, 839. 60 days. Piquant flavor, use as "professional" touch to your soups and salads. Sow thinly in drills a foot apart in early spring and thin to stand 6 to 7 inches apart. 1 pkt. for 15 ft.; 1 oz. for 100 ft. Pkt. 15¢; ½ oz. 40¢; oz. 75¢.

Swiss Chard

Healthful greens, all summer, from one short row of Swiss Chard. Same culture as for Beets. Have you tried cooking the mid-ribs as Asparagus? One packet for 30 ft., one ounce for 100 ft. of row.

POSTPAID: Pkt. 10¢; oz. 25¢; ¼ lb. 70¢; ½ lb. $1.25.

GIANT LUCULLUS, 167. 60 days. Curly green leaves of mild Spinach-like flavor and a white mid-rib of moderate size.

Perpetual Spinach, Beet, 168. 50 days. Stands continuous cutting, slender, pale green leaves.

Green Lyons, 169. 60 days. Large, dark green, heavily crumpled leaves with broad white mid-rib.

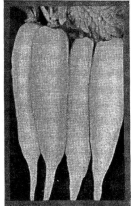
Radish—White Icicle

Squashes

Summer Squash

Squash is easy to grow, delicious to eat and the yield is heavy. Add to the variety on your table with baked, boiled, or fried squash. Rich in vitamins. Sow in hills 3 to 4 feet apart each way as soon as the ground is thoroughly warmed. 1 pkt. for 6 hills; 1 oz. for 25 hills.

EARLY PROLIFIC STRAIGHTNECK, 864. 55 days. Fruits 10 inches long and 2½ inches thick, smooth with light yellow skin. Pkt. 10¢; oz. 30¢; ¼ lb. 90¢; lb. $3.00.

Early Golden Summer Crookneck, 883. 50 days. Long bright orange yellow fruits densely covered with warts. Sweet fine-grained flesh of rich buttery flavor. Pkt. 10¢; oz. 30¢; ¼ lb. 90¢; lb. $3.00.

Cocozella Bush, 862. 60 days. Oblong dark green variety speckled lighter green. Fruits 10 to 12 inches long. Pkt. 10¢; oz. 35¢; ¼ lb. $1.00; lb. $3.00.

Early White Bush, (Patty Pan), 873. 54 days. Flat, scalloped fruits of greenish white color when young, and white when mature. Pkt. 10¢; oz. 30¢; ¼ lb. 90¢; lb. $3.00.

BLACK ZUCCHINI, 860. 62 days. The cylindrical fruits grow 12 inches long and 3½ inches thick. For finest flavor, use when quite small. Pkt. 10¢; oz. 30¢; ¼ lb. 90¢; lb. $3.00.

Yankee Hybrid, 882. 50 days. Oblong creamy yellow fruits of splendid quality. Early, reliable, and a prolific yielder. Pkt. 15¢; oz. 75¢; ¼ lb. $2.25; lb. $7.50.

Table Queen or Acorn, 879. 80 days. Vining, dark green fruits 5 inches long and 4 inches across with thick tender yellow flesh of sweet flavor. Just the right size for baking. Pkt. 10¢; oz. 35¢; ¼ lb. $1.20; lb. $3.25.

Golden Table Queen, 866. 83 days. Vining, 5 inches long and ideal for individual servings. Golden yellow skin and clear yellow flesh which is sweet and fine-grained. Pkt. 10¢; oz. 40¢; ¼ lb. $1.50; lb. $4.95.

Uconn Squash 886
1950 Gold Medal Winner
All America Selections
Uconn Squash instead of running all over the place is a bush variety scarcely taking a space 3 feet by 3 feet. Fruit is the same as Acorn and the yield is heavy. Perfect for small gardens. Pkt. 25¢; oz. 75¢.

Squash—Hubbard

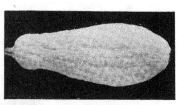
Squash—Early Prolific Straight Neck

Winter Squash
Vining

Sow vining Winter Squashes 5 seeds to a hill spaced not less than 4 feet apart each way. Cover seeds ½ inch deep.

Boston Marrow, 858. 100 days. Similar to Hubbard, 15 inches long and 12 inches in diameter. Has hard, rough, dull orange skin and thick, golden-orange fine-grained sweet flesh. Pkt. 10¢; oz. 25¢; ¼ lb. 75¢; lb. $2.55.

Buttercup, 885. 100 days. Turban-shaped fruits of medium size weighing 3 to 4 lbs. each. Yellow skin with silver-grey mottling. Pkt. 10¢; oz. 40¢; ¼ lb. $1.50; lb. $4.95.

Golden Delicious, 887. 105 days. Top-shaped fruit 8 to 9 inches long, weighing about 8 lbs. Golden yellow shell, fine-grained, rich orange flesh. Pkt. 10¢; oz. 40¢; ¼ lb. $1.10; lb. $3.75.

Blue Hubbard, 870. 105 days. Similar to other Hubbards, but skin is slaty blue. Fine textured orange flesh. Pkt. 10¢; oz. 40¢; ¼ lb. $1.10; lb. $3.60.

Golden Hubbard, 871. 100 days. Earlier and smaller than Hubbard. Deep orange red fruits. Flesh is deep orange yellow, fine grained and dry. Pkt. 10¢; oz. 40¢; ¼ lb. $1.10; lb. $3.75.

Improved Hubbard, 872. 108 days. The standard winter squash. The large dark green fruits are slightly warted and have deep orange-yellow flesh. Pkt. 10¢; oz. 40¢; ¼ lb. $1.10; lb. $3.60.

BUTTERNUT, 881. 85 days. A new squash, delicious for pies and superb for baking and boiling. Thick bottle-shaped fruits, 10 inches long and 5 inches wide. Smooth golden-brown skin, yellow, dry, sweet flesh of delicious flavor. Pkt. 15¢; oz. 60¢; ¼ lb. $2.25; lb. $7.50.

Squash—Butternut

Squash—Acorn

Vegetable Spaghetti, 880. 60 days. Vining squash with fruits the size of an eggplant. Boil whole for 30 minutes. Cut open and serve the spaghetti-like flesh with salt and butter. Pkt. 10¢; oz. 35¢; ¼ lb. $1.00; lb. $3.50.

Sunflower Seed

Mammoth 838. 60 days. Produces immense heads measuring 12 to 20 inches across. Grow it for winter food for birds and poultry. Pkt. 10¢; oz. 15¢; ¼ lb. 35¢; lb. $1.00.
SUNFLOWER FEED, 6212. For the birds. lb. 60¢; 5 lbs. $2.75, postpaid.

TOMATO — *America's Favorite Vegetable*

Tomato—Bonny Best

A POUND OF FOOD TO EVERY SQUARE FOOT OF GARDEN

Sow seeds in the house about the middle of February. When they are 4 inches tall, transplant into flats or a hotbed to stand 4 inches apart each way, or into small pots (clay or paper). Plant outdoors, 3 feet apart each way, about the end of May. Use individual plant stakes, a fence or inverted "V" wooden slat supports — or mulch the ground and let the vine run. Pinching back to one good stem will increase size of individual tomatoes. Plant soon as weather is settled. One ounce of seed will produce about 2500 plants. You can now plant **Pelletized Tomato Seed** right where you want your plants.

Bonny Best, 894. 113 days. Extra early, old but one of the best. Scarlet fruits are almost round, and are produced in abundance. Pkt. 10¢; ½ oz. 45¢; oz. 80¢; ¼ lb. $3.00.

BREAK O'DAY, 896. 110 days. The fruits are similar to Marglobe, being round, smooth, solid and of a fine scarlet color. Highly resistant to disease. Pkt. 15¢; ½ oz. 45¢; oz. 80¢; ¼ lb. $3.00.

Pelletized Break O'Day, P896. Pkt. 20¢.

Crimson Cushion or Beefsteak, 897. 128 days. One of the largest of the rich crimson tomatoes, very solid and smooth makes juicy beefsteak-like slices. Pkt. 15¢; ½ oz. 70¢; ¼ lb. $4.50.

Golden Ponderosa, 912. 126 days. Very large fruits of splendid quality. Solid, rich golden yellow flesh, minimum acid. Beautiful sliced. Pkt. 15¢; ½ oz. 70¢; oz. $1.25; ¼ lb. $4.50.

ITALIAN CANNER, 915. 110 days. The paste tomato. Medium-sized oblong fruits about 2¼ inches long and 1¼ inches in diameter. Serve whole or halved in salads. Pkt. 20¢; ¼ oz. 50¢; ½ oz. 90¢; oz. $1.75.

John Baer, 917. 106 days. Similar to Bonny Best but a little earlier. Pkt. 10¢; ½ oz. 45¢; oz. 80¢; ¼ lb. $3.00.

JUBILEE, 919. 112 days. Add color to your salads with this bright orange tomato; perfectly smooth round fruits weighing about 6 ounces each and orange-colored tomato juice, too! Pkt. 15¢; ¼ oz. 50¢; ½ oz. 75¢; oz. $1.40.

Marglobe Certified, 923. 115 days. Large, smooth, meaty, globular red fruits which ripen evenly and are completely free from cracks. This is your best "stuffed" tomato. Very productive and remarkably wilt-resistant. Pkt. 15¢; ½ oz. 45¢; oz. 85¢; ¼ lb. $3.00.

Michigan State Forcing, 928. 115 days. Splendid wilt-resistant variety with attractive, deep smooth globular scarlet fruits for forcing. Pkt. 25¢; ½ oz. 60¢; oz. $1.15.

Penn State Earliana, 938. 104 days. Standard extra-early with bright red fruits and solid tasty flesh. Pkt. 15¢; ½ oz. 45¢; oz. 80¢; ¼ lb. $3.00.

Ponderosa, 930. 125 days. Profitable and popular late sort for the home garden. Tasty, purplish-pink fruit of large size. Pkt. 25¢; ½ oz. $1.35; oz. $2.25; ¼ lb. $7.85.

Pritchard or Scarlet Topper, Certified, 941. 115 days. Fine early tomato with large, smooth, globular fruits ripening to a clear scarlet right up to the stem end. Pkt. 15¢; ½ oz. 45¢; oz. 80¢; ¼ lb. $3.00.

RUTGER'S CERTIFIED, 937. 113 days. Uniform, globular, smooth very solid fruits averaging 8 ounces each. Ripens evenly, sparkling red color. The best canning variety. Pkt. 15¢; ½ oz. 45¢; oz. 80¢; ¼ lb. $3.00.

Pelletized Rutger's Certified, P937. Pkt. 20¢.

Selected Stone, 942. 125 days. Very dependable and will produce a large crop of solid, deep red fruit. Pkt. 10¢; ½ oz. 45¢; oz. 80¢; ¼ lb. $3.00.

Stokesdale Certified, 950. 110 days. Bright scarlet color with fruits weighing 5½ to 6 ounces each. Smooth, globe-shaped, solid, and of splendid quality. Pkt. 15¢; ½ oz. 45¢; oz. 80¢; ¼ lb. $3.00.

Valiant, 947. 110 days. Large, deep globe-shaped, scarlet-red fruits free from cracks and blemishes. Pkt. 15¢; ½ oz. 55¢; oz. $1.00.

Tomato—Rutgers

Hot Kaps, 25 and Setter, 85¢, postpaid.

Miniature Tomatoes

Full flavored very small tomatoes borne in clusters like grapes. The name describes size and type; All are ¾" to 1" in diameter except the Peach which is about 1½" in diameter. Serve whole in your dish of appetizers and salads; a neat hors d'oeuvres addition. Delicious for tomato conserve or pickled whole.

115 days	Pkt.	½ oz.	oz.		115 days	Pkt.	½ oz.	oz.
931 Red Cherry	$0.15	$0.55	$1.00		934 Red Pear	$0.15	$0.70	$1.25
953 Yellow					955 Yellow Pear	.10	.55	.95
Cherry	.15	.75	1.35		935 Red Plum	.15	.70	1.25
933 Red Peach	.20	.80	1.50		956 Yellow Plum	.15	.70	1.25

Miniature Tomatoes

Turnip—Purple-Top White Globe

TURNIPS *For All the Year*

Culture—For an early crop sow thinly ½ inch deep in the open in spring, in drills 18 to 20 inches apart. Thin out seedlings to stand 3 to 4 inches apart. For succession, sow every two weeks until May 15. For fall and winter use, sow in July and August. 1 pkt. for 50 ft.; 1 oz. for 300 ft.; 2 lbs. for an acre. Use Pelletized Seed and space plant 2 inches apart. See Purple-Top White Globe.

POSTPAID: Pkt. 10¢; oz. 20¢; ¼ lb. 50¢; lb. $1.50.

Extra-Early White Milan, 975. 40 days. Flat roots 4 inches across and fine-grained, mild, tender, white flesh.

All Season Foliage Turnip, 961. 42 days for roots; 20-30 days for greens. The tender tops of this turnip yield repeated cuttings of "greens." The large white roots are fine quality.

Golden Ball, 962. 60 days. Small tops and medium-sized roots which are round and smooth. Firm, crisp, amber flesh.

Seven Top, 970. 45 days. Grown for its leafy tops which make excellent greens. Does not produce edible roots.

Snowball, 972. 40 days. Roots have smooth white skin and are nearly round.

Yellow or Amber Globe, 977. 57 days. Forms large, globular, smooth roots 5 to 6 inches in diameter. Yellow skin tinted green at the top, fine grained, sweet, tender flesh.

Early White Flat Dutch, 976. 50 days. Tender, fine-grained, sweet roots measuring 4 inches across and 2 inches deep.

PURPLE-TOP WHITE GLOBE, 966. 55 days. Globular roots, smooth bright purplish-red above the soil level, and white below.

Pelletized, Purple-Top White Globe, P966. Pkt. 20¢.

Purple-Top Strap Leaf, 969. 55 days. Flattened roots, purple tops, white below. Fine quality.

Large White Globe, 965. 75 days. Globe-shaped, pure white roots.

White Egg, 974. 55 days. Egg-shaped roots 3 to 4 inches long with sweet, white flesh.

Ruta Baga

Improved Purple-Top Yellow, 985. 100 days. Smooth skin, yellow flesh fine-grained, Pkt. 10¢; oz. 20¢; ¼ lb. 65¢; lb. $2.00.

HERB GARDENS *for Flavor* — Seeds or Plants

Your herb garden may consist of a few pots on the window sill, an odd corner by the kitchen door or could stretch over acres. No matter the space or location, your herb garden is an endless source of interest and taste thrills.

The seeds and plants below will give you a good start and from there you can go on and on and encompass, in your own yard, plants from the four corners of the earth, and from antiquity to the present day. We'll be glad to send free on request our own leaflet on "Herb Culture."

Anise, 5010. Aromatic seeds. Pkt. 15¢; ½ oz. 65¢.

Balm, 5012. Used medicinally. Pkt. 15¢; ½ oz. 90¢.

*****Balm, Lemon.** Scented leaves. Plants only.

Basil, Sweet, 5014. Used for seasoning. Pkt. 15¢; ½ oz. 45¢.

Borage, 5018. Used for seasoning. Pkt. 15¢; ½ oz. 55¢.

*****Caraway, 5020.** (Biennial.) Aromatic seeds. Pkt. 20¢; ½ oz. 50¢.

Catnip, 5022. Excellent tonic for cats. Pkt. 15¢; ½ oz. $1.00

Chervil, 5025. Aromatic foliage for flavoring. Pkt. 15¢; oz. 50¢.

*****Chives, 5023.** Mild onion-like flavor. Pkt. 15¢; ½ oz. $1.15.

Coriander, 5024. Seeds used in confectionery. Pkt. 10¢; ½ oz. 35¢.

Celery Seed for Flavoring, 5027. Oz. 10¢; ¼ lb. 25¢.

Dill, 5028. For dill pickles. Pkt. 10¢; oz. 25¢; ¼ lb. 75¢.

Fennel, Sweet, 5030. Used in sauces. Pkt. 15¢; ½ oz. 35¢.

Horehound, 5032. For seasoning. Pkt. 20¢; ½ oz. $1.15.

*****Lavender, 5034.** English Lavender. Pkt. 25¢; ½ oz. $1.70.

Marjoram, Sweet, 5036. For seasoning. Pkt. 15¢; ½ oz. 80¢.

Pennyroyal, 5038. Used for seasoning. Pkt. 25¢; ¼ oz. 65¢.

*****Peppermint, 5040.** The leaves and young tips are used for flavoring. Pkt. 25¢; ¼ oz. $1.00.

*****Rosemary, 5042.** The fresh leaves are used for seasoning. Pkt. 25¢; ½ oz. $1.70.

*****Rue, 5044.** An old-fashioned herb used in home remedies. Pkt. 25¢; ½ oz. $1.35.

Saffron, 5046. (Carthamus tinctorius.) For flavoring and coloring. Pkt. 15¢; ½ oz. 40¢.

*****Sage, 5048.** The most popular of all herbs. Pkt. 15¢; ½ oz. $1.10.

Savory, Summer, 5050. Used for flavoring. Pkt. 15¢; ½ oz. 53¢.

*****Savory, Winter.** Plants only.

Tansy, 5054. Young leaves used for seasoning. Pkt. 25¢.

*****Tarragon.** For making tarragon vinegar. Plants only.

*****Thyme, English, 5056.** For seasoning. Pkt. 20¢; ½ oz. $1.10.

*****Wormwood, 5060.** For flavoring, medicine, and liqueurs. Pkt. 25¢; ½ oz. 70¢.

PLANTS: Varieties marked with star (*) can be supplied in plants at: $1.00 for a single plant; any 3 for $2.00; any 12 for $7.00, postpaid.

Dill   Thyme   Horehound   Anise   Tarragon   Sweet Marjoram   Fennel

A HAND-PICKED LIST OF VEGETABLES

Especially selected for (1) Quality, (2) Productiveness, (3) Adaptability to the Home Garden and (4) Popularity. A selection from this list is sure to prove satisfactory.

BEAN, Green Bush, Bountiful, 023. 48 days. Light green, tender, brittle oval pods. Stringless and disease-resistant. Pkt. 15c; ½lb. 35c; lb. 60c; 2 lbs. $1.10; 5 lbs. $2.55.
BEAN, Green Bush, Tendergreen, 061. 53 days. Light green Beans, meaty and entirely stringless. Six inches long, rust-resistant; delicious flavor. Pkt. 15c; ½lb. 35c; lb. 60c; 2 lbs. $1.10; 5 lbs. $2.55.
BEAN, Yellow Bush, Sure-crop Stringless Wax, 084. 53 days. Handsome, rich yellow pods 6 to 7 inches long, very meaty, flat but thick. Pkt. 15c; ½lb. 35c; lb. 60c; 2 lbs. $1.10; 5 lbs. $2.55.
BEAN, Yellow Bush, Pencil-Pod Black Wax, 065. 54 days. The round, nearly straight pods are 6 to 7 inches long and entirely stringless. Clear yellow. Pkt. 15c; ½lb. 35c; lb. 60c; 2 lbs. $1.10; 5 lbs. $2.55.
BEAN, Green Pole, Kentucky Wonder or Old Homestead, 028. 65 days. Pods are 7 to 8 inches long, deeply saddle-backed, and very fleshy. Pkt. 15c; ½lb. 35c; lb. 60c; 2 lbs. $1.10; 5 lbs. $2.55.
BEAN, Bush Lima, Fordhook, 107. 75 days. The standard of excellence for Limas. Beans are large, plump and of the finest eating quality. Pkt. 15c; ½ lb. 40c; lb. 75c; 2 lbs. $1.40; 5 lbs. $3.10.
BEET, Detroit Dark Red, 149. 60 days. Deep red flesh showing no light zones. Delicious, fine-grained and tender. Pkt. 10c; oz. 25c; ¼lb. 75c; ½lb. $1.35.
SWISS CHARD, Giant Lucullus, 167. 60 days. Curly, dark green leaves of mild spinach-like flavor with a white midrib which may be used the same as asparagus. Pkt. 10c; oz. 25c; ¼lb. 70c; ½lb. $1.25.
CARROT, Chantenay, Improved Red-Cored, 232. 70 days. Large, thick, stump-rooted Carrot tapering toward the bottom. Smooth orange skin; crisp, tender flesh. Pkt. 10c; ½oz. 25c; oz. 45c; ¼lb. $1.50.
CELERY, Golden Plume, 274. 110 days. Full solid hearts of a golden yellow color. Easy to blanch, crisp and brittle, with delicious flavor. Pkt. 15c; ½ oz. 70c; oz. $1.25; ¼ lb. $4.50.
SWEET CORN, Golden Bantam, 318. 80 days. Sweet, distinct buttery flavor. The 8-inch ears are just the right size for eating off the cob. Pkt. 15c; ½lb. 30c; lb. 45c; 2 lbs. 85c; 5 lbs. $1.95.
SWEET CORN, Golden Cross Bantam, 335. 84 days. Fourteen rows of delicious light yellow grains. Often bears 2 ears per plant. Pkt. 15c; ½lb. 40c; lb. 70c; 2 lbs. $1.30; 5 lbs. $2.95.
CUCUMBER, Clark's Special, 365. 62 days. Dark green fruit, 9 to 10 inches long, tapering at both ends. Clear white, crisp, firm flesh with few seeds. Ideal for slicing. Pkt. 10c; oz. 40c; ¼lb. $1.30.
ENDIVE, Green Curled, 414. 95 days. Beautifully curled and fringed leaves. Crisp and tender even when not blanched. Pkt. 10c; oz. 35c; ¼lb. $1.00.
KOHLRABI, Early White Vienna, 431. 55 days. Skin and flesh white; best quality when 1 inch in diameter. Pkt. 10c; ½oz. 40c; oz. 75c; ¼lb. $2.25.
LETTUCE, Black-Seeded Simpson, 442. 45 days. Large, loose-leaf plants with attractively crumpled and fringed light green leaves. Always crisp and sweet. Pkt. 10c; oz. 25c; ¼lb. 85c.
LETTUCE, White Boston, 458. 76 days. Uniform light green. Forms solid heads with a tightly folded heart. Pkt. 10c; oz. 30c; ¼lb. 90c.
LETTUCE, Bibb, 444. 78 days. Solid heart of rich yellow-green. Does best in early summer or fall. Has a delightful, mild flavor. Pkt. 15c; oz. 40c; ¼lb. $1.20.
ONION SETS. The easiest and quickest way to raise either green Onions or large Onions for cooking.
White Onion Sets, 6302. ½lb. 30c; lb. 50c, postpaid.
Yellow Onion Sets, 6304. ½lb. 25c; lb. 40c, postpaid.
PARSLEY, Extra Triple Curled, 607. 75 days. Densely curled and deeply fringed leaves of beautiful rich green. Pkt. 10c; oz. 25c; ¼lb. 75c.
PARSNIP, All American, 609. 150 days. Sweet, tender, clean white roots free from fiber and hard core. Pkt. 10c; oz. 35c; ¼lb. $1.00; lb. $3.00.
PEAS, Little Marvel, 654. 64 days. Three-inch pods full of large, dark green, sweet Peas. Grows 18 inches tall and bears several good pickings. Pkt. 15c; ½lb. 30c; lb. 55c; 2 lbs. $1.00; 5 lbs. $2.20.
PEAS, Laxtonian, 648. 60 days. Five-inch pods filled with 7 or 8 rich green Peas. Vines 18 inches tall, with deep green foliage. Pkt. 15c; ½lb. 30c; lb. 55c; 2 lbs. $1.00; 5 lbs. $2.20.
RADISH, Early Scarlet Globe, 813. 23 days. Tops medium to small, with deep scarlet roots. Remains crisp and tender until an inch in diameter. Pkt. 10c; oz. 25c; ¼lb. 75c; lb. $2.00.
RADISH, White Icicle, 786. 30 days. Icy white roots 5 inches long and ¾ inch across. Withstands hot weather. Pkt. 10c; oz. 25c; ¼lb. 75c; lb. $2.00.
SPINACH, Bloomsdale Long Standing Savoy, 849. 45 days. Savoyed and crumpled, glossy green leaves, very slow to go to seed. Pkt. 10c; oz. 25c; ¼lb. 75c; lb. $2.10.
SQUASH, Table Queen or Acorn, 879. 80 days. Dark green fruits measuring 5 to 6 inches across, with thick tender yellow flesh. Fine flavor, ripens early and is a good winter keeper. Pkt. 10c; oz. 40c; ¼lb. $1.20; lb. $3.25.
SQUASH, Black Zucchini, 860. 62 days. Green-black skin with flavorful, greenish white flesh. The fruits are blunt ended and generally somewhat fluted. Pkt. 10c; oz. 30c; ¼lb. 90c; lb. $3.00.
TOMATO, Rutgers, 937. 73 days. Uniform, smooth, globular fruits, bright red and averaging 6 ounces each. The best Tomato for home gardeners. Pkt. 15c; ½oz. 45c; oz. 80c; ¼lb. $3.00.
TURNIP, Purple-Top White Globe, 966. 55 days. Roots are smooth, bright purple-red above the soil level and white below. Good table quality and a fine winter keeper. Pkt. 10c; oz. 20c; ¼lb. 50c; lb. $1.50.

Dreer's Money Saving Vegetable Garden Collections

We did the selecting for you. All varieties were selected for quality, ease of growth, and productiveness and to give you the **most food per square foot.**

Bungalow Collection

$1.70 Value for $1.25 postpaid

One packet each of 15 varieties, sufficient seed for a space 20 x 30 and to yield quantities of the finest garden fresh vegetables through summer and fall. **Order No. 5100.**

Bush Bean, Bountiful
Bush Bean, Sure-Crop Stringless Wax
Beet, Detroit Dark Red
Carrot, Red-Cored Chantenay
Sweet Corn Golden Bantam
Cucumber, Clark's Special
Lettuce, Black-Seeded Simpson
Lettuce, Big Boston
Onion, Yellow Globe
Parsley, Extra Triple Curled
Peas, Laxton's Progress
Radish, Scarlet Globe
Spinach, Bloomsdale Long-Standing
Swiss Chard, Lucullus
Turnip, Purple-Top White Globe

Suburban Collection

$4.25 Value for $3.50 postpaid

If you have a space 50 x 50 or 40 x 60 you can raise all the vegetables for a family of five from early summer, through the fall, with enough left over to can, store or freeze for winter use. Remember! All Dreer's Seeds are Guaranteed to satisfy or your money back. **Order No. 5102.**

½ lb. Bean, Bountiful
½ lb. Bean, Sure-Crop Stringless Wax
½ lb. Bush Lima, Fordhook
1 oz. Beet, Detroit Dark Red
1 pkt. Cabbage, Copenhagen Market
1 oz. Carrot, Red-Cored Chantenay
½ lb. Sweet Corn, Golden Bantam
1 pkt. Cucumber, Clark's Special
1 pkt. Lettuce, Black-Seeded Simpson
1 pkt. Lettuce, Big Boston
1 pkt. Onion, Ebenezer
1 oz. Spinach, Bloomsdale Long-Standing
1 pkt. Parsley, Extra Triple Curled
½ lb. Peas, Pedigree Extra-Early
½ lb. Peas, Laxtonion
1 pkt. Radish, Scarlet Globe
1 pkt. Tomato, Marglobe
1 pkt. Squash, Early White Bush
1 oz. Swiss Chard, Lucullus
1 pkt. Turnip, Purple-Top White Globe

"Henry A. Dreer, Inc., warrants to the extent of the purchase price that seeds or bulbs sold are as described on the container within recognized tolerances. Seller gives no other or further warranty, expressed or implied."

Seed Beds—Pots—Flats—*For an Early Start*

Green Thumb Seed Bed. New Improved. Made of corrosion-resistant 98.8% pure aluminum with hail-and-shatter-proof Vimlite glazing. Also includes four ground supports for corners of the seed bed to anchor it firmly to the ground.
Standard model. 3 ft. by 6 ft. (shipping weight 17 lb.)...$20.95
Junior model. 3 ft. by 3 ft. (shipping weight 11 lb.) $12.75

Cable-Thermostat. For 6 x 6 ft.
No. S80A $9.00
Cable only for 6 x 6 ft. No. S80. ....$4.50
Cable-Thermostat. For 6 x 3 ft. J40A. $6.75
Cable only, for 6 x 3 ft. No. J40, postpaid $2.25

Dibbles. Iron point, wood handle, $1.15, postpaid. Brass point, wood handle, $1.60, postpaid.

Watering Can No. 101. Practical, decorative watering can with long tapering spout and gracefully curved handle. Reaches those "hard to get at" places. Red, Green, Blue or White. Qt. $1.50; 2 qts. $2.50. Solid Copper, qt. $4.00. Add 20c for postage.

Plant Fountain Sprinkler. Most practical for watering plants in the home. Correct amount of water where you want it. No spilling. Gardeners also say it's ideal for watering seeds. $1.00 each, postpaid $1.15.

Garden Flat

GARDEN FLATS

Removable front to permit sliding out pots without root disturbance.
No. 1 Garden Flat with 36 two-inch pots $1.00 each, postage 20c; 6 for $5.75 by Express collect.
No. 3 Garden Flat with 16 three-inch pots $1.00 each, postage 20c; 6 for $5.75 by Express collect.
Kraft Board Pots sold separately if desired. 2 inch, 100 for $1.00; 1000 for $9.00 prepaid. 3 inch, 100 for $1.35; 1000 for $12.50, prepaid.

Metal Seed Flat. No drowning of delicate seedlings with this patented flat. Inner plate permits watering from bottom. Drainage plug is provided to draw excess water. Rust-proofed steel, painted grass-green. 12 x 14 x 2¾ in. deep, $2.25. (postpaid $2.50).

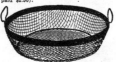

Handy Sifter. A necessary gardening aid for sifting soil to be used in vegetable beds, seed flats, window boxes, etc. 13½ in. top diameter. Available in fine or coarse screening, green enamel finish. Fine screening is 8 meshes per inch; coarse screening is 2½ meshes per inch. $1.35 each, postpaid $1.60.

Sprayer, Capson Hand. Strictly first-quality sprayer for indoor and outdoor use. Pint glass jar with nickel-plated brass pump; operates with one hand. Handy for sprinkling clothes. $2.95 each. Add 20c for postage.

Wik-Fed Flower Pot. Especially designed for African violets or any plant that should be watered from the bottom. The base is a reservoir for water, which is carried directly to the roots by a special wick. Made of non-warping, unbreakable plastic; will last for years. Colors: Ivory, Yellow, Red and Pink. 4 in. $1.15 ea.; 2 for $2.00. 5 in. $1.65 ea.; 2 for $3.00. postpaid.

Glaswik. The scientific way to water house plants. Supplies a constant, even amount of water. ¼-in. diam., for 4 to 6-in. pots, 25c per ft. ⅜-in. diam., for 7 to 12-in. pots, 35c per ft., postpaid. The ⅜-in. size is best for seed flats.

PLASTIC FLOWER POTS

Similar in shape to clay pots, but unbreakable. Decorative as well as useful. Colors: Red, Green, Yellow and Ivory. Please specify color and second choice.

Top Diam.	Pots per doz.	Saucers per doz.
2¼ in.	$1.00	
3 in.	1.50	$0.75
3½ in.	2.00	.90
4½ in.	3.00	1.10
7¾ in.	7.50	

If wanted by parcel post, add 10% for postage.

Rubber Saucers. Unbreakable, non-sweating saucers for jardinieres, vases or flower pots. Will not mar finely finished surfaces.
No. 1 Size, 5-in. diam., up to 6-in. pot, 30c each...............................$3.00, doz.
No. 2 Size, 7½-in. diam., up to 8-in. pot, 55c each...............................$6.00, doz.
No. 3 Size, 10¼-in. diam., up to 12-in. pot, $1.10 each.......................$12.00, doz.
Buy six at the dozen rate.
If wanted by parcel post, add 10% for postage.

Ferto Pots. Made of compressed manure, roots grow right through pot. Put seeds in Ferto Pots about six weeks before garden is ready for planting. Then plant pot and all. Plant eats Pot, also adds organic Humus to soil.
2¼ in. 60c per doz...................$3.50 per 100
3 in. 75c per doz...................$4.50 per 100
Potting Soil. Sterilized potting soil, reinoculated with growth organisms. Revive your plants with fresh soil. 1½-lb. bag 50c, postpaid.
Vermiculite. Excellent for starting seeds, cuttings, and for lightening heavy soil. Perfectly sterile; moisture retentive. 4 qts. 45c, postpaid 60c; ½ bus. 85c, postpaid $1.10; 2 bus. $1.75. By express collect.
Hyponex. Perfectly safe for house plants. Oz. 10c; 3 ozs. 25c; 7 ozs. 50c; 1b. $1.00, postpaid.

Labels—Stakes—Supports—Twine

PERFECT GARDEN LABELS

When marked with an ordinary lead pencil the writing will remain legible through all kinds of weather. Gray color of the labels blends well with the foliage and soil.

Border Size. 5 in. long for garden use. 25 for $2.40; 100 for $9.25, postpaid.
Rock Garden Size. 4 in. long for small plants in the rock garden. 25 for $2.00; 100 for $7.90, postpaid.
Show Garden Size. 7 in. long, a more conspicuous label for taller growing plants. 25 for $2.90; 100 for $11.25, postpaid.
Tie on Label. 3½ in. x ¾ in. for roses, shrubs, etc., fitted with copper wire. 100 for $3.60, postpaid.
Pot Label. 4 in. x ¾ in. for pots, seed frames, etc., 100 for $3.00, postpaid.

Wired Wood Label

Wood, Wired, 3½ x ⅝ inches, for trees, shrubs, Dahlias and similar plants, 100 for 60c; 1000 for $5.00, postpaid.

Pointed Pot Label

Wood, Pointed and Painted Labels. For pot and garden plants, prices are postpaid.

SIZE	100	1000
4 x ⅝	$0.50	$4.50
5 x ⅝	.55	4.85
6 x ⅝	.65	4.95
8 x ⅝	.85	7.75
10 x ⅝	1.10	9.00
8 x ⅞	1.25	11.00
10 x ⅞	1.40	12.00
12 x 1⅛	2.25	20.00

Label Pencils. Special rainproof, 15c each; 12 for $1.50, postpaid.

TWINE—RAFFIA—TAPE

Green Cotton. Light weight but strong. 20c per ball; pound (12 balls), $1.75.
White Cotton. 3 ply. Pound (6 balls), $1.00.
Jute. 2 or 3 ply, state which, 40c per ball; pound (2 balls), 75c.
Jute. 5 ply, in one pound balls, 70c per ball. All twine postpaid.

RAFFIA

Unsurpassed for tying plants. Natural color, pound $1.00, postpaid.
Dyed green, pound $1.25, postpaid.

TAPE

Cotton Fabric. 5/16 inch wide, dyed green. Excellent for heavy plants such as Dahlias. 275 feet $1.00, postpaid.
Garden Rule. A substantial aluminum yard stick showing at a glance the proper depth and spacing for all popular vegetables. 2 in. wide; 36 in. long. $1.25, postpaid.

Plant Props. No tying needed; simply slip top loop around stem. 16 in., doz. 60c; (Postpaid 80c). 30 in. doz., $1.25 (Postpaid $1.45). 42 in. doz., $1.50 by express. 66 in. doz., $2.50 by express.

Pointed Dowel Stakes. Round, straight, painted green. ½-inch diameter.

Length	Doz.	100
3 ft.	$0.55	$4.00
4 ft.	.70	5.25
5 ft.	.80	6.00

Heavy Dahlia Stakes. Pointed, painted green. 15/16-inch in diameter. A very substantial stake. Add 10% for postage.

Length	Doz.	100
4 ft.	$1.50	$12.75
5 ft.	1.75	14.25
6 ft.	2.00	16.50

Stakes, Bamboo Dyed Green. About pencil thickness, very fine for staking Delphinium, Hardy Chrysanthemums, Gladiolus, etc. Add 10% for postage.

Length	100	1000
18"	$0.75	$7.00
24"	.90	8.50
30"	1.25	11.75
36"	1.50	14.00
42"	1.65	15.50
48"	2.00	18.50

FRUIT SACKS. Perfect protection for grapes, apples, etc. Admit correct light and air for perfect ripening of fruit. Special fastening device makes it easy and quick to apply. 55 for $1.00; 1000 for $18.00, postpaid.

BEAUTIFY and PROTECT your flowers and lawn

with *stikit® wikit*

the modern fencing

Easy to hammer into hard ground

Easily installed, each unit is 21" high, 12" wide, white or green baked enamel on ¼" hardened steel. Carton of two dozen makes 24 feet of fence, enough for the average flower bed.

WHITE OR GREEN $1.89 PER DOZEN (FORMERLY $2.40)

Germaco Hotkaps
New Method of Plant Protection

Paper wax cones to protect young seedlings against frost, rain, insects, and ground crusting. Ideal for early sowing. Trial set of 25 Hotkaps and setter, 70c; Postpaid .85c. 100 Hotkaps with a special garden setter. $2.75. Postpaid $2.95. 250 Hotkaps with special garden setter. $4.65. Postpaid $4.90. Standard package of 1000 Hotkaps. $14.65—by express. Extra Steel Setter $1.95.

TRAIN-ETTS

Weatherized Trellis Netting

Ideal supports for sweet peas, garden peas, pole beans, cucumbers, tomatoes, etc. Easily suspended between stakes. Will not rot like string, or rust like wire.

No. 160 x 72 in. $ .75 each postpaid.
No. 260 x 96 in. $ .95 each postpaid.
No. 360 x 180 in. $1.40 each postpaid.

'TWIST-EMS'

Trademark Reg. U. S. Pat. Office

Save the tedious work of tying plants with twine or raffia. Simply put around the stems and supports, twist, and the plant is securely fastened.
8 inch: 100 for 25c.—Postpaid 35c. 1000 for $2.25; 16-inch, 100 for 50c.—Postpaid 60c; 1000 for $3.90, postpaid.

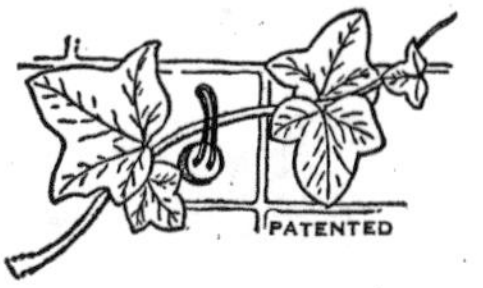

Wayward Vine Guide and Support. A new and easy way to train all kinds of vines to brick, stucco, stone, cement and wood walls. The vines are held in place by wire loops which may be easily bent. Brick red, gray, or white. State color wanted. Per box of 25 including cement $1.00, postpaid.

Vine Support, English Wall Nail. For securing fruit trees, roses and climbing plants to the wall. The head of the iron shank projects through the clip to receive hammer blows and after being driven into the wall, the lead clip can be turned over the branch. A box of assorted sizes 5 1" nails, 10 1¼" nails and 5 1½" nails—75c, postpaid.

Good Tools For Good Gardens

GARDEX TOOLS

Cultivator and Weeder. A 3-prong cultivator for loosening the soil combined with a blade which cuts off weeds quickly. A two-in-one tool. $1.60, postpaid $1.85.

Speedy Cultivator No. 1514. No collection of garden tools would be complete without this popular tool. The curved tines are sharply pointed and short enough for working under low bushes, flowers, and plants. $1.60, postage 20c.

Straight Tooth Rake No. 252. A good quality steel rake with 14 polished teeth and green-painted head. $1.45, postpaid $1.80.

Garden Rake No. 251. Same as above except that the teeth are curved. $1.45, postpaid $1.80.
Floral Rake No. 253. A small light steel rake with 10 teeth and a 3¼ ft. handle. Suitable for ladies who prefer a lighter rake with teeth closer together. Excellent for work in small flower beds. $1.00 each, postpaid $1.25.
Dandelion and Clean-Up Rake No. 415. Gardeners who have never tried this type of rake will find it indispensable around the home. Ideal for removing dandelion blossoms before going to seed, raking up dead grass, leaves and miscellaneous debris. $1.60 each, postpaid $2.00.

Bow Pull Hoe. Narrow 7 in. steel blade supported on both ends. $1.35.

Pull Hoe Weeder. A favorite with many gardeners. Has a "U" shaped steel cutting plate. 5 in. wide with one share. $1.85, postpaid $2.10.

Gardex Hand Seeder No. 270. Has adjustable hopper for spacing and adjusting of holes from small flower seeds up to cucumber size. A very practical small seeder. $1.50, postpaid.

Garden Hoe No. 906. A very popular all-purpose hoe. width of blade 6½ inches. 4¼ ft. handle. $1.10 each, postpaid $1.35.

Disston Lawn Rake. This tool, fitted with teeth, made from flat spring steel, is so well constructed and of such superior material that we believe it to be the best lawn rake available. 18 teeth $2.25; 24 teeth $3.00.

Disston Lawn Rake

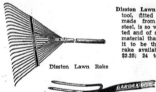

Gardex Spading Fork. Forged from one piece of high carbon steel, the 11" tines are round pointed and triangular shaped for easy soil penetration. $2.25, postpaid, $2.50.
Garden Spade GSUD. A sturdy, well-made, square-point garden spade with substantial metal D-handle. $2.25, postpaid $2.50.
Shovel, Round Point, Long Handle. Has a blade measuring 9 x 12 in. and a long handle. $2.25, postpaid $2.50.
Shovel, Round Point, D-Handle. Of the same proportions as the preceding but with a D-handle. $2.25, postpaid $2.50.
Shovel, Square Point, D-Handle. The blade measures 9¾ x 12 in. Equipped with a D-handle. $2.25, postpaid $2.50.

Kneepron. A Kneeling Apron. Made of heavy duty tan canvas that is pre-shrunk and water-resistant. The rubber knee inserts will not absorb moisture or soil and are easily removed when laundering Apron. The large pocket is cut on a bias and is ideal for holding Trowel, Pruning Shears, etc. The small center pocket is for keys and cigarettes. Fits any person from 5' 2" to 5' 10". $3.95. By mail add 25c.
Knee Pads. Constructed of top quality molded rubber. Soft rubber on the inside gives positive protection against aching knees. Easy to put on and comfortable when kneeling, standing or walking. $2.25 pair. By mail add 20c.
Hand Cleaner. Instant acting. Rub on and wipe off. Use without water. Removes stubborn dirt, grime, grease and stains. 3 Oz. tube, 35c; postpaid 45c, 3 for $1.00, postpaid.

Garden Club Hoe and Cultivator. Two of the most important of garden tools on one handle. Three tines one side, and 3 inch hoe on the other, made of cadmium plated "rust-proof" high grade carbon steel, 51 in. hardwood handle. $2.00 each, postpaid $2.25.

THE GARDEN CLUB *Model*

Dreer Trowel. A flat-bladed professional tool which is exceptionally strong and serviceable. $1.40, postpaid.

English Pattern Trowel. Forged from a single piece of high-grade steel with polished blade. $1.25, postpaid.

Transplanting Trowel. Has a narrow steel blade which speeds up the work. 35c, postpaid.

Hand Spading Fork

Hand Spading Fork. A strong, serviceable tool for weeding or loosening the soil between plants. 80c, postpaid.
Garden Tool Set No. 104. Trowel, cultivating fork and transplanting trowel. These tools have the patented finger-rest to prevent finger slipping on the handle. Feather-weight aluminum alloy of highest quality, hand polished and buffed to a brilliant mirror-like finish. $3.45 per set postpaid.

Garden Tool Set

Hole-in-One Bulb Planter. Makes a neat round hole which permits planting bulbs without disturbing the surrounding soil. An indispensable garden tool. 75c, postpaid.

Weeding Knife. A good tool for lawn weeding and very useful throughout the garden. 60c, postpaid.

Ideal Weeder No. 200. A very popular style of hand weeder made of forged steel and both edges are well sharpened. 75c each, postpaid.

Magic Weeder. Made of heavy galvanized, flexible wire with flattened ends.
No. A. Short handle, 35c, postpaid 50c.
No. B. 18 in. handle. 3 tines. 50c, postpaid 65c.
No. F. Long handle, 48 in. 4 tines, $1.00, postpaid $1.25.
No. G. Long handle, 57 in. 4 tines. $1.25, postpaid $1.60.

Magic Weeder

Tools — Pruning — Grass Trimming

Shrub and Tree Pruner

Shrub and Tree Pruner. A practical pruner for a long reach. Ideal for high climbing roses, shrubs, young fruit trees. Clean slicing stroke does not injure bark, cuts ¾" branches with ease. This pruner is light weight, sturdily built, and extremely serviceable. 4 ft. $5.00 (postpaid, $5.35); 6 ft. $6.00 (postpaid, $6.50).

Tree Pruner, Disston D-3. A popular "Waters Pattern" general purpose pruner, tempered, smooth cutting steel blade connects to operating lever with wire. Cuts branches up to 1" diameter. 8 ft. $4.00; 10 ft. $4.50; 12 ft. $6.00. By express.

Pruning Compound, Trefix. An antiseptic, durable, and elastic dressing for pruning wounds and cavities. Pt. 75c (postpaid, 90c); qt. $1.25 (postpaid, $1.50); gal. $2.40.

Pruning Saw, Disston No. 31. An excellent hand pruning saw with a 20-inch blade. $4.25, postpaid.

Saw, Disston No. D27. Used by expert tree surgeons and others who prune in a scientific manner. Made of steel with special beveled teeth, 6 points to the inch. Cuts on push stroke. Length of blade, 26 in. $6.10, postpaid.

Pruning Saw, Pacific Coast Type, No. 15. Built like a hacksaw. The blade is 14 in. long and interchangeable, $3.25, postpaid.

Pruning Saw, California Pattern No. 166. A popular type with taper ground, curved, steel blade and 8 point teeth cutting on the draw stroke. $2.25, postpaid.

Pruning Saw, Double Edge K-40. Has 8 point teeth on one side and "Lightning" style teeth on the other. A very fine double purpose saw. $2.35, postpaid.

Pruning Saw and Shear No. 55. A combination tree pruner combined with a curved, taper-ground 9½ inch pruning saw cutting on draw stroke. Hook, frame, and socket of malleable iron. Shear blade hardened, tempered steel. $5.75, postpaid.

Pruning Shears, Disston No. 201. A good quality shear for general use, keen cutting blade is hardened and tempered to stay sharp. Strong malleable iron handles. 9 in. $1.50, postpaid $1.65.

Pruning Shear, Snapcut No. 119. Unequalled for ease of operation making a clean, sharp cut which leaves no ragged edges. A favorite with the ladies as well as with many men gardeners. 6 in. $1.76; 8 in. $2.25, postpaid.

Forester Lopping Shears. A heavy-duty tool for brush cutting and heavy pruning. No. 2 for 1½ in. cut of greenwood $8.50, postpaid $8.75. No. 3 for 2 in. cut of greenwood $9.75, postpaid $10.10.

AS CUT FROM BUSH

Flower Holding Shear No. 615. Stainless cutlery steel blades. Cuts and holds stems with one snip. $2.50, postpaid.

Pruning Shears No. 419. Light-weight aluminum body with keen "V" blade working against a soft metal anvil giving an effortless action. $2.75, postpaid.

Hedge Shear, Disston No. 180. A good moderate priced hedge shear. Blades are hollow ground and polished. Hardwood handles are securely riveted. 8" $2.50, postpaid.

Hedge Shear, Disston No. 160. A small hedge shear for light work, popular with ladies for trimming hedge, grass, and shrubbery. 6" blade, $1.50, postpaid.

Hedge Shear

Sunbeam
Electric
Hedge Trimmer

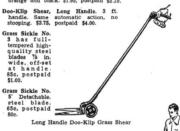

A powerful electric trimmer connected with the house current with specially designed 12-inch long cutlery steel blades, hardened and precision ground. Well balanced, of sturdy construction, yet of light weight. With convenient on-and-off switch right in the handle. May be used on AC or DC current. $37.50, postpaid.

Grass Shear, Doo-Klip. A splendid tool with cadmium-plated cold-rolled steel blades with serrated edges. The blades are 5¼ inches long and the zinc-alloy non-rusting handles are finished in orange and black. $1.95, postpaid $2.10.

Doo-Klip Shear, Long Handle. 3 ft. handle. Same automatic action, no stooping. $3.75, postpaid $4.00.

Grass Sickle No. 3 has full-tempered high-quality steel blades ⅞ in. wide, off-set at handle. 85c, postpaid $1.00.

Grass Sickle No. 5. Detachable. steel blade. 65c, postpaid 80c.

Long Handle Doo-Klip Grass Shear

Grass Whip. No. 165. Blade sharpened along both edges and concaved for strength. Overall length 37 inches. $1.00, postpaid $1.15.

Graswip. Improve the golf swing and cut down on the weeds at the same time. Big tough weeds go down easily before its heavy double-edged steel blade. Ideal for trimming along sidewalks or flower beds. $1.79, postage 25c extra.

Sprayers and Dusters

Banner

Bantam

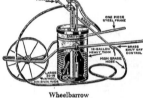

Wheelbarrow

Jim Dandy

COMPRESSED AIR SPRAYERS

Smith Banner. Four gallon zinc-grip steel tank compressed air sprayer complete with a fixed nozzle, two spray discs and extension rod. $9.95.

Bantam Sprayer No. 8. The ideal Home Gardeners' Sprayer, big enough to do a thorough job and small enough to handle easily. Holds 2 gals. Comfortable aluminum carrying handle. 12 in. extension rod, 3 ft. of hose and adjustable nozzle are included. $9.10; (postpaid $9.45).

F-Z Knapsack Sprayer. 5-gal. zinc-grip steel tank; 4 ft. hose; 2 ft. brass extension. Adjustable nozzle. $26.95.

Wheelbarrow Sprayer, Smith No. 60SG. Has an 18-gal. oval tank and a capacity of 2½ gal. per minute. 12 ft. of hose, 2 ft. extension rod and automatic nozzle. Single wheel truck. $33.25.
No. 60BPG. Same, with high-pressure tank and balloon tire. $59.00.
No. 60SPG. Same, with high-pressure tank and two steel wheels. $49.00.

Jim Dandy Cart Sprayer. This Sprayer is entirely new and is especially recommended for liquid applications of 2,4-D Weed Killer on the lawn. Zinc-grip steel tank, balloon tire wheels on roller bearings, runs free and smooth. Equipment consists of 12 ft. Spray Hose; automatic nozzle and 2 ft. extension rod. Shipping Weight 34 lbs. $32.00.

Arnold Sprayer

Pestmaster

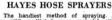

Hayes Jr.

The **Arnold Garden Hose Sprayer** attaches to the garden hose, and as the water passes through the cartridge chamber, the insecticide is dissolved and discharged from the nozzle in a fine spray. Chrome finish, adjustable nozzle. $5.50. Postpaid.

Chrome Extension. 36 inches long, $1.75.

Cartridges. Sulph O-Spray, Arsen O-Spray, P-R (Pyrethrum-Rotenone), Rot-O-Spray, Pyr-O-Spray, DDT Spray, Fungus Spray, Nic-O-Spray, and Weed-O-Spray (2,4-D). 35c each; 6 for $2.00.

Blizzard Continuous Sprayer. One-quart copper tank with brass pump and nozzle for under-foliage spraying. An excellent small sprayer $4.25, postpaid.

Pestmaster Garden and Tree Sprayer. This is a brand new sprayer for 1950 and is unexcelled for spraying gardens, roses, shrub and fruit trees. It is light in weight and very easy to operate. The brass adjustable nozzle throws a long distance or short spray. 2 qt. size $8.50, postage, 25c; 1 gal. size $9.00, postage 35c.

Continuous Sprayer No. 10-G (UTK). A heavy tin one-quart sprayer delivering a continuous fog-spray straight ahead. $1.50, postpaid.

Dustmaster No. 36-D. A heavy tin duster with glass jar holding about 25 ounces of dust. Has non-clog adjustable angle nozzle. 40 inches long. $1.50, postpaid.

HAYES HOSE SPRAYERS

The handiest method of spraying. Fill jar with undiluted spray material, attach to hose and you are ready to work. Water as it passes through jar and nozzle is properly mixed with the spray material.

Hayes-ette Sprayer. BantamWeight sprayer, operates on 20 to 150 pound water pressure. Makes 1½ gallons of mixed spray material. $3.45, postpaid.

Hayes Jr. Spray Gun. Operates 30 to 170 pounds of pressure. Makes 3 gallons of mixed spray at one time. $6.95, postpaid.

Dobbins Hand Duster. Capacity one pound. A uniform discharge with every stroke of the gun down to the last particle of the dust in the chamber. New, two-way dust cap will dust over and under leaves. $1.85, postpaid.

Use Sprayer-Kleener after using 2,4-D, lb. 25c.

Blizzard

Dustmaster

Dobbins Hand Duster

Insecticides—Fungicides

Sprays—*A Spray in time beats the bugs*—Dusts

NAME	PRICE	USE ON OR FOR	BASIC INGREDIENTS
Ant-Killer, Cyanogas	4 oz. can, 39c	Ants	Cyanide
Ant Traps	25c ea. or 5 for $1.00	Ants	Thallium Sulphate
Arasan	¾ oz. 25c; 8 oz. 80c	Seed Protectant	Special Formula
Arsenate of Lead	Lb. 60c; 4 lbs. $1.75	Chewing Insects	As Named
Black Leaf 40	Oz. 35c; 5 oz. $1.05; lb. $2.42	Aphids, Thrips	Nicotine
Bordeaux Mixture (Powder)	Lb. 45c; 4 lbs. $1.25	Fungus Diseases	Copper and Lime
Ced-O-Flora Plant Spray	3 oz. 50c; qt. $1.50; gal. $3.50	Mealy Bug, Red Spider. Adds Lustre	Essential Oils
Ceresan	4 oz. 35c; lb. 90c; 4 lb. $3.00	Seed Protectant	Ethyl Mercury
Ceresan, New Improved	4 oz. 45c; lb. $1.00; 4 lbs. $3.40	Grain Protectant	Ethyl Mercury Phosphate
Chaperone	4 oz. 60c; 8 oz. can, $1.00	Dog & Rabbit Repellent	Special Formula
Chlordane Dust 6%	Lb. 50c; 4 lbs. $1.40	Ants, Snails, Cinch Bugs	Chlordane
Cyanogas, Grade A	Lb. 98c; 5 lbs. $3.75	Moles, Woodchucks, Rats	Calcium Cyanide
Cyanogas Foot Pump	$11.00 each	For Using Cyanogas	
D. D. T. Wettable	Lb. 75c; 4 lbs. $2.00	General Insecticide	50% D. D. T.
Du Pont Floral Dust	Lb. $1.15; 4 lbs. $3.50	Insects, Diseases	Rotenone, Methoxychlor, Fermate
Du Pont Rose Dust	Sifter-top can, lb. $1; 4 lbs. $3	Black Spot, Mildew, Rust	Sulfa, Fermate
Du Pont Spreader Sticker	Pt. 90c; gal. $6.00; 5 gals. $28.75	Spreader For Sprays	Spreading and Sticking Agents
Du Pont Vegetable Dust	Lb. $1.15; 4 lbs. $3.50	Garden Diseases and Insects	Methoxychlor, Parzate, Rotenone
D-X Nicotine	1½ oz. 50c; ½ pt. $1.75; qt. $5.50	Contact Spray for Sucking Insects	Nicotine, Rotenone
D-X Spray	1½ oz. 50c; pt. $1.75; qt. $5.25; gal. $13.50	Sucking and Chewing Insects	Rotenone, Pyrethrum
Endopest Applicator Gun	98c; Refill cartridge 75c; 2 lb. pkg. $1.98	Insects and Fungus Diseases	Rotenone, Sulphur
Fermate	8 oz. can 75c; 3 lbs. $2.75	Fungus Diseases on Trees, Plants, Roses	Fermate
Fungtrogen	½ pt. 75c; pt. $1.25; qt. $2; gal. $6	Mildew and Black Spot	Copper Solution
Gladiolus Dust	1 lb. $1.50	Gladiolus Thrip	Spergon, D. D. T.
Japonex	½ lb. can $3.00	Japanese Beetle Grubs	Milky Spore Disease
K.R.O. "Kill Rats Only"	2 oz. pkg. 75c	Rats	Red Squill
Lime Sulphur Powder	1 lb. 50c; 5 lbs. $2.00	Dormant Spray for Scale, Blight	Lime, Sulphur
Lime Sulphur Liquid	Qt. 60c; gal. $1.50	Dormant Spray for Scale, Blight	Lime, Sulphur
Loro	Pt. $2.10; gal. $11.20	Aphids, Thrips, Red Spider, Plant Mites	Aliphatic Thiocyanates
Mole Nots	Small size 35c; large size $1.00	Moles	Strychnine Sulphate
Mologen	½ lb. 50c; 1½ lbs. $1.25; 5 lbs. $4.00	Moles	Ricine
Mouse Nots	Small size 25c; large size $1.00	Mice	Strychnine Sulphate
Naphthalene Flakes	Lb. 25c; 5 lbs. $1.00; 25 lbs. $4.50	Gladiolus and Cyclamen Thrips	Naphthalene
NNOR Garden Spray	Oz. 35c; 6 oz. $1.00; 16 oz. $2.15; gal. $13.50	Insects, Chewing and Sucking	Rotenone
Pomo Green with Nicotine	Lb. $1.05; 5 lbs. $3.85	Gen. Plant Diseases; Good for Roses	Nicotine, Sulphur Arsenate
Phygon-Wettable	2 oz. 50c; 4½ oz. $1.00	Seed Protectant	Special Formula
Pratt's Fruit Tree Spray	Lb. 65c; 3 lbs. $1.25	Insects, Blight, Scale	Sulphur, D.D.T., Lead Arsenate
Pratt's Vegetable Dust or Spray	Lb. 65c; 3 lbs. $1.25	Insects and Fungus	Rotenone, Copper
Rabbit Scat	6 oz. $1.00; lb. $2.50; 5 lbs. $10.00	Repels Cats, Rabbits, Dogs	Special Formula
Rat Nots	Small size 25c; large size $1.00	Rats	Red Squill
Red Arrow	Oz. 35c; ¼ pt. $1.00; pt. $2.85; qt. $5.00; gal. $18.20	Chewing, Sucking Insects	Rotenone
Rotenone Dust, Black Leaf	Lb. 35c; 4 lbs. $1.25; 25 lbs. $5.25	General Insecticide	Rotenone & Sulphur
Scalecide	Qt. $1.00; gal. $2.40; 5 gal. $8.10; 15 gal. drum $19.00	Dormant Spray for Orchard Pests	Veg. Oils, Naphthalene Resin Soap
Semesan	2 oz. 60c; 12 oz. $2.40; 4 lbs. $11.00	Seed Disinfectant	Mercurial
Semesan Bel	2 oz. 50c; lb. $2.00; 4 lbs. $6.33	Seed Disinfectant	Mercurial
Semesan Jr.	12 oz. 62c; 25 lbs. $13.85	Seed Protectant	Mercurial
Semesan, Special	Lb. $2.00; 4 lbs. $6.92	Brown Patch, Dollar Spot, On Lawns	Mercurial
Slug Shot	Lb. 40c; 5 lbs. $1.65	General	Rotenone, Sulphur, Copper
Snarol	Lb. 35c; 2½ lbs. 75c; 6 lbs. $1.50; 50 lbs. $10.00	Snails, Cutworms, Sowbugs	Special Formula
Spergon	Oz. 25c; 5 ozs. $1.00; lb. $2.25	Seed Protectant	Special Formula
Spray Catalizer	2 lbs. 75c; 50 lbs. $13.50	Spreader-Sticker for Lime, Sulphur, etc.	Calcium Casenate
Sprayer-Kleener	Lb. pkg. 25c	Cleans Sprayers	Special Formula
Sulphur Wettable	2 lbs. 50c	Mildew, Black Spot, Rust	Sulphur
Sunoco Spray Oil	Gal. $1.50; 5 gal. $6.00	Dormant Spray	Essential Oils
Tobacco Dust	5 lbs. 75c; 25 lbs. $2.50	Cinch Bugs, Aphids	Nicotine
Tomato Dust	Lb. 50c; 4 lbs. $1.25	Insects and Fungus	Copper, Calcium Arsenate
Torch, Caterpillar	$1.00 each	Burning Caterpillar Nests	
Tree Tanglefoot	Lb. $1.00; 5 lbs. $4.75; 25 lbs. $20.00	For Banding Trees	Special Formula
Triogen Dust	Lb. 85c; 5 lbs. $3.50	Dusting Roses	D.D.T., Rotenone, Fermate
Triogen	E Kit (for 12 Roses) $1.35	Complete Rose Spray	Combination
Triogen	A Kit (for 20 Roses) $2.25	Complete Rose Spray	Combination
Triogen	B Kit (for 80 Roses) $6.00	Complete Rose Spray	Combination
Triogen	C Kit (for 160 Roses) $9.00	Complete Rose Spray	Combination
Triogen	D Kit (for 600 Roses) $30.00	Complete Rose Spray	Combination
Volck Nursery & Garden Spray	4 oz. 35c; 16 oz. 70c; gal. $2.85	Red Spider, Aphids, White Fly, etc.	Emulsified Petroleum Oils
Wilson's O.K. Plant Spray	Qt. $1.15; gal. $3.50; 5 gals. $13.50	Soft-bodied Insects	Soap, Nicotine
Worm Rid	Lb. $1.25; 4 lbs. $4.00	Earth Worms	Special Formula

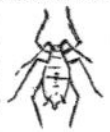

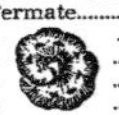

Handy Helpers For Home Grounds

Gardenade
A combination of a soft rubber kneeling pad and a convenient rack for garden tools, with upright handles for lowering or lifting yourself with a minimum effort. $4.50, postpaid.

Dandelion and Clean-Up Rake No. 415. Gardeners who have never tried this type of rake will find it indispensable around the home. Ideal for removing dandelion blossoms before going to seed and for raking up dead grass, leaves and miscellaneous debris. $1.60 each, postpaid $2.00.

Dreer's Animal Repellent Rope. Repells dogs, cats, rabbits, rats, etc. All animals detest the odor. It is a special absorbent rope saturated with the repelling agent. Vegetable gardens that had been overrun with rabbits can now be protected with Repellent Rope. Packed in cans of 100 ft. $1.50, postpaid.

Havahart Animal Traps Humane, simple effective all-metal traps; harmless to animals and humans. Easy to bait and easy to set.
No. 2. For Squirrels, Rats Rabbits, Chipmunks, etc. 7 x 7 x 24 in. $4.50.
No. 3. For Cats, Woodchucks, Opossum, Raccoon, etc. 11 x 11 x 36 in. $10.50.
Write for Catalog describing larger sizes.

Mole Trap, Stenton. An efficient metal trap with pointed spears to destroy the moles. $3.50, postpaid.

Mologen. Non-poisonous (to humans) Mole Killer. ½ lb. 50c; 1½ lbs. $1.25; 5 lbs. $4.00.

Handi Cart
Every gardener needs one. Makes a thousand odd jobs less tiresome and will last for many years. Strong steel body with solid steel axle and rubber-tired 10-in. disc wheels.
No. 18. Holds 3 cu. ft. $8.95.
No. 20. For the larger garden; holds 3½ cu. ft. $13.95.

Gloves, Eezy Wear. Soft, all-leather, dirt-proof, washable. The ideal garden glove. Sizes 6, 7, 8, 9, 10. $1.50 per pair, postpaid.

Shrub-Gard
Protect your shrubs against harm by dogs. The flexible steel spring wires will not tear clothing and are harmless. Each has 3 prongs. Enough for 2½ lineal feet. Carton of 12, $3.00, postpaid.

SCARE AWAY— Modern Scarecrow
A modern scarecrow, rids gardens, orchards, and berry patches of destructive birds and small wild animals. Scientifically designed metallic strips drive out garden marauders with a frightening combination of crackling noise, flashing and fluttering motion. Easy to hang from string or wire. Package of 10 units. 25c; 5 pkgs. for $1.00, postpaid.

Planet Jr. No. 17 Single Wheel Hoe. The most popular of all wheel hoes, light, easy to handle and has the most needed equipment. 1 pair of 6 in. hoes, 3 cultivator teeth and a large garden plow. Does half a day's work with a hand hoe in half an hour. $11.65.

Bird Feeders—*Recommended by Audubon Societies*

Wild Bird Banquet. (Wild Bird Feed). Everything except Suet and Nuts. Small grains, for small birds—cracked corn for larger birds—a generous helping of Sunflower for Cardinals, Jays and Titmouse. Lb. 35c; 5 lbs. $1.25; 10 lbs. $2.00, postpaid.

Community Diner. Aerial picnic grounds for climbing and perching birds such as chickadees, nuthatches, and juncos. Filled with assorted seed suet and pressed peanut suet, molded into paper cups. No. CDD, $1.65. Box of twenty-four extra cups $1.25. Illustrated at right. Postage, 25c.

Clymer Bird Feeder

This attractive bird feeder is easily suspended from any tree branch and therefore accessible to birds only. It comes complete with a grain-suet mixture of food. $1.50. Postage, 25c.

Grain-Suet Refills, 45c each; 3 for $1.25, postage, 15c.

Gridiron. Made of rust-resistant metal. Ideal for cardinals, blue jays, catbirds, mocking-birds, etc. Filled with seed suet cake, $1.75. Extra Suet Cakes, 40c each; 3 for $1.15, postage 25c.

Gridiron

Ready Reference Chart For Fertilizers

NAME	Apply lbs. per 100 sq. ft.	INGREDIENTS—USE	100 lb.	50 lb.	25 lb.	10 lb.	5 lb.
Aluminum Sulphate	2 lb.	To make soils acid	$5.00	$2.75	$1.50	$0.85	$0.50
Ammonium Sulphate	2 lb.	20% Nitrogen, quick acting, acid	5.00	2.75	1.50	.85	.50
Blood, Dried	2-4	12% Nitrogen quick acting, organic	11.00	5.75	3.00	1.50	.85
Bone Flour	3 ll.	.82% Nitrogen, 29.7% Phos. slow, organic	6.00	3.70	2.25	1.10	.60
Bone Meal	5 lb.	3.7% Nitrogen, 21.5% Phos. slow, organic	6.00	3.25	1.75	.90	.55
Bovung (500 lb. $21.25)	5-10	Cow Manure & Peanut Shells, 97%, organic	4.50	2.25	1.30	.75	.45
Cotton Seed Meal	5 lb.	Nitrogen & Potash, acid, organic	8.50	4.50	2.50	1.25	.70
Cow Manure, Dried, (500 lb. $19.75)	5-10	Manure from the feeding pens, organic	4.50	2.50	1.50	.85	.50
"Electra" (5-10-3)	4-lb.	80% Organic, for greenhouses	10.50	6.00	3.75	....	1.00
Hollytone (4-6-4)	3-lb.	Organically balanced food, acid	7.00	4.00	2.50	1.25	.75
Hyper Humus	40-50	Lightens heavy soil, organic	2.50	(500-1b. $11.25; 1000 1b. $22.50)			
Lawn Bilder (8-8-4)	1-lb.	For Lawns, contains 2,4-D, Weed Control	....	4.85	2.75	1.29	....
Lime Hydrated (500 lb. $6.75)	5 lb.	Quick acting, soil sweetener	1.45	.95	....	.30	....
Limestone Pulverized	5-10	Slow acting, soil sweetener	(80-lb. bag $1.00; 6-80 lb. bags $4.80)				
Michigan Peat	1 Bu.	Soil conditioner, organic	(3 bu. $3.50; 30 bu. $30.00)				
Muriate of Potash	1-2	40% Potash, intensifies colors	5.00	2.75	1.50	.85	.50
Nitrate of Soda	1-2	16% Nitrogen, quick acting, sweet	5.00	2.75	1.50	.85	.50
Peatmoss, Horticultural	1 Bu.	Soil lightener, moisture holder, organic	(Bale $6.00)				
Sheep Manure, Dried	5-10	Natural dried weed-free Manure	4.50	2.50	1.50	.85	.50
Superphosphate (20%)	5	20% Phosphate, most soils need it	2.50	1.45	1.00	.60	....
Tobacco Mulch, Coarse Ground	20-30	Insect repellent, some fertilizer value	....	2.50	....	....	....
Vigoro (500 lbs. $20.00)	3-5	5-10-5, General fertilizer	4.25	2.65	1.60	.90	.50
Wood Ashes	2½	Natural source of Potash	6.00	3.25	1.75		

Special Foods

Adco. Scientifically compounded bacterial powder that transforms waste vegetable matter into valuable manure in a few months. Use 2 lbs. to a wheelbarrow load of refuse. 5 lbs. $1.00; 20 lbs. $2.00; 150 lbs. $12.00 by express.

Activo. Promotes bacterial growth in waste vegetable matter which quickly turns "waste into the wealth" of richly activated plant food. No. 2 size for 425 lbs. of waste matter, $1.00, postpaid $1.15. No. 7 size for 1400 lbs. of waste matter $2.00, postpaid $2.25.

Triogen Rose Food. A special food for your Roses, combining organic (long lasting) and inorganic (quick acting) plant foods. 5% Nitrogen 10% Phosphorus and 5% potash. Economical too, only 4 lbs. for 25 bushes 5 lbs. $1.00 (postpaid $1.25); 10 lbs. $1.60 (postpaid $2.00); 25 lbs. $3.00 (postpaid $4.00).

Bovete. Deodorized cow manure for home use. No odor but all the fertilizing properties retained. Use freely on all house plants for stronger, sturdier growth. 12 oz. 39c; postpaid 54c.

Plantabbs. Complete plant food and Vitamin B-1, combined in convenient tablet form. Easy to use, safe and odorless. 30 tablets 25c; 75 tablets 50c; 200 tablets $1.00; 1000 tablets $3.50, postpaid.

Hyponex. Complete plant food, primarily for growing plants in water, but largely used as a plant food for potted plants. Excellent for African Violets. Teaspoonful to a gallon of water. 3 oz. 25c; 7 oz. 50c; 1b. $1.00 postpaid. 10 lbs. $8.00; 25 lbs. $15.00 by express.

Hy-Gro. Completely water soluble, all the plant foods including Vitamin B. Simply mix with water per directions and apply. 3 oz. 30c; 20 oz. $1.00; 2 lbs. $1.50; postpaid. 10 lbs. $4.00 by express.

Hormones

Rootone. Root producing plant hormone to use on cuttings, roots, bulbs, and tubers. Promotes quicker, better growth. ¼ oz. 25c; 2 oz. $1.00; 1b. $5.00, postpaid.

Transplantone. Hormone powder to over come shock due to root disturbance in transplanting. Use for all transplanting from tiny seedlings to full grown shrubs and trees. One level teaspoonful to a gallon of water. ½ oz. 25c; 3 oz. $1.00; 1b. $4.00, postpaid.

Rosetone. Combination of Vitamins and Hormones to promote root growth on Roses. Use when planting or on establishing plants. ½ oz. 25c; 3 oz. $1.00, postpaid.

Fruitone. Plant Hormone spray, prevents blossom drop and premature fruit drop. Sprayed on blossoms of tomatoes, produces nearly seedless fruit. Increases yield of berried shrubs. 2/5 oz. (makes 5 gallon) 25c; 2 oz. (makes 25 gallons) $1.00; 12 oz. $5.00, postpaid.

Floraglow. Beauty treatment for potted plants. Spray or dab on the leaves, gives added lustre and promotes vigorous growth. 6 oz. bottle with spray top 75c; 32 oz. bottle with spray top $1.85, postpaid.

Hormodin No. 1. General purpose root promoting Hormones for Florist or home gardener. ¼ oz. 25c; 1¾ oz. 50c; 1b. $3.00, postpaid.

Hormodin No. 2. For semi-woody species and shrubs. 1¾ oz. 75c; 1b. $4.50, postpaid.

Hormodin No. 3. For hard to root cuttings such as evergreens and dormant leafless cuttings. Oz. $1.00; ½ 1b. $4.50, postpaid.

Combination Package of Nos. 1, 2 and 3, 75c postpaid.

Weed Killers

CRAB GRASS KILLER, Weedone. Contains potassium cyanate, proved by nation wide tests over a period of 2 years to be the most efficient chemical for the control of Crab Grass. 5 ozs. (enough for 500 sq. ft.) $1.00; 20 ozs. (3200 sq. ft.) $3.00

Atlacide. Chlorate weed killer, apply dry or liquid form on the soil. Kills all plant life for 6 months or more. One pound per 100 sq. ft. 5 lbs. $1.50; 10 lbs. $2.50; 100 lbs. $16.00.

Ammate. Non-poisonous. Kills all vegetation including poison ivy. Apply as spray on foliage. Use 1 lb. to a gallon of water. 2 lbs. 95c; 6 lbs. $2.55.

Fairmount Weed Killer. Concentrated liquid weed killer. Mix with 40 parts of water and apply to soil. Kills all vegetation for 6 months or more. 1 qt. 70c; gal. $2.00; 5 gal. $9.00.

Weedone, New Improved. 2, 4-D plus the new powerful 2, 4, 5-T. The most effective chemicals for killing weeds without harming lawn grass. Non-poisonous to animals or humans. 8 oz. $1.00; (postpaid, $1.15); Qt. $2.75 (postpaid $3.00); gal. $6.95 (postpaid $7.30); 5 gal. $25.00, by express.

Weedone Applicator. Fits any standard screw top gallon or half gallon jug. Economical, puts Weedone right where you want it. 49c (postpaid 64c.)

End-O-Weed. Selective weed killer to be sprayed on foliage. Kills by absorption. Will not harm lawn grass. 8 oz. treats 2000 sq. ft. 8 oz. $1.00; 32 oz. $3.25.

Zotox Crab Grass Killer. Zotox kills crab grass plants and seed and checks reinfestation. 8 oz. treats 1000 sq. ft. 8 oz. $1.00; (postpaid $1.15); 16 oz. $1.50 (postpaid $1.75); 32 oz. $2.50 (postpaid $2.85); 5 lbs. $4.50 (postpaid $5.00).

Soil Test Kits

It is easy and inexpensive to test your own soil with Sudbury Soil Test Kits. You can quickly test for nitrogen, phosphorus, potash, and acidity, and adjust your soil to the crops you want to grow. Home garden size (20 tests) $2.50. Horticultural Model (100 tests) $12.50. De Luxe Model (200 tests) $22.50.

Jr. Professional (50 tests) $4.75.

Spring Fertilizer Special

$8.00 Value—3 bus. Michigan Peat, $3.50; 100 lbs. Bovung, $4.50................for $7.50

The Ideal Fertilizer for Spring

Humus in its finest form, Michigan peat, plus the best organic fertilizer, dried cow manure. Mix them together and apply liberally (10 lbs. per 100 square feet), on lawns, roses, shrubs and perennial borders.

Delivered free in our delivery zone; or shipped by freight collect.

Where To Find What You Want

Pelletized Flower and Vegetable Seed—Page 7

GENERAL INDEX

LAWN TOOLS AND SUPPLIES

Lawn Trimmer and Edger. Just half a lawn mower, cuts to within an inch of walls, trees, fences, etc. Saves hours of hand trimming. Width of cut 6 in. 8 inch rubber tired wheel. $19.95, by express. Shipping weight 26 pounds.

Lawn Mower, "Great American". Tops in quality Lawn Mowers. Self sharpening (cuts easier), easy to adjust (cuts more uniformly) ball bearing (long wearing), rubber tires (will not mar the lawn), lipped cutting edge (longer life). 15 inches $25.75; 17 in. $27.50; By express.

Salem Real-Reel. Attaches to faucet and water runs through reel and then hose. You only unreel as much hose as you need. Reel or unreel while water is running. Holds 150 ft. $14.95. By express.

Erosionet. Paper twine netting for use on banks and terraces to prevent seed and soil from washing. 45 in. wide, 25c per lineal yard.

Wingfoot Garden Hose. A Goodyear product. Made from special heavy rayon cord and covered with Neoprene. The highest quality hose for lawn and garden sprinkler service. Guaranteed for 15 years normal service. 25 ft. ⅝ in. $5.95; 50 ft. ⅝ in. $10.95 complete with brass couplings.

Weathermaster Garden Hose. Goodyear. Light weight flexible and easy to handle. Ideal for the "Lady Gardener". Special rayon cords covered with Venyl. Guaranteed for 10 years normal service. 25 ft. ½ in. $5.50; 50 ft. ½ in. $10.25 complete with brass couplings.

Nozzle, DeLuxe Fan-Shaped No. 301. Five rows of fine holes give a fan-shaped spray. Waters the corners, will not wash tender seedlings. $1.25, postpaid.

Nozzle, Rain King No .N1. Precision built, chromium plate, adjustable nozzle. Fine or coarse spray will not leak. $1.50 postpaid

Ross Root Feeder. Fertilizes and waters your trees and shrubs at the roots without disturbing the lawn. Complete with 12 plant food cartridges. $3.50 (postage 25c). Extra cartridges, doz. $1.20 postpaid.

Soil Soaker. The perfect way to water. Porous canvas hose that puts the water where you put the hose, water oozes out evenly throughout the entire length. No sprinkling of passersby, minimizes loss through evaporation. No. 0. 12 ft. $1.75; No. 1. 18 ft. $2.25; No. 2. 30 ft. $3.50; No. 3. 50 ft. $5.50.

Fertilizer Spreaders

E-Z Fertilizer Spreader. Inexpensive fertilizer spreader, saves its cost in one application of fertilizer. Made of treated heavy cardboard with metal wheels. 16 inches wide $1.25. Postpaid $1.50.

Vigoro Spreader. The new Vigoro Spreaders have been modernized and redesigned to give perfect distribution of Vigoro, Grass Seed, Lime, etc. Rubber tires, ball bearing, force feed and rate of application dial.

Model B. 16 in. spreader, capacity 20 lbs. $7.50 (shipping weight 15 lbs.).

Junior. 16 in. spread, capacity 40 lbs., $11.35 (shipping weight 26 lbs.).

ROTOTRIM LAWN EDGER

After mowing your lawn, trim the edges with a ROTOTRIM. Rotary slicing action makes edging easy.

$**4**⁹⁵

Naturain. Portable Irrigation System. Lifetime aluminum. 5 ft. sections (weight 12 ozs.). Sprays from 2 inch trickle to 25 ft. shower. 5 ft. primary section $2.95; 5 ft. extension section $2.75.

Naturain
"Right as Rain"

Better Lawns. (Howard B. Sprague). The best book on lawns. $2.00, postpaid.

Metco Wave Sprinkler. For years of trouble-free service. Powerful water motor, that never requires lubrication, throws a huge water curtain slowly back and forth over a rectangular area 40 x 50 ft. Mounted on smooth tubular runners to protect the lawn. Easily adjusted to smaller areas. $16.95, postage 25c.

Rain King K   Rain King H

Rain King K. Lawn Sprinkler. Fingertip control for circle from 5 to 50 ft. in diameter. Chrome-plated brass mounted on sturdy green enamel base. $7.25.

Rain King H. Lawn Sprinkler. Two nozzles adjustable for spray or stream and to determine the size of area to be sprinkled. $6.25.

Rain King D. Lawn Sprinkler. Similar to Model H but smaller. $5.25.

"Your Lawn"—from Clay to Turf

The Foundation for a "Good Lawn" is as important as the foundation for a House. There should be six to eight inches of top soil or at least soil with sufficient humus (decayed vegetable matter) to permit the ready flow of water down when it rains, up when it is dry.

HEAVY CLAY SOIL can be broken up and made more porous by mixing in:

1. **Michigan Peat.** (Page 71.) Natural 97 per cent organic Peat that holds moisture, increases bacteria action and has some fertilizer value. On good soil use 1½ bushels per 100 sq. ft.; on poor soil, 3 bushels per 100 sq. ft.; 3 bushel bags $3.50; 10 bags or more, $3.00 per bag.

FERTILIZERS. (Page 71.) You can take your pick but apply sufficient to keep the grass growing through the summer. We like the organics such as:

1. **Pulverized Sheep Manure.** Apply 10 lbs. per 100 sq. ft. $4.50 per 100 lbs.; 500 lbs. $19.75.
2. **Bovung.** Cow manure with pulverized peanut hulls. 75 per cent organic. 10 lbs. per 100 sq. ft. 50 lbs. $2.25; 500 lbs. $21.25.
3. **Bone Meal.** Raw not steamed. 5 lbs. per 100 sq. ft. 50 lbs. $3.25; 100 lbs. $6.00; 500 lbs. $25.00.

Or the chemical or inorganic fertilizers will give excellent results without quite so much bulk.

1. **Vigoro** (5-10-5). Use 2 to 4 lbs. per 100 sq. ft. 25 lbs. $1.60; 100 lbs. $4.25.

PREPARATION. Spade (GSUD, $2.25, page 66) or fork (Garden $2.25, page 66) the ground to a depth of 6 or 8 inches, a Rototiller does a wonderful job if you can hire one. Rake roughly with a steel garden Rake (Gardex Rake, $1.35, page 66) to remove coarse rubble. Permit the ground to settle for 10 days and apply the fertilizer as above and rake again.

SEEDING. Sow plenty of seed, 1 pound to 200 sq. ft. Use a Seeder if possible or, if you sow by hand, divide the seed in half and go over the plot twice, making the second sowing at right angles to the first.

COVERING THE SEED. Lawn Seeds are quite fine and should be barely covered. Use a light garden or a flexible spring tooth rake (Disston Rake, 18 teeth, $2.25; page 66).

WATERING. Water only when absolutely necessary and when you water, do a thorough job. Get the water down 4 to 5 inches. Really good LAWN SPRINKLERS are: (See page 73.)

1. Rain King "K" Lawn Sprinkler, $7.75.
2. Rain King "H" Lawn Sprinkler, $6.75.
3. Metco Sprinkler, $16.95.
4. Soil Soaker, 12 ft. $1.75; 18 ft. $2.25; 30 ft. $3.50; 50 ft. $5.50.

MOWING. Mow as soon as grass is 3 inches high. Mower may be set to cut 1½ inches in May and early June but for summer set to cut not less than 2 inches.

1. **GREAT AMERICAN LAWN MOWER, 15 IN. WIDTH, $28.20; 17 IN. WIDTH, $30.00; 19 IN. WIDTH, $32.95.** (See page 73.)

Mow often enough so you do not have to use a grass catcher. But if you need one they are $2.00 (fits 12-18 in. mowers).

ROLLING. Established lawns should be rolled with a medium weight roller, as soon as the ground is dry enough not to pack, to push the roots that have been heaved by freezing and thawing back into the soil.

FEEDING. Grass grows during ten months of the year. Be sure to have sufficient plant food in the ground to nourish it. The new "Lawn Bilder" Lawn food (10 lbs. 1000 sq. ft.) is a combination of all that is best in Lawn fertilizers and also contains 2,4-D Weed Killer to help control the weeds. Or use the foods listed under fertilizers but only one-half the amounts.

RESEEDING. Reseed established lawns in spring and fall, using one pound to 400 sq. ft. For summer baldness, use Dreer's Summer Patching Mixture, $1.00 per pound, for temporary relief.

BANKS AND TERRACES require special care and special grasses. See TERRACE LAWN MIXTURE or use TAILOR MADE LAWN.

"Lawn Bilder"

Complete (8-8-4) plant food combined with the latest 2,4-D Weed Killer. Promotes luxuriant, verdant growth and kills noxious weeds at one application. Safe to use spring, summer, or fall, but do not use on newly planted lawns or Bent grasses. Economical, 25 pounds for 2500 square feet. 10 lbs. $1.29; 25 lbs. $2.75; 50 lbs. $4.85.

Tailor Made Lawn

Finest grade lawn seed, fertilizer and root hormones are incorporated in pure cellulose wadding. Supplied in rolls 2½ ft. wide by 20 ft. long. Prepare ground the same as for sowing seed, unroll Tailor Made Lawn, anchor with pegs or light covering of soil. Especially fine for banks and terraces. Roll 50 sq. ft. $2.00 Postpaid.

Separate Varieties of GRASSES AND CLOVER

PRICES ARE SUBJECT TO MARKET CHANGES

	Postpaid		Not Postpaid	
	1 lb.	5 lbs.	25 lbs.	100 lbs.
Bent, Astoria, 6151. Seed of high purity	$1.65	$8.00	$38.75	$150.00
Bent, Velvet, 6149. This is the finest of the Bent Species	6.30	30.80	150.50	600.00
Blue Grass, Kentucky Fancy Recleaned, 6153. (Poa pratensis) Permanent	1.20	5.75	26.75	100.00
Alta Fescue, 6161. For Athletic fields, fairways, pastures	1.25	6.00	28.75	110.00
Fescue, Chewings New Zealand 6158. (Festuca rubra fallax). For fine lawns	1.05	4.90	23.75	90.00
Fescue, Meadow, 6160. (Festuca pratensis). For hay and pasture	.70	3.30	15.50	60.00
Red Top Grass, Extra Recleaned Seed, 6166. For lawns and golf courses	1.20	5.75	26.75	100.00
Rye Grass, Domestic, 6170. Extra fine, heavy seed	.45	2.00	8.00	30.00
Rye Grass, Perennial, 6172. (Lolium perenne)	.60	2.80	13.00	49.00
Wild White Clover, 6122. A true perennial of dwarf growth, well suited to lawns and pastures.				
1 to 2 ozs. per 100 sq. ft. Oz. 25c; ¼ lb. 65c; ½ lb. $1.20	2.20	10.45	50.75	200.00

Permanent Pasture Grass Mixture, 6119. Specially recleaned grass and clover seeds including perennial varieties which insure at all times an abundant and nutritious food supply for all kinds of stock. 50 lbs. per acre. Includes Ladino Clover. Lb. $1.00; 5 lbs. $4.75; 10 lbs. $9.25; 25 lbs. $22.50; 100 lbs. $35.00, delivered.

The Perfect PERENNIAL GARDEN

FOUR MONTHS OF FLOWERS from easy-to-plant, easy-to-care-for, hardy, field-grown plants. Once planted they bring you perennial beauty year after year and provide continuous color in your outdoor living room from June to frost.
Plant this permanent garden for only **$7.00, postpaid.** One each of the 12 varieties (enough for a bed 3 ft. x 10 ft.) below to flower in:

JUNE	JULY	AUGUST	SEPTEMBER
Canterbury Bells	Coreopsis	Platycodon	Helenium
Delphinium Hybrids	Geum	Monarda	Anemone
Columbine	Dictamnus	Liatris	Aconitum

$15.00 for 3 of each (36 plants). Enough for a border 3 ft. by 30 ft. Postpaid

Aster Frikarti

Hardy Verbena

Flame. Brand-new and fiery-red. This hardy creeping plant blooms all summer. Wonderful for rock gardens or tops of walls. 3 for $1.75; 6 for $3.25.

Aster Frikarti

Something blue to bloom all summer? Here it is; blue as blue can be, in continuous bloom from July until frost. 2 feet tall. 3 for $1.75; 6 for $3.00.

NO
C.O.D.
ORDERS
PLEASE

Verbena, Flame

Indoor Gardens Are Fun!

Start spring right now with these colorful, easily grown plants and flowers. Brighten your windows with the breath of spring.

Lily-of-the-Valley

These lovely, fragrant flowers will bloom in three weeks from our specially prepared pips. Ready planted in unbreakable plastic pots in decorator colors—or by the dozen, for you to plant. No magic—just keep watered in a bright sunny window. After blooming save for planting outdoors when the weather moderates.

Six pips in a plastic pot, $1.85; 3 pips in a plastic pot, $1.00. Pips not planted, $2.40 per doz.; 25 for $4.50; $16.00 per 100.

Or place a standing order for delivery every two weeks.
6 pips in a pot; 6 shipments, $9.95
3 pips in a pot; 6 shipments, $5.45
Postpaid—of course

Amaryllis, Giant Red, 40-002. $1.25 each; $12.50 per doz.

Giant Amaryllis

So easy to grow and so long lived (one of Dreer's customers' Amaryllis was 25 years old last March) that no flower lover should be without them. Plant bulbs in pots, half covering them with soil; water thoroughly. What could be simpler? Stems 12 to 20 inches tall, bearing four to six lily-like flowers up to 10 inches across.

DREER'S GOLD MEDAL HYBRIDS. The finest giant strain from California, with huge, round-petaled flowers. Assorted colors only from white to red.
Mammoth Bulbs, 40-009. $1.25 each; $12.50 per doz.
Extra Large Bulbs, 40-008. $1.00 each; $10.00 per doz.
AMERICAN HYBRIDS, 40-001. 3-inch bulbs. A nice assortment of colors, reasonably priced. 75c each; $7.50 per doz.

What Better Gift for an Invalid?

Golden Yellow Calla

The leaves with transparent spots are almost as decorative as their golden yellow flowers.
Mammoth Roots, 40-053. 65c each; $6.50 per doz.
Extra Large Roots, 40-052. 45c each; $4.50 per doz.

Gloriosa Lily

40-258. (The Climbing Lily.) You need a sun porch for this one, but it's a beauty. Bright red and yellow, lily-like blooms on vines that grow 6 to 10 feet tall. $1.00 each; $9.00 per doz.

Gloriosa Lily

Fancy-Leaved Caladiums

For window sills in early spring, for porch boxes or shaded patio spots during the summer. Colorings of the leaves stagger the imagination. White, cream, pink, yellow, green in unending variation. Height 15 to 18 inches. Barely cover the bulbs in 4 or 5-inch pots, and water moderately. **45-185.** 45c each; 3 for $1.20; 12 for $4.00.

Gloxinia

Ideal house and porch plants, with open-throated, trumpet blooms of velvety texture. Barely cover bulbs in 4 or 5-inch pots, and water sparingly until growth starts. Finest imported bulbs guaranteed to bloom. Height 10 inches.

Emperor Frederick, 47-018. Brilliant scarlet with broad white border.
Emperor William, 47-021. Deep violet-blue with contrasting white edge.
King of the Reds, 47-023. Carries an abundance of brilliant red blooms.
Mont Blanc, 47-025. Vigorous plants; large, pure white flowers.
Violacea, 47-030. Glorious flowers of a rich velvety dark blue.
Mixed, 47-033. All varieties are represented in this assortment.
Any of the above: 40c each; 3 of one variety $1.00; 12 of one variety $3.75

German Varieties Mixed, 47-020. Wide range of colors, producing 30 to 40 blooms at one time. 50c each; 3 for $1.25; 12 for $4.25.

Calla Lily

Gloxinia

X

City Yard • Country Plot • Suburban Home
YOUR LAWN COMPLETES THE PICTURE

Just for fun, cut out a piece of brown paper and cover the grass in the photo above. See the difference!

Dreer's Lawn Seed Mixtures are made from the finest turf grasses only. They contain no timothy. You get more coverage per dollar from more seed per pound.

Dreer's Lawn Mixtures are the result of over a century's experience in compounding formulas that meet all requirements from city yard to the largest airfield, and almost all kinds of soil and climatic conditions.

Your *permanent* Dreer Lawn will pay for itself many times over in upkeep and property value. You'll be proud of your Dreer Lawn!

Choose the formula that meets your needs.

"THE DREER" LAWN GRASS
Tops in Fine Grass Seed

"The Dreer" Lawn Grass produces a smooth, even sod of finest texture. All grasses in this mixture are permanent, fine bladed, and of a rich green color. Includes Bent Grass and White Dutch Clover. Can also be supplied without Clover, if you wish. **6100.** Lb. $1.20; 2 lbs. $2.35; 5 lbs. $5.75; 10 lbs. $11.25; 25 lbs. $26.25; 100 lbs. $100.00, delivered.

"Fairmount Park" Lawn Grass

An economy mixture, excellent for general use. Will give a quick lawn on poor soil. White Dutch Clover included. **6104.** Lb. 90c; 2 lbs. $1.75; 5 lbs. $4.25; 10 lbs. $8.25; 25 lbs. $20.00; 100 lbs. $75.00, delivered.

White Dutch Clover

For an extra-heavy stand of Clover in the lawn, sow 1 pound per thousand square feet. **6120.** Oz. 20c; ¼lb. 50c; ½lb. 90c; lb. $1.50; 5 lbs. $6.85, delivered.

"Shady Place" Lawn Grass

A carefully formulated mixture of grasses that grow in the shade where ordinary grasses do not thrive. The best seed to plant under trees or on the shaded side of walls or buildings. **6110.** Lb. $1.20; 2 lbs. $2.35; 5 lbs. $5.75; 10 lbs. $11.25; 25 lbs. $26.25; 100 lbs. $100.00, delivered.

"Terrace" Lawn Grass

A special mixture of long-rooted, drought-resistant grasses, ideal for slopes, terraces and extremely dry locations. Contains White Dutch Clover. Produces a thick sod; stops wash-outs. **6112.** Lb. $1.20; 2 lbs. $2.35; 5 lbs. $5.75; 10 lbs. $11.25; 25 lbs. $26.25; 100 lbs. $100.00, delivered.

Seashore Lawn Grass

Lawns at the shore present a special problem. Dreer's Seashore Lawn Grass gives you deep-rooting varieties that take hold and grow with a minimum of topsoil and minimum care. **6114.** Lb. $1.20; 2 lbs. $2.35; 5 lbs. $5.75; 10 lbs. $11.25; 25 lbs. $26.25; 100 lbs. $100.00, delivered.

For Fertilizers and Cover Crops see General Catalog.

California Centennial

World-Famous Varieties
World-Famous Quality

When you buy Roses from Dreer's, you buy the finest quality possible to obtain. Select from the most recent introductions or the time-tested old favorites. For "the best buy in Roses" pick the famous Dreer Dozen. Modern Roses are easy to grow—and helpful hints and simple directions come with each order.

Dreer's Roses Are Guaranteed (1) To Arrive in Perfect Condition. (2) To Grow. (3) To Bloom. And (4) Most Important—to Satisfy You. All Dreer Roses are No. 1 Grade—2-year, field-grown, grafted on the hardiest stock.

Your order will be shipped at proper time for planting in your location, or on date you specify. Some varieties are in short supply. **Order Early.**

HYBRID TEA ROSES
Varieties in Red New for 1950

BABE RUTH. Pat. applied for. This fine new Rose performs like a champion. Strong plants with leathery, clean green foliage. Long, heavy-petaled buds are copper-salmon, deepening to rose-pink as the petals unfold. $2.00 each; 3 for $5.00.

California Centennial. Propagation rights reserved. Vigorous and upright, with coppery green foliage. Very few thorns. The long spiral buds are rich glowing crimson, which holds until the flower is full blown. Intensely fragrant. $2.00 each; 3 for $5.00.

CAPISTRANO. Pat. applied for. All-America Award Winner for 1950. Just to see this Rose is to know it is a prize-winner. Strong, vigorous plants, producing unusually large buds and flowers heavy with fragrance. Deep, glowing rose-pink in the bud and open flower. $2.50 each; 3 for $6.25.

Charlotte Armstrong. Pat. 455. All-America Award Winner. Tall, upright bushes covered with long, slender, deep red buds opening to brilliant red blooms which change to cherry-red. $1.50 each; 3 for $3.75.

Condesa de Sastago. Magnificent two-toned flowers; inside of petals a glowing orange-scarlet, outside a pleasing contrast of bright yellow. Very substantial and exquisitely fragrant. $1.25 each; 3 for $3.50.

22 Prize-Winners $33.33

Selecting the best of this prize-winning group is impossible, so all 22 Roses on these two pages (except the Dreer Dozen) are included in this money-saving collection. You can close your eyes and with confidence put your finger on one of the finest Roses of today.

Order one of each 22 ROSES on these two pages for **$33.33**.

We shall not only prepay the shipping charges but include a FREE $1.00 size package of Rosetone (Root-producing hormones) to give them a running start.

Countess Vandal. Pat. 38. Well known as the finest of all pink Roses. The long, tapering buds are salmon-pink shaded with copper, and the large, fragrant blooms show a glint of salmon and gold. $1.35 each; 3 for $3.60.

Crimson Glory. Pat. 105. The choice of thousands as the finest red Rose of today. Plants are vigorous and bear quantities of large, urn-shaped buds which open into beautiful crimson blooms with the texture of fine velvet. $1.35 each; 3 for $3.60.

Douglas MacArthur. Pat. 581. Long, graceful buds opening slowly into a glorious shade that combines the burnished rose, gold, and salmon of autumn foliage. Strong, free-blooming plants. $1.50 each; 3 for $3.75.

Etoile de Hollande. Splendidly formed, richly fragrant, crimson flowers on strong stems. Classed with the best of red Roses; free blooming and a sturdy grower. $1.25 each; 3 for $3.50.

Forty-niner. Pat. 792. 1949 All-America Award Winner. A magnificent Rose in all stages of bloom. The shapely, long-pointed buds show only the deep chrome-yellow on the outside of the petals; as the flower unfolds the vivid orient red of the inside of the petals is disclosed. Mildly scented. Vigorous plants with dark green foliage. $2.00 each; 3 for $5.00.

Mme. Chiang Kai-shek. Pat. 664. All-America Award Winner. Long spiral buds expanding into light, clear canary-yellow flowers of perfect form. Pleasantly fragrant. Plants are strong and upright growing. $1.50 each; 3 for $3.75.

Mme. Jules Bouche. Long-pointed, pure white buds opening to full-centered, white blooms with the faintest trace of primrose at the center. Fragrant and a continuous bloomer. $1.25 each; 3 for $3.50.

Peace. Pat. 591. 1946 All-America Award Winner. Vigorous growth, abundance of blooms, good substance, and a color progression that has no equal make this today's outstanding Rose. Buds are rich yellow, softening to paler yellow with a trace of pink which grows as the flower ages. $2.00 each; 3 for $5.00.

Poinsettia. Bright, rich scarlet buds are long pointed, opening semi-double. Vigorous, fairly tall-growing plants with glossy foliage. Spicy Tea Rose fragrance and in constant bloom. $1.25 each; 3 for $3.50.

ROSES BY MAIL. If wanted by parcel post, add to your remittance 10% (15% west of the Mississippi) of the prices quoted to cover postage and special packing. Minimum charge 15c. Otherwise shipped express collect.

Douglas MacArthur

XII

DREER'S *World-Famous* ROSES

THE FRONT COVER
The Roses in the actual home-garden natural-color photograph on the front cover are Pink Dawn, at the back; the red one is McGredy's Scarlet; the yellow, Mrs. E. P. Thom; salmon on the left, Talisman; salmon on the right, Condesa de Sastago; and the beautiful pink in the foreground is The Doctor. Yours—all six—for $6.75; 2 of each for $12.50; 3 of each for $18.00.

San Fernando. Pat. 785. 1948 All-America Award Winner. Fine large, bright scarlet blooms. Full double, with high centers and delightfully fragrant. Bushes are vigorous and grow upright; heavy bloomers. $2.00 each; 3 for $5.00.

Sleigh Bells. Pat. applied for. A white Rose that blooms and blooms and blooms. Large, ovoid buds, opening to full double, extra large blooms borne on long stems. Excellent for cutting. Color is pure glistening white with just a trace of primrose at the base of the petals. Fragrant, of course. $2.00 each; 3 for $5.00.

BUTTERSCOTCH
Pat. 613. Long graceful buds and blooms, a delightful combination of yellow tones, penciled with orange-buff. A strong grower with clean foliage. $1.50 each; 3 for $3.75.

Butterscotch

MISSION BELLS
Pat. applied for. All-America Award Winner for 1950. Deep salmon-pink buds opening to a clear shrimp-pink. Plants branch heavily, to bear full-centered blooms on long stems with few side buds. Delightfully tea scented. $2.50 each; 3 for $6.25.

Mission Bells

SUTTER'S GOLD. Pat. 885. A twofold prize winner: All-America Award Winner for 1950 and Gold Medal at the International Bagatelle Contest in Paris. Long-pointed, bright yellow buds shading to red and opening to various shades of yellow and orange, depending on the weather. Clean, glossy green foliage, highly resistant to mildew and blackspot. $2.50 each; 3 for $6.25.

Talisman. The forerunner of the multicolored Roses. An exquisite blending of rich scarlet, gold and deep pale yellow. Delightfully fragrant and free blooming. $1.25 each; 3 for $3.50.

Tallyho. Pat. 828. 1949 All-America Award Winner. The inside of the petals is a delightful shade of phlox-pink and the outside varies from crimson to cardinal-red. Ovoid buds with spicy fragrance; robust plants with rich green foliage. $2.00 each; 3 for $5.00.

TOM BRENEMAN. Pat. applied for. The happiness, laughter and gaiety that Tom Breneman brought to the world over the radio could not be better exemplified than in the new Rose that bears his name. The long, coral-rose buds unfold into beautiful, long-lasting, intensely fragrant blooms. $2.00 each; 3 for $5.00.

"The Best Buy in Roses" THE DREER DOZEN

If they rate a place in the "Dreer Dozen" you know they're good!

Autumn. A typical autumn burnt-orange! Buds are ovoid and open full double.
Christopher Stone. Bright scarlet. Fragrant; free flowering and strong growing.
Golden Rapture. Clear golden yellow; double. Old-time Rose fragrance. Vigorous; glossy green foliage.
Kaiserin Auguste Viktoria. Perfect snow-white blooms slightly lemon tinted at the center; fragrant.
Margaret McGredy. Blooms almost continuously. Extra large, non-fading orange-scarlet.
McGredy's Ivory. Shapely, large blooms, borne profusely on tall, well-branched plants. Ivory-white.
McGredy's Scarlet. Strong, healthy plants, almost constantly in bloom. Crimson-scarlet.
Mrs. E. P. Thom. Long-pointed, canary-yellow buds opening lighter. Perhaps the best of all yellow bedding Roses.
Pink Dawn. Deep rose opening lively pink. Full double.
President Herbert Hoover. Tall growing, with flowers on long stems. Orange-scarlet to lighter orange. Foliage glossy and leathery.
Red Radiance. Vigorous; free blooming. Full double, bright cerise-red.
The Doctor. Enormous (5 to 6 inches across); pleasing soft silvery pink. Very fragrant. Vigorous, bushy growth.

THE DREER DOZEN ROSES are $1.25 each; 3 of a variety for $3.50 or for "The Best Buy in Roses"

All 12 for $12.00 $13.00 Postpaid

THE PROPAGATION OF PATENTED ROSES IS PROTECTED BY U. S. PATENT LAW

DREER'S *World-Famous* ROSES

Pink Rosette

ROSETTE ROSES

A new distinct type of Rose similar in growth to the Polyanthas and Floribundas, with flower size midway between the two. Bloom almost continuously.

Pink Rosette. Pat. applied for. Dainty camellia-like flowers of the most delightful shade of pink. $1.50 each; 3 for $3.75.

Crimson Rosette. Pat. applied for. The striking crimson-scarlet of these lovely blooms is enhanced by the deep glossy green of the foliage. Flowers are full double and borne five or six to a truss. $1.50 each; 3 for $3.75.

POLYANTHA ROSES

Smaller flowered than the Rosette or Floribunda types but make up in mass of bloom what they lack in size.

Cecile Brunner. Also known as Sweetheart Rose. A dainty variety with small double blooms of perfect form, in many-flowered, graceful sprays. Rosy pink on a creamy white ground. Fragrant.

Gruss an Aachen. Vigorous plant with rich green, leathery foliage. Flowers are large, double and delicately fragrant. Orange-salmon, lightening to white at the edges.

Mrs. R. M. Finch. Large, impressive clusters, each a bouquet in itself. Flowers are a deep rosy pink.

Orange Triumph. A delightful combination of salmon-red with orange shadings. Flowers are semi-double, cup shaped, with a pleasing fragrance.

Triomphe Orleanais. Vigorous growing, with heavy, glossy foliage. Flowers semi-double, in large clusters. Bright cherry-red.

$1.25 each; 3 for $3.50

SHRUB ROSES

Lipstick. Vigorous plants that grow like shrubs, large and full. Produces showy, large flower clusters all season long. Individual blooms are medium size, single, clear cerise shaded salmon. $1.25 each; 3 for $3.50.

Skyrocket. Vigorous bushes, excellent for hedges. Large, full double, unfading dark red blooms. Honey scented. Blooms intermittently from June through October. $1.25 each; 3 for $3.50.

> **HOW TO GROW ROSES.** (McFarland and Pyle.) The key to sucessful Rose growing. 192 pages of authoritative information. $2.50 postpaid. We shall be pleased to send a Membership Application for the American Rose Society on request.

FLORIBUNDA ROSES

To know Floribunda Roses is to love them. Blooms are smaller than the Hybrid Tea Roses but are borne in clusters on sturdy, vigorous bushes. They are produced without interruption from early summer until late fall.

FASHION. Pat. 789. This enchanting Rose, coral suffused with rose, took the country by storm last fall and as a result we are completely sold out until the 1950 crop comes in. Place your order now to insure delivery this fall. $2.00 each; 3 for $5.00. (Fall Delivery.)

Baby Chateau. Clean-growing plant with glossy, bronze foliage. Crimson buds are ovoid in shape and borne in clusters. Full-blown flowers are red, shaded garnet. Very fragrant. $1.25 each; 3 for $3.50.

Dagmar Spaeth. Very vigorous plants with green, glossy foliage. Flowers are alabaster-white flushed pink, fading to pure white. Large for a Floribunda. $1.25 each; 3 for $3.50.

Improved Lafayette. Brilliant flowers of medium size, borne most abundantly on sturdy plants. The deep glowing red blooms are vividly suffused with crimson and large clusters of them given an impressive display. $1.25 each; 3 for $3.50.

World's Fair. Pat. 362. Large, semi-double flowers of spicy fragrance. Deep crimson in the bud, lightening to scarlet as the flower ages. $1.25 each; 3 for $3.50.

HARDY CLIMBING ROSES

Climbing Roses will transform a plain wall into a bower of beauty. They are traditional covering for an arbor, a fence, a wall, a doorway. Perfectly hardy—grow lovelier as the years go by.

Blaze. Pat. 10. Ablaze all summer with vivid scarlet blooms. The most free-blooming Climbing Rose. $1.50 each; 3 for $3.75.

High Noon. Pat. 704. Double, loosely cupped flowers, lemon-yellow tinted red. Clean, spicy fragrance. A strong grower with glossy foliage. $2.00 each; 3 for $5.00.

Mermaid. Extra-large, single, light sulphur-yellow flowers. In constant bloom, especially heavy blooms in the fall. $1.25 each; 3 for $3.50.

Mme. Gregoire Staechelin (The Spanish Beauty). Well known as one of the most desirable of all Climbing Roses. Very hardy, with large, semi-double, fragrant flowers, pearly pink tipped with light crimson. A fine variety for cutting. $1.25 each; 3 for $3.50.

Mrs. Paul J. Howard. Pat. 450. Vigorous growth and profuse bloom make this one of the finest crimson climbers. Buds are long, pointed, opening full double. $2.00 each; 3 for $3.50.

New Dawn (Everblooming Dr. W. Van Fleet). The first patented Rose. Vigorous climber with dark glossy foliage. Long-stemmed. Double, blush-pink blooms. $1.25 each; 3 for $3.50.

Paul's Scarlet Climber. The plants are completely covered with large, vivid scarlet blooms in June. There are from three to twenty large flowers to each cluster. $1.25 each; 3 for $3.50.

Silver Moon. A delightfully different climber. Buds are large and pale yellow, opening to semi-double, creamy white flowers. Rapid grower with deep green, glossy foliage. $1.25 each; 3 for $3.50.

Paul's Scarlet Climber

BROWNELL *Sub-Zero* ROSES

In response to popular demand, Dreer's now offer you Brownell's famous Sub-Zero—"*unconditionally guaranteed through two winters*"—Roses.

Sub-Zero Roses are different. Their hardy New England ancestry is coupled with a new beauty and new shades obtainable only in this fine strain.

If you have ever lost Roses from freezing, these are a "must" and are worthy of a trial in every Rose garden.

Supply is limited. Order now for years of Rose satisfaction.

$1.75 each; any 3 for $5.00; any 12 for $18.00

SUB-ZERO HYBRID TEAS

Break O'Day. Propagation rights reserved. Shading from orange to apricot, in many delightful combinations. Full double blooms.

Curly Pink. Propagation rights reserved. A delightfully different, pure pink. As the flower opens, the outer edges roll back, giving a charming form.

Early Morn. The pastel pink of the sky at dawn; large, full double blooms.

King Boreas. Propagation rights reserved. King of the Sub-Zero family. Lemon-yellow, completely double and very free blooming.

Lily Pons. Pat. 420. Large, well-formed blooms; white with yellow centers. Vigorous and free blooming.

Pink Princess. Pat. 459. Bright red buds opening to deep pink flowers. Holds its foliage into late fall.

Queen O' The Lakes. King Boreas's lovely queen gowned in regal crimson velvet. Large; full bloom.

Red Duchess. The keynote of this delightful Rose is fragrance, a delightful tangy fragrance. The color, true rose-red.

Shades of Autumn. Pat. 542. A combination of red, yellow and blush, as brilliant as autumnal foliage.

Tip Toes. Red, orange and pink tints, building a flower of delightful form and grace. Spicy fragrance.

V for Victory. Pat. 543. Extra large, extra double, extra yellow, extra fragrant and one of the longest-lasting Roses.

Red Duchess

Golden Climber

Sub-Zero Floribundas

Anne Vanderbilt. Pat. 504. Semi-double, coppery orange. Lovely clusters in an unending stream from June until autumn.

Lafter. A cheerful bushful of sparkling orange and yellow. In constant bloom.

Sub-Zero Climbers

Apricot Glow. Pat. 200. Coppery pink. A vigorous climber or abundant creeper, as you wish.

Golden Climber. Pat. 28. The yellow climber supreme. Blooms are borne in large clusters on long stems, fragrant and ideal for cutting.

Golden Glow. Pat. 263. Remember the New York World's Fair and Rose Court with that delightful climber with its masses of yellow blooms? That climber was Golden Glow, pure rainbow yellow.

Pearly White. A splendid, semi-double, pure white. Nicely formed buds for cutting, opening into graceful flowers.

TRI-OGEN ROSE FOOD. The perfect food for Roses, the proper foods in the proper proportions to keep your Roses at their best. Economical too, 4 pounds per 100 square foot (25 Roses). 5 lbs. $1.00 (postpaid $1.25); 10 lbs. $1.60 (postpaid $2.00); 25 lbs. $3.00 (postpaid $4.00).

Shades of Autumn

PRINTED IN U.S.A.

Single Frilled Begonia
Collection: One each of 7 colors, $1.90

Imported Tuberous-Rooted

Begonias

(See page 66, January issue of House Beautiful)

Each plant a prize! A bed of them breath-taking! Our special importation from Belgium's most expert growers. Jumbo bulbs, 2 inches and up in diameter. Bloom their best in half shade, in light, crumbly soil that will hold moisture without becoming soggy. For early bloom start indoors in pots in February or March. Or plant bulbs outdoors after weather has become settled in May. Try them as summer pot and box plants on porch or patio. Bloom from June to heavy frost. Height 12 to 15 inches.

Each 30c; $3.00 per doz.; $22.00 per 100. Buy 25 at the 100 rate.

SINGLE FRILLED

Waxy-textured, single blooms as large as saucers. Delightful for floating in shallow bowls.

Orange, 45-085	White, 45-091	Yellow, 45-095
Scarlet, 45-087	Pink, 45-093	Mixed, 45-100
Dark Red, 45-089	Salmon, 45-094	

COLLECTION: One each of the 7 colors $1.90

DOUBLE CARNATION-FLOWERED

Huge, full-double blooms that far outshine their namesake in beauty. Delicately frilled.

Orange, 45-104	White, 45-110	Yellow, 45-114
Scarlet, 45-106	Pink, 45-112	Mixed, 45-120
Dark Red, 45-108	Salmon, 45-113	

COLLECTION: One each of the 7 colors $1.90

DOUBLE CAMELLIA-FLOWERED

All the charm of the finest camellias; full-double, well-formed blooms 4 to 5 inches across. Large, overlapping petals in iridescent colors.

Orange, 45-121	White, 45-126	Yellow, 45-130
Scarlet, 45-123	Pink, 45-128	Mixed, 45-135
Dark Red; 45-125	Salmon, 45-129	

COLLECTION: One each of the 7 colors $1.90

Any 2 Collections $3.50   3 Collections $4.95

Carnation-Flowered Begonia
Collection: 1 each of 7 colors, $1.90

Begonia Pendula
The Trailing Tuberous Begonia. Plant in wall pots, hanging baskets or porch boxes. Hundreds of full-double, 1-inch blooms throughout the summer. Fine for shaded rock gardens. Mixed colors only. Each 30c; $3.00 per doz.

Camellia-Flowered Begonia—Collection: One each of 7 colors, $1.90

CPSIA information can be obtained
at www.ICGtesting.com
Printed in the USA
BVHW091126271118
534110BV00023B/947/P